A MEXICAN ULYSSES

JOSÉ VASCONCELOS

A MEXICAN ULYSSES

AN AUTOBIOGRAPHY

TRANSLATED AND ABRIDGED BY

W. REX CRAWFORD

INDIANA UNIVERSITY PRESS

BLOOMINGTON

CONTENTS

JOSÉ VASCONCELOS—
AN APPRECIATION

The death of José Vasconcelos on June 30, 1959, marks the close of a career noted for its contradiction and color even in Mexico, a land abundantly blessed with these traits.

History has recorded many a remarkable *volte-face*, but perhaps none which affected so many different kinds of people in twentieth-century Latin America as that performed by Vasconcelos in the early thirties.

Before that time, as author of *La raza cósmica*, he gave many young intellectuals, made uneasy by Rodó, a sense of confidence by affirming the mixed blood of Latin America as the stock of a great future race. As minister of education, nurtured by the idealism of the Ateneo de la Juventud, he set a nation, numb from a decade of unrestricted violence, about the task of educating the *raza cósmica*. The fact that Mexico's budget for education is still larger than her military expenditure is due principally to Vasconcelos, who made the country education-conscious. Also, as minister of education, he gave the *raza cósmica* a chance to express itself when he turned over, metaphorically, the walls of Mexico to Diego Rivera. As head of the National University, he left this inspiring, albeit somewhat enigmatic motto: "Por mi raza hablará el espíritu" ["My race will give voice to things spiritual," EDITOR'S NOTE]. These are the deeds that earned Vasconcelos the title of Maestro de la Juvendad and the profound respect of more than half of the western hemisphere.

Daniel Cosío Villegas wrote in *Extremos de América* that it was too bad Vasconcelos' life could not have ended there. These may be unkind words, especially now, but there is a ring of truth to them. For the *maestro* spent the remainder of his life repudiating the deeds which had given him fame, affection, and admiration. He spurned *La raza cósmica* as a "librecillo de error" ["an insignificant little book filled with error," EDITOR'S NOTE]. He dismissed Diego Rivera, Siquieros, and Orozco as Communist dupes. (In retrospect, his ideological quarrels with the Big Three of Mexican painting seem to have been partly justifiable. The reaction against official Indian painting in

Mexico is now widespread. The domination of these three artists in the end proved stifling.)

At about this same time, he returned whole-heartedly to the Church, and the *volte-face* was complete. He now worried privately about the harm the Americans and Jews were doing to Mexico. He favored the cause of Franco, and, what is more important in Mexico, became a strong supporter of Cortés. Interpretation of Mexican history is often made along pro-Spanish or pro-Indian lines. Officially, Mexico does not recognize much value in Spain's contribution to her heritage. Vasconcelos in his *Breve historia de México* (which one wag remarked was "ni breve, ni historia, ni de México" ["neither brief, nor history, nor about Mexico," EDITOR'S NOTE]) hailed Cortés as the bearer of civilization to Mexico, and denounced the heritage of Huichilobos as a weight which kept Mexico constantly on her knees. The truth, of course, lies somewhere in between, but this theory was an explicit negation of his earlier *indigenismo*. In the same book, he branded Juárez and *la reforma* as a wholesale delivery of Mexico into the hands of Masonry.

He will also be remembered as a fine stylist. His four-volume autobiography, of which *Ulises criollo* is the first and the best, offers enviable examples of Spanish prose. It is also a frank statement about the author's personal life and a valuable record of his connection with the Mexican revolution. . . .

As a philosopher, he was known in the United States and Europe. Had he lived, he would have attended the International Congress of Philosophy in India, for he had recently been designated president of that group. His interest in philosophy goes back to those days in the first decade of the present century when he met with Antonio Caso, Alfonso Reyes, and Pedro Henríquez Ureña (what a remarkable group the Ateneo really was!) to discuss Plato and Bergson.

The record of this brilliant and contradictory man will now be gone into extensively—both superficially and thoroughly—as is the wont in Hispanic culture when one of the great flames is extinguished. Some people will see in his life no contradiction at all, merely the subjective truth of an impulsive individual. No one can doubt his high moral stature. His abhorrence of violence in an age of great and seemingly useless bloodshed was genuine. Many times he was on the point of resigning as Obregón's minister in protest against some method of repression employed by one of his colleagues. In the end, he finally did.

Officially, all Mexico mourned his passing: "México consternado por Vasconcelos," proclaimed the banner headline of *Excélsior*. In recent years, he had firmly maintained the ideological position assumed after his defeat for the presidency by Calles in 1929, had often appeared on TV, where he was known for his individual reaction, and came faithfully to his desk at the Biblioteca, where he was often available to visiting North Americans, whom he always treated with the utmost courtesy, despite his distrust of their country as a whole. Against the advice of his doctors a week before he died, he attended the funeral of philosopher Samuel Ramos (b. 1897), whose death on June 20 really created *un mes infausto para la cultura mexicana* [a fateful month for Mexican culture, EDITOR'S NOTE].

Even in death his rugged nature asserted itself. The newspaper carried a copy of a letter written to his son-in-law, leaving explicit instructions about his remains. He carried his sense of outraged justice with him to the grave. The letter, as it appeared in *Novedades*, July 1, 1959, is worth quoting:

"My dear Herminio:

"I confirm our recent conversation. The months of January and February turned out to be true to their reputation in that they brought about a positive weeding out of old men. In the last few months three members of the Colegio Nacional have passed on, and all three wound up in the Pantheon of Illustrious Men. I do not criticize the intention of rendering all homage possible to outstanding men from the intellectual world; but in view of the fact that it is becoming the practice to place in a single rotunda persons of the most diverse tendencies, should it occur to anyone to seek such an honor for me as a member of the Colegio Nacional, I beg you to make public my most violent disapproval.

"In the first place, as you know, and as I have repeated to several friends, I have never consented to accept noisy honors because I feel that our countrymen have no right to honor me as a writer until they recognize me as a politician. I have not even accepted friendly banquets because justice still must be done to those who died in the electoral campaign of 1929 and to many others. The nation's conscience knows, or should know, that we won the elections of 1929, and as long as this is not recognized publicly, and perhaps officially, I could not accept any honor without feeling that I was betraying truth and justice. . . . Consequently, if, out of its fear of acknowledging the truth, my country does not decide to honor me properly as a politician, I prefer that it not be concerned with me in any other way.

"Besides, a burial in the Rotunda would be for me almost an insult. There lie, among others, the remains of a certain aviator who owes his official acclaim to persecutions perpetrated against my friends of the Vasconcelos movement. Moreover, the author of the *Brief History of Mexico* has no business in a cemetery dedicated especially to the heroes of the Masonic reform carried out by Juárez and his group.

"A thoroughly humble burial in any village cemetery and perhaps later removal to some modest Catholic chapel is all that I request of my family. . . . (Signed: José Vasconcelos)"

The Sunday after his death, *Novedades* carried a long interview by Emmanuel Carballo, reportedly granted two weeks before. It is overflowing with special *sal amarga de Vasconcelos* [bitter salt of Vasconcelos, EDITOR'S NOTE]: "What we have done so far arouses in me more nausea than admiration." *"In present circumstances, what do you think of the Mexican people?"* "They are a people made up overwhelmingly of cowards." "I consider myself a sub-philosopher because I am a Mexican, and I don't pretend to be any better than my compatriots."

The intransigency of Vasconcelos was both his strength and his weakness. Now that he has dictated the resting place for his mortal remains and deprecated his country for the last time, he enters the realm of ideas, where everyone can make of him what they will. One may be sure that Penelope will weave the thread again for this *Ulises criollo*.

HOWARD T. YOUNG
POMONA COLLEGE

This article was reprinted from *Hispania* (published by The American Association of Teachers of Spanish and Portuguese) XLII, December 1959, pp. 570–72. Vasconcelos' letter and interview were translated by Professor Merle E. Simmons.

TRANSLATOR'S INTRODUCTION

TRANSLATOR'S INTRODUCTION

"Why do Anglo-Saxons write so many excellent biographies and autobiographies, and Latin Americans so few?" The distinguished Latin American who posed this question in my presence continued, "Why, we have only two first-rate ones in my country—my father's and my sister's life of my father." Whether that judgment is true or not, the life story of José Vasconcelos (1882–1959), told by himself in four stout volumes (some 2,500 pages, a million words), remains one of the few notable memoirs to come out of the southern republics, and is commonly regarded as the great Mexican autobiography.

The first volume, bearing the title of the series, *Ulises Criollo* (A Creole, or Mexican, Ulysses), appeared in 1935, published by Editorial Botas. By 1958, when the new publishing house, Editorial Jus, brought out the first expurgated edition, the four volumes were numbered respectively the eleventh, eighth, sixth, and fourth editions. To be sure, the number of volumes per edition was relatively small, but nonetheless these publishing figures affirm its position as a classic in Mexican literature.

The expurgated edition is said to have been provided because parts of the text were hardly proper reading for young people and were profoundly upsetting even to adult Catholics. I am glad, however, that I worked from the complete text, with its revelation of the total life of a passionate intellectual. Some readers may object to the inclusion of certain passages as they might to parts of the Confessions of St. Augustine or Rousseau, and to our daily fare in contemporary fiction. Others will lament the inevitable curtailment of a long and detailed story that, even in original, ends before the author's mellowing, less bitter last twenty years. I have tried to satisfy these readers with personal, political, and philosophical selections in a proportion which mirrors the man. At the same time I have kept in mind the American reader and have attempted in my selections to link Vasconcelos' early experiences and first meetings with later activities and reflections which are their outgrowth, or sometimes a rebellion against them. If the result is jumpy, it should be noted that transitions are often abrupt or nonexistent in Vasconcelos' own massive volumes and that the only organization is the juxtaposition of many facets of one man's personality. Although the book is not exactly a journal—Vasconcelos did not keep a diary—it should be read as if it were; transitions are really no more to be expected than they would be in the diaries of André Gide.

It cannot be over-emphasized that Vasconcelos cared very little for our demands for a careful, dated narrative; the terms, clear, informative, logical, I have often found, tend to be used as mildly pejorative by Latins, damning with faint praise the Yankee who cannot rise to rhetoric, poetry, and philosophy. He cared less about his immediate environs than for his feelings, the ambitions that stirred him, the reflections that crossed his mind. For us, it is the exactitudes that matter, for him, the *inquietudes* (concerns with universal and philosophical problems) of which Latin Americans believe us to be almost totally devoid.

A second warning to the reader: do not expect Vasconcelos to be monolithic, all of a piece. He is disconcertingly and all-too-humanly inconsistent. Dissenting, he is a Catholic—or at the very least, no sympathizer with Protestants. From the sins of the flesh he turns to rhapsodic prayers. The friend and frequent beneficiary of Americans, he displays bitter hostility toward many of our policies. Writing on race, he has nothing but scorn for scientific work on the subject from the Smithsonian Institution. Flaunting his musical sensitivity, he dismisses Debussy and Ravel as unintelligible; parading names of the best-known painters, he visits Toledo and does not mention El Greco. He expects to be invited to occupy a chair of philosophy, although he has never taken a university course in the field, and his reading strikes one as less than organized. Almost madly a Mexican patriot and foe of imperialism, he is harshest on his own people, is contemptuous of the Aztec and the Inca strain, and idealizes the Spanish influence. It is indeed difficult to understand this Mexican.

And yet, it is just there that the fascination lies—there and in the question of his representativeness. I cannot overcome the feeling that there is more here than a puzzling individual. In many ways, he symbolizes the Latin American intellectual; perhaps if more North Americans had been familiar with this revealing autobiography, the ascendency of such leaders as Fidel Castro might have been less surprising.

The reader will profit not from attempting to extract from this volume an exact chronology of journeys, meetings, and departures, but from coming to know the man who experienced them and was endlessly reacting and reflecting. Nevertheless, Vasconcelos devotes so much space to that key period in Mexican history—the Revolution, which continues today—and his part therein after a relatively apolitical youth, that a brief outline of its events and actors may serve as an aid to those readers unfamiliar with the highly confusing recent Mexican history and as a refresher to others.

Díaz ruled Mexico as a Presidential dictator for a quarter of a century, and Vasconcelos, whose attitudes toward other political figures often shifted with the political climate, remained firmly opposed to his rule. Soon after Díaz's fall from power in 1911, Madero, whom Vasconcelos served and eulogized, but later came to judge less enthusiastically, became President; but by February 1913, his weak hold of the government could be exploited by his enemies. Victoriano Huerta imprisoned and later caused the assassination of Madero and Vice-President Pino Suárez. By mid-1914 Huerta was in trouble, domestically and with the United States. He yielded to pressure to resign, and, with the aid of Obregón, First Chief Carranza came into power. Other revolutionary leaders held authority in their regions; chief among them were Villa in the north and Zapata in the south. The situation between the divergent forces continued to deteriorate until it became imperative to reach some agreement. On October 10, 1914, the revolutionary generals and a few civilians began the long and troubled Convention of Aguascalientes, which was finally resolved with the "election" of Gutiérrez as provisional president. Carranza refused to resign as First Chief and, again aided by Obregón who returned to his side and by the American withdrawal from Veracruz, where he took refuge, he was able to maintain himself against the weak Gutiérrez and the divided and politically inept revolutionary generals. His end came in flight and violent death in 1920, after Obregón had turned against him. Obregón, recognized by the United States in 1923, was able to accomplish some of the objectives of the Constitutionalist leaders. It was during this period that Vasconcelos did his notable work as Minister of Education.

The chosen successor of Obregón was Plutarco Elías Calles. Adolfo de la Huerta led an unsuccessful revolt against the imposition of Calles on the country, and Calles became President in 1924, to be followed at the end of 1928 by Portes Gil. Morgan partner, Dwight Morrow, the "proconsul" so distrusted by Vasconcelos, so highly praised by most American historians and political scientists, was ambassador during this time. Vasconcelos subsequently ran for President against Ortiz Rubio as he recounts and, according to the official count, lost disastrously. This hasty survey brings us to a point at which Vasconcelos, "the young philosopher-revolutionary," at last felt justified in turning from politics to philosophy. A fuller account of the complicated story of the revolution can be read in two recent and admirable books by Robert E. Quirk [1] and John Watson Foster Dulles,[2] who strive to be objective and to bring order to a confused Time of Trouble. Each book also includes maps useful to those who feel the beginning of wisdom is cartography.

Vasconcelos never ceased to regard his mission as that of living, feeling, and transmitting a philosophy. But *A Mexican Ulysses,* which relates some of the ambitions, plans, and way of writing, reveals little of the content of this most original of Latin American philosophers. For a brief introduction, the curious reader may turn to secondary sources in English.[3]

His trilogy is Metaphysics, Ethics, Aesthetics. His approach is original in that he began with the last, and at least a glimpse of a monistic philosophy is achieved in his intuition that true beauty is conformity to divine order. Vasconcelos, who had never shown much understanding or enthusiasm for scientific method, finds that aesthetics, not science, is the way to truth, for it is super-intellectual. It is the proper way to comprehend the nature of things, it is divine, or participation in the divine. The hierarchy of knowing parallels the hierarchy of existence; the highest form of knowing deals with reality itself. There is amazingly little faith in reason, intelligence, or what we have historically known as logic. His logic—he calls it organic—coordinates wholes. As psychologically we perceive or experience wholes, so in the highest thinking we coordinate wholes. We do this when we experience the true aesthetic emotion. If the aesthetic method is better than the intellectual or scientific method, it seems also true that for Vasconcelos it is higher than the ethical quality. Romanell summarizes, "to him the sense of beauty is superior to the sense of duty." Looking forward to a volume called *Mística,* which he apparently planned to write, Vasconcelos exclaimed, "Mysticism is the belief in the intuition of the absolute, its method is an art which no longer manipulates forms, but content."

The importance of this personal account of a thoughtful man and his beloved country may be seen most sharply from the perspective of

1. Robert E. Quirk, *The Mexican Revolution, 1914–1915: The Convention of Aguascalientes* (Bloomington: Indiana University Press, 1960).

2. John Watson Foster Dulles, *Yesterday in Mexico: A Chronicle of the Revolution, 1919–1936* (Austin: The University of Texas Press, 1961).

3. Patrick Romanell, "The Aesthetic Monism of José Vasconcelos," *Making of the Mexican Mind: A Study in Recent Mexican Thought* (Lincoln: The University of Nebraska Press, 1952), chapter 4. W. Rex Crawford, *A Century of Latin American Thought* (Cambridge: Harvard University Press, 1944 and 1961), pp. 260–276.

Mexico today.[4] Is the Mexican culture nearer the ideals that were Vasconcelos' fervent hope? While the answer to this is not clear, it is important that Mexico has undergone a transformation since 1940 with the change in emphasis of governmental goals. Whereas Vasconcelos and his contemporaries were deeply concerned with the mentally and materially impoverished common man, the leaders today are concentrating on raising the level of production and industrialization. With a stable government and large foreign investment, Mexico has achieved a rapid and steady growth in national income. Despite this achievement, Dr. Lewis notes that Mexico has failed "to realize fully many of the social objectives of the Mexican Revolution. In 1960, over 60 per cent of the population are still ill fed, ill clothed, and ill housed, over 40 per cent are illiterate and some 45 per cent of the nation's children are not being schooled." Whether more even income distribution will follow this economic development is not certain. It is clear, however, that United States influence will continue to be prominent, through capital investments, tourist traffic, and imports of American consumer goods. English is the second language of the country and North American advertising can be seen everywhere. However disturbing these outside cultural influences and lagging welfare programs may have been to Vasconcelos in his declining years, he must have viewed with pride his nation's growth and leadership among the Latin American countries. As Mexico comes more and more into its own, some of the dreams of this devoted countryman may well become reality.

W. Rex Crawford

University of Pennsylvania
January, 1963

4. For an excellent picture of Mexico since 1940, I would recommend an article written in 1956 by the brilliant anthropologist, Oscar Lewis. See "Mexico Since Cárdenas," in *Social Change in Latin America Today* (New York: Council on Foreign Relations, 1960), pp. 285–345 for a revised and updated version of the original article.

PART ONE

A MEXICAN ULYSSES

A MEXICAN ULYSSES

I felt like a physical extension, a mere part of a warm, protective presence, of something almost divine. My mother's deep voice gave direction to my thoughts, determined my impulses. One might say that I was bound to her by an invisible, psychological umbilical cord which endured for many years after the breaking of the physical bond.

I cannot remember what the town of Sásabe was like in my early days. My memory of concrete things has never been good. On the other hand, memories of feelings come back to me easily. Little of that period of infancy remains with me. It seems that for some months, when we lived in the capital, I went to the kindergarten of the Normal School. I remember a patio which is probably the very one in which I afterward set up the University Press.

I suspect that fate was kind to us in the first years of our stay on the frontier. A child can appreciate this, even though he does not understand. My mother wore light dresses, she went about happily and seemed young. One day she put on mourning, but I did not ask why. Time passed, and one afternoon, at the hour when we usually read, she made me repeat a passage from a book called *Un hombre honrado* [*An Honored Man*]. It describes the marvelous way in which a man serves his country in evil days; he retires to private life when normal times return, wins the respect of all good men, and dies in tranquility, enjoying general esteem.

Mother's sobs interrupted my reading. When she had pulled herself together, she asked, "Who deserves such praise?" I hesitated and then said, "Juárez." "Yes," she said, "and so does your grandfather."

In Piedras Negras business was good. Public buildings were going up, the railroad shops were being mechanized, shops dealing in luxury goods and jewelry and big stores were numerous, but there was no decent school. In search of one, we moved for a while to the neighboring American town of Eagle Pass.

My first experience in the school there was a bitter one. There I saw

North American and Mexican children sitting in front of a teacher whose language I did not understand. Suddenly my nearest neighbor, a bilingual Texan, stuck his elbow into my side and said, "Hey you! How many of them can you lick?" I didn't understand, and he went on, "Can you take on Jack?" and he pointed to a red-haired boy. After looking him over, I replied modestly that I couldn't. "And Johnny, and Bill?" Finally, worn out by his insistence, I answered at random, "Yes." The boy in question was more or less my size.

As soon as we went out for recess, they formed a circle. Some boys came over to take a close look at me; others grabbed my books; one shook hands, and several gave me a push. Then my benchmate shouted, "This guy says he can lick Tom!" They put us face to face; they drew a line on the ground between us; the first to step over it was the braver. We rushed at each other, not at the line, and we fought. We stepped back and looked each other over; we fought again; after a while they pulled us apart. "O.K.," said my neighbor, "you come after him," and to me, "You're number seven." Puzzled and offended, I couldn't do anything but submit. The whole episode made me angry and I withdrew further into myself. I was a timid, sad child, subject to sudden fits of rage.

Anxious fears would come over me; for no good reason, I became profoundly sad; for long hours I stayed alone, wrapped in the darkness of my own mind. Paralyzing fears overwhelmed me, and then suddenly I would be a prey to reckless, frenetic impulses. "Go slow about making a decision, because when you do, you will be its slave." If someone had whispered this advice in my ear, it might have made life a lot easier for me. Darkness, helplessness, terrible fears, self-centeredness, such is the summary of the emotional life of my childhood.

As soon as we could find a decent place to live, we went back to Piedras Negras. It is in this house that my conscious life begins. I must have been about ten. We were glad the time in Eagle Pass was over. My mother had suffered a great deal from neuralgia there. Then, too, she was bothered by one of those things that leads to jealousy and recrimination. My father never failed to come home to sleep, but he began to arrive late at night.

My mother's elder brother, Esteban, was paying us a visit at the time, and he managed to calm her down. He had just finished his engineering course, and he spent a lot of time with books. He impressed me so much that I thought his learning quite unlimited. He used to discuss religion with mother, and they would both get worked up. Uncle soon returned to the capital. A few days after he left, mother sent me to gather some kindling. I lit a big fire and then I helped her throw into it a lot of bound and paperback books. A whole pyre of print went up in flames. "These books," explained my mother, "are heretical books!"

The most innocent of the games, and the most often played, was baseball. It never attracted me. I kept away from it, or contented myself with watching. At the most, if no one else was available, I undertook to be a fielder.

School had been winning me over gradually. Now I would not have exchanged it for any pastime. I never missed a class. All things considered, the school was very permissive and the teachers fair. The year we had a woman teacher I got my first punishment. I don't remember what I had done, but I was forced to hold out my hand. The blow I received was given with a will, but still without anger.

The fair-mindedness of the teachers stood out in connection with the arguments arising from Texas history. The independence of Texas and the war of 1847 divided the class into rival camps. We Mexicans in the class were not numerous, but we stood our ground. When I say Mexicans, I include the many who lived in Texas, and whose fathers had become naturalized, but who made common cause with us because of their descent. And if they had not, it would have turned out just the same, since the Yankees put us all in the same category. When it was said in class that a hundred Yankees could put to flight a thousand Mexicans, I got up and said, "That isn't so!" And it made me still more angry if some pupil compared the customs of the Mexicans to those of the Eskimos, and said, "Mexicans are a semi-civilized people." At our house, on the other hand, we believed that Yankees had just recently acquired culture. I would get up in class to argue, "We had printing before you did." And the teacher would chime in, "Yes, look at Joe: he's a Mexican. Isn't he civilized? Isn't he a gentleman?"

For the moment, this fair observation established a cordial relationship, but soon our passions were aroused again. We made a date for recess; blows were exchanged. The fight became a personal one. We went to the neighboring field. A large group followed us. We began to fight in earnest. From the beginning, I got the worst of it. My opponent beat me up methodically. Next day, at lunch time, while I was brooding over my defeat of the previous day, a Mexican fellow-student, one of those born and brought up beside the river, came up. "Here, take this," he said, handing me a sharp razor. "I'm lending it to you. These gringos are afraid of the blade. Keep it for this afternoon."

When we came out of school, my foe took up a position in front of his gang. I came closer, with my friends. I made him a sign, inviting him to fight, and at the same time showed the open blade in my right hand. "Not that way," said Jim, "the way we did yesterday." "No, not like yesterday," I said, "like this." My Mexican friend told me, "Now these gringos won't bother you." It was lucky that I managed to make myself respected in this way, for I loved the classes.

"Mama, what is a philosopher?" I asked; and she, as laconic as the catechism, replied, "A philosopher is a man who by the light of reason tries to find the truth." The word philosopher sounded to me full of satisfaction and mystery. I wanted to be a philosopher. When would I become a philosopher?

It began to be fashionable to buy one's clothes in Eagle Pass, on the other side of the border. It was cheaper than ordering them from Mexico City. And while the tables in the Mexican restaurants were deserted, in Eagle Pass new restaurants were being opened, with white tablecloths and silver-plated table service.

In the old days, taverns served their patrons individual glasses of red wine out of barrels imported from France or Spain by way of Galveston. At home we drank white Bordeaux. Now suddenly, beer won out. The bars offered whiskey or bock beer. At the beginning, people of taste preferred a good Madeira or Port or Sherry. But cheapness, abundance, the offer of beer mugs, the heat—all conspired to defeat wine.

Certain scholastic triumphs and the isolation forced upon me by my work had made me not only the best read boy in town but the most famous as a good student. So on one of the holidays, the Patriotic Committee decided to include me among the orators.

In short pants and with a few sheets in my hand, feeling very important, I marched in the procession beside my father. It seemed obvious to me that when I reached the years of those about me, I would be immeasurably superior to them. Even as a boy, I regarded myself as something apart. Visions of future glory appeared and disappeared, kicked up by the dust of our feet. The hour of my debut was at hand; my hands were cold, and I had a lump in my throat.

At the same hour, with the very same patriotic trappings, the same oratory, the same popular "enthusiasm," similar ceremonies were being celebrated in every village and city of the country. No wonder that I, too, felt moved. My weak, dull voice counted against me. An exaggerated timidity inhibited my movements and was in painful contrast to my inner conviction about the value of what I had written. In reality, the audience did not worry me; but gradually, as I read my composition, I lost interest in it; I saw defects in it and was mentally correcting them. I wanted to say, "This isn't good; it must be done over." But somehow or other I kept on reading, in a hurry to get it over, since no one was listening and the hisses were beginning. My father began to make signs, telling me to cut it short, but I didn't know how. I felt a flame burning in each ear. At last I finished. What I had written was not too long, but I had not known how to deliver it; perhaps it was just not in the right style for a speech. One thing was sure, I lived through agony. The crowd soon forgot me, but I kept thinking of my failure. My mother, hours later, found some consoling words, "You are not made for oratory; you'll be a writer, and that is better."

We left there, you might say, without any apparent reason except an unspoken agreement within the bosom of the family. The pretext may have been dissatisfaction with the new boss. The dominant motive, however, was our desire to find better schools for my sisters and to prepare me for a professional career. Taking advantage of the two months of paid vacation which the regulations allowed my father after I don't know how many years of work, we decided to move without knowing exactly where we would go. We wanted a job in the customs office in a place where there were good secondary schools. In this way, the family could remain united without standing in the way of our educational progress. By consulting our geography, we found that only two ports filled the bill: Vera Cruz and Campeche. No use thinking about Vera Cruz; only the pets of the government went there, and my father was not cast in that role. With absolute conviction, father began to assert, "We are going to Campeche."

Although I was very eager to go, to broaden my horizons and my destiny, I used to wake up at nights crying; I dreamed of returning to Piedras Negras after years of absence. I could see the streets transformed; people I did not know would look at me with indifference. Hanging around in the shade of the doorways, not a single friendly face. Bigger and higher buildings, but I hardly recognized the places I had loved. Showy construction, smooth pavements, a new and sumptuous Piedras Negras, no longer mine, had replaced the city of my childhood, a part of my soul forever lost.

I wept from the homesickness I expected to feel in the future. I did not suspect the delight which years bring. My psyche was bound to my environment, but actually it hurt little to leave people behind; it hurt much more to be torn away from the everyday sights. The trip would allow me to brag to my acquaintances as one who is going to the capital to achieve a glorious future.

One afternoon, at the close of school, a tall, correct, serious, kindly gringo called me. I walked with him the several blocks to his house. "It's too bad," he said, "that you should leave now, and interrupt your career with us. If your father would only leave you in the care of some family . . . you are thirteen now . . . when you are fourteen and have finished the course, I could get you a scholarship in the State University at Austin. Speak to your father about it, and if he is willing, tell him to see me. It will be easy to work out."

At first my father was offended; then he realized that such a disinterested offer deserved a courteous reply, a grateful one, and he went to give it.

So I let slip the opportunity to become a Yankee philosopher. A Mexican or Texan Santayana? Grown up, I might have become a university professor, teaching philosophy. But in those days I didn't go in for such modest futures.

My deceased grandfather left a widow and six children who lived in Tacubaya. They were experiencing hard times, but I hardly noticed this, as I did not have the habit of dividing humanity into the rich and the poor. My unawakened curiosity, my inclination to affection led me to like my relatives without prying into their economic level and without criticizing their peculiarities. Besides, it was not easy to make exact comparisons, since we were not on friendly terms with any rich people.

My Aunt María involved me in arguments which left me thoughtful. She was going through a free-thinking period. The teaching of Comte had infiltrated into the Normal Schools. I accepted without questioning the divinity of Jesus. My aunt listened and seemed to be in harmony with me, but discreetly she put into my hands the book that was the bible of her crowd, Spencer's *Education*. She urged me to read Rousseau's *Émile*, too. The novelistic form of *Émile* set me against it. María and I got into hot arguments on religion. My mother listened and came to my support, reinforcing my naïve arguments.

Auntie, firm in her college erudition, overwhelmed us with quotations and facts. Mother was worried; probably she consulted some confessor; it is certain that she, too, began to provide herself with books. Through my aunt I discovered ideas that were unknown in Piedras Negras, and my vanity decreased.

Then, too, my talents took a beating in the process of rubbing up against metropolitan sophistication. The carelessness of one of my sisters allowed my notebook of travel observations to fall into the hands of my Normal School aunt. I don't know how many people read it with delighted comments.

The move from Piedras Negras met with some obstacles; the two months' vacation with pay was extended without salary, and no other course was left to my father but to return to his job and wait for the slow unrolling of the red tape. Since he had not given up hope, he decided to return alone. But it did not seem to him a good idea to have us spend the time of waiting in a big place like Mexico City, with no friends to help us, and scanty financial resources. Near the capital, he thought, was Toluca; and its Institute was a well-known school. By exceptional good luck, the governor was interested in improving the schools. And there was the additional advantage that lodging and food were cheap there.

I enrolled in the Institute. My younger brothers went into the annex for children. The Institute provided such deficient teaching that it discouraged me immediately. I was taking, as I remember it, the last year of grammar school. There were forty or fifty of us in a classroom with a brick floor, laid on loose earth. The unpainted benches had been rubbed smooth by many generations of students. The teacher, half-Indian, slovenly and grumpy, was mainly concerned with impressing us with his superiority. From the first lessons I became convinced that the teaching was on a par with the furniture. Some of the textbooks were just questions and answers, and we were expected to memorize them. I started to be rebellious, and that only got me the black looks of the teacher. My patriotism was humiliated by having to recognize the superiority of the little town school of Eagle Pass. Could it be that a North American village school was better than the annex of an Institute that boasted of having produced Ignacio Ramírez and Ignacio Altamirano? Still, I made the best of my opportunity to strengthen my command of written Spanish. Doing so much in a foreign language had made me slow in learning my own.

In the geography class, I could not contain myself. It was all right to tax your memory in Latin or grammar; at least, I knew no other system. But in geography, so well taught in Eagle Pass, I would not take it lying down.

The sanctuary of the Institute was the library. I used to enter it with the same kind of feeling that churches produced in me. The room was not large, but you felt at home in it. From that day on I cherished the idea of some day building a bigger library on the same plan.

The right to use the library was a more precious thing than going to classes. I had never had such a number of books within my reach. I read everything with the avidity of a man acquiring a vice which dominates him completely. One thing led to another. Learning to read French was like an open sesame to new spiritual worlds. A history of astronomy fell into my hands; from that I went on to astrology and magic. It was not the techniques of the sciences that interested me, but the conclusions that were reached. In science I sought neither the abstract thesis nor the practical recipe, but the affirmation and the way to a concrete, living truth.

When the school year ended with examinations, relaxed by my facile success, I was able to give more time to reading. Usually I passed the mornings shut up in the library. It was my mother who put into my hands the book that was the main event of that whole period of my life; Chateaubriand's *Genius of Christianity*. We kept coming back to it as a leitmotif.

The intellectual life of Campeche was indifferent to religion rather than irreligious. The professors of the Toluca Institute would have felt dishonored if anyone had seen them at Mass. Many professors of the Campeche Institute, on the other hand, went to the Cathedral on Sunday, but they always stayed at the door, watching the girls go by. They would have been incapable of becoming interested in a theological argument. Their minds were not concerned with anything more than a line with the women and wisecracks. Their ambitions were limited to economic well-being and sensuality.

Once, on returning from the country, some of us students passed the part of town which we imagined as desirable and fearful, without daring to visit it. Imagination, whether I was waking or dreaming, added to the mysteries of the flesh, to my awakening sensuality.

It did me little good to go to confession once every two or three months. "Go and say an 'Our Father'," was all I got out of the confessor. It would have helped a lot more if he had said, "You will weaken your body, undermine your health, deprive yourself of future satisfactions." And so I had to wage alone the only struggle with which my mother could not help me. And yet, even in this matter,

she did give me a relatively useful remedy. Penitence for her was
not a word but a practice. She had accustomed us from childhood to
think of the punishment of the body as a useful mortification of the
soul, so it was hardly necessary to consult her in this particular case;
when at night a violent desire awoke me, I stuck myself with a pin,
which I had previously hidden in the hammock, and fought furiously
against the tempting images. But at other times, of course, nature won
the battle and I gave in with hopeless cynicism.

Campeche kept its distance from the confused reform movements
of the capital. It did not have to bear the burden of the proletarian
masses that fall prey to the demagogue, nor did it suffer the plague of
gilded youth. It had no racial problem, for, aside from sailors and Indian workmen, the white inhabitants had no contact with the Negro.
When I talked of "us Mexicans" my companions had their reservations. They were Campechans, and I was a *guacho*, that is, a man
from up there, on the tablelands, not fond of water, and vaguely suspect in his way of life. The national festival was to them the anniversary of their separation from Yucatán. The fifteenth of September
was the Mexican holiday. The State of Campeche had its flag, which
was unfurled on solemn occasions, beside the national tricolor. My
aggressive patriotism was so aroused that I turned imperialist: If necessary, we Mexicans would hang on to Campeche by force. What could
they do alone? Would they ask to be annexed to the United States as
Yucatán had once done? Would they, too, be traitors?

The Yankee peril, the great concern of my youth, did not affect
them. They had no idea of life on the frontier and of the intense conflict occasioned by a strong neighbor. They were not able to frater-
nize with the frontier Mexican, stubborn and masculine, but characterized by a lack of culture bordering on barbarism; not only on the
coast, but also in the center of the country, the frontiersman was
thought of as living in a kind of desert that Spanish culture had not
reached. Altogether, the necessity of always being on the defensive, in
which the men of the North found themselves, gave them a patriotic
point of view which the people of Campeche, in their disdain, lacked.
The lesson of nationalism reaches the people's heart only when they
feel the effect of economic rivalry.

When war broke out between Spain and the United States, rival
groups were formed in school, and the majority were for what they
called "the Cubans." I organized the group of "the Spaniards,"
and argued, "The same thing will happen that happened with Texas,
which, under the pretext of independence, became North Ameri-

can." And we fought with sticks and stones. The idea that we were preparing ourselves against a possible invasion by the United States made us indifferent to rain and sun, hardened our muscles, and made us insensitive to fatigue.

"Don Patricio wants to see you in his office," they told me.

I hurried to the headmaster, and the good old man told me that his daughter Sophia had been studying English for some time, but that she needed practice.

"Would you like to come to the house from time to time to read with her and converse with her?"

My parents jumped at the invitation. So I presented myself the first afternoon, quite bashful, my hair still wet from the bath, and worried because my shirt sleeves stuck out too far. Don Patricio made the introductions, talked a little, and then left me with the two ladies, my future pupil, who was not more than eighteen, and her mother. The good lady, perhaps aware of my timidity, touched upon the chord of Chateaubriand, and I broke into enthusiastic and complicated talk.

Gradually the three-cornered conversation about how we should go about our studies was converted into practice between the two of us. Soon we went from boring translations into reading together works more suited to our youthful interests. She put into my hands *Paul and Virginia* by Saint Pierre, always a classic for us tropical folk. Lamartine was also a much read author at that time. But the one sure thing is that it was Jorge Isaács' *María* that led to my first feelings of amorousness toward the young lady. Reading aloud one of the pages leading up to the tragic dénouement, she broke off because her eyes were filling with tears. I went on with the reading, my voice, too, uncertain, without thinking of the text, and disturbed by that living María. Without my knowing what was happening, I fell in love with the pallid oval face and loving eyes, the thin lips and smooth forehead, the abundant black hair falling to her neck, the perfumed fragrance of the tender maiden. I hardly looked at her when I was with her; but alone, I recreated her image and idealized her. Her thoughts, her gestures carried me away like the sound of haunting music. With this new love, the name of which I dared not say, a need of physical nearness was added to my habitual state of admiring ecstacy.

I owe to Sophia my introduction to the knowledge of life and humanity. From her I acquired that romantic illness which is never cured, from her I learned that mystery which makes bodies attractive to each other, whether or not the souls become united. This memory of her coincides with my sentimental awakening. Distracting me from dry philosophical and polemical reading, she touched me with the moving, the human; she enlarged my perspective on the world.

Examinations approached, and with them my last year at the Campeche Institute. On the wall of the corridor in the school I read over the parchments with the names of the winners of the first prize in each graduating class. Although my ambition was to be a star in the larger constellation of the Preparatory School in the capital, I did not want to go without leaving my mark here. My great desire was to be sure of the first prize this year. It was generally known that the first prize lay between Lino Gómez and me. Even more, it was common knowledge, and Gómez himself admitted, that I had the better chance. If I lost out, it was because of overconfidence. From the first year of the Institute, they had given us music lessons. My terrible voice never managed to hit the right notes; but the theory of music had an extraordinary interest for me. I turned the pages of treatises on composition in the library. In the meantime, my rival Gómez worked hard on his horn. He got the highest possible grade in music (and they were giving supplementary points for performers), while I came off with a merely decent "Good," in spite of all my hard studying. When they made the calculations, my lower grade in music cost me the first prize, which was fairly awarded to Lino, while I received honorable mention. My name was not engraved on the parchments that recorded immortality in Campeche.

Home had become sad. The absence of my father had already lasted several months and the whole family was making plans to join him in Piedras Negras, where he had gotten his job back. My mother hid as well as she could her distress at leaving me in the metropolis. In order not be separated from her, I then thought of giving up my studies. On the border it would have been easy to find work on the railroad or in business; she was not willing to give her consent, nor did I push very decidedly for this choice.

We tried not to speak of our pain and anxiety. The cold shivers of fever shook my body every night, and mother's fever lasted all night. As often happens with a change of climate, my malaria, latent on the coast, had reappeared. What she had was worse, but she would pay no attention to it. And it was not at the doctor's, but at the altar of the Virgin that she sought health—health, and also the strength necessary for me to overcome the perils to which she was abandoning me at the hands of the enemies of Heaven. She was worried about the dangerous situation that an education not merely secular, but positively hostile to the beliefs in which she had raised me, would create for me.

Before the tie between us was broken, it almost choked us, and we tried to relieve the intolerable tension, she by convincing herself that I was going to an heroic destiny; and I, by clinging to my ambitious yearning for a quick and brilliant success in the world. Still, the trial was a bitter one. During the final weeks, in order that we might talk more freely and late into the night, I put my bed into her bedroom. Like one who listens to sacred music, I heard her counsel and advice, not suspecting that they would be her last.

Classes took all day; but it was hard to fill the cruel hours of solitude between five or six—when classes ended—and dinner time. After dinner, homework kept me busy until midnight. The solution for those solitary twilight hours was finally the library of the Preparatory School. More than twenty thousand volumes were there for me to use, not to mention the six hundred thousand in the National Library, which I could also consult as I wished. That's why I was in the capital! At last, I was a member of the group that enjoyed the privilege of utilizing the vast resources of knowledge!

On religious holidays or on afternoons when I had no classes, I took one of the chairs in what used to be the Church of St. Augustine, badly made over to serve the purpose of a National Library. I was to catch the enthusiasm for science so characteristic of college students, and I read Humboldt's *South American Travels* and Reclus' *Man and Land*. The latter's opinions on the coexistence of races in America were the germ of what I was later to write on the same subject. I also went in for Buffon and Cuvier. But even in that period of love of science, I remained antiscientific without knowing it, in the sense that what interested me were not the details of investigation nor what was later called "behavior in the animal realm," but rather what science cannot explain in the meaning of the zoological in relation to the fate of man. I got along well in the field of natural history; on the other hand, my troubles and dissatisfactions with respect to mathematics grew daily.

My anti-mathematical temperament seemed to find a way out in mechanics; forms and masses lose their rigidity and take on a creative form, freeing themselves from crystalization into something finite. I read in my French textbook of mechanics that the world is not a matter of lines and of solids in movement through a Cartesian space of pure extension, but is rather the interplay of forces. It is dynamics, not statics, a sort of evolution of the objective world which is action. The whole world of objects ceased to be immutable and geometrical and became provisional, indeterminate. There would be objects as long as the soul needs them to find its way in the cosmos. Objects would disappear as soon as the soul found the truth—which is its last and supreme end—and made its jump, as it were, from the objective to the essential, from the human to the divine. This was the heart of the teaching of mechanics. And its symbol was not the sphere of the Pythagoreans, but the spiral which carries man upward and onward, or passes by way of man, broadening and progressing as it moves toward the absolute.

My glorious liberty lasted only a month. My mother, alarmed by my deserting the boarding house of the Misses Concha, where she had arranged for me to board, got in touch with some friends of hers and ordered me to take up residence with them. So I moved to the modest, but rather distinguished pension which two old maids from Oaxaca kept in the capital; their name was Orozco. In spite of their economic straits they maintained their contact with the colony of Oaxaca people in the capital; in those days, this was a powerful group. It was the boast of the elder sister, Miss Lupita, that she had gone to the ball given for Porfírio Díaz, Governor of Oaxaca.

"He bears the stamp of the hero," she said.

"Of the assassin," I interrupted.

"What do you know about it, boy?" she answered. "He is a hero!"

Why my violent reaction against the Mexican caudillo? I had not thought it out. Perhaps I merely absorbed my hatred from my surroundings. He was never publicly attacked, but you breathed in the very air a violent dislike of him. Still, politics was not yet part of my way of feeling; not even of my vocabulary. My world was the world of the spirit, and I had no time to look at what was around me.

Weeks went by, weeks of hard work but free from worry, and then suddenly, disaster came. I was entering my room whistling one evening, just as on so many others, when the maid said the Orozco sisters wanted me to come to the parlor. I found them quiet and serious; they asked me to sit down and handed me a telegram: "Carmita seriously ill; no hope." When I proposed to telegraph to ask for later news of my mother, they added, "Another message has come . . . Be resigned . . . What can we do for you? . . . We feel for you." Almost without a word, I retired to my room. An icy sensation ran down my spine and I threw myself on the bed, covering my face. My temples were beating so hard that I held them in both hands. I wept disconsolately.

An hour passed and they called me to dinner. I made my excuses and the maid brought something which I left untouched. Through the whole house there was a considerate silence which frightened me.

Later I took my hat and went out into the street. Like a condemned man I sought out the places where I had walked with her.

Thinking of the bed which would offer rest to my weary body, I was just going into my room when at the back of the corridor the face of my fiancée appeared. She approached quietly and had me sit down on the bench beside her. All the neighbors had closed their doors and there was no light. Her hand pressed mine, trying to convey some comfort. Overcome with gratitude and tenderness, I committed the stupidity of swearing to love her for eternity.

I can only blame silly romantic literature, without entirely excusing my naïve initiator, Sophia from Campeche, for this error which was to plague us both all our lives. The fact is that, feeling no support from heavenly powers, I took refuge in the flesh which intoxicates and brings forgetfulness, although really it is only using us as part of that absurd chain of passion which perpetuates the generations of human life.

It was September, two months before examinations. To give up and lose the year would have betrayed the very sacrifice my mother had made for me; it was a matter of honor to make her sacrifice worth while. At first I could not concentrate on my studies. But it was impossible to turn up in Piedras Negras with a disaster as the outcome of my year.

When I got my grades, swallowing my tears because I had no one to show them to, I looked upon certain top grades as completely natural, something that was due me. Nevertheless, a kind of childish vanity whispered inside me, "Well, you see, it isn't only in Campeche!"

The end of the school year brought changes of importance in the life of our house. During the vacation months the Misses Orozco went to Oaxaca, and my future brothers-in-law left with my fiancée. The last days I spent alone in the house with the maid. She often appeared in my room to chat. I paid little attention to her stories until once she said, "You ought to be named Castellanos . . . your father is a son of the priest Castellanos." I woke up to the fact that at home they never talked about my paternal grandfather. Whether it was true or false, the story worried me. It was not until many years later that I learned the truth: my father had been a bastard, not the son of a priest, but rather of a Spanish business man, well-off and even of noble blood.

My vacation was almost over when my father got a raise. They moved him from Piedras Negras to the same position, Inspector of Customs, but with a higher rank, in Ciudad Juárez. He must have been glad to be able to get his family out of a place which could bring them only sad memories. Hurried preparations were made to move the whole family.

The beginning of the school year was lively. Every professor unloaded on us an opening speech in which he gave an overview of all the subject matter he was going to cover. The classes were pleasant. On the other hand, outside the classroom the school was a poor imitation of a garrison barracks. For Director we had a Porfirista colonel, assisted by a dozen prefects who played the part of sergeants. They never allowed us to congregate in the patios or around the college, and when the main auditorium was opened, the watchfulness of the employees was increased. The fear that tyranny has of public assembly was very keen, even if we got together for nothing more than to read poetry or plan some social event. If there were more than five of us around a column in the corridor, right away a prefect would come along to disperse us. On the other hand, nobody stopped the student body from patronizing bars, houses of prostitution, and pool halls that were established right beside the institution.

Science was offered us not as a means to increasing human happiness, but as an end in itself, a neutral and beautiful thing which was worthy of one's entire devotion. This scientific enthusiasm I found attractive. It gave a new orientation and a concrete goal to my disenchantment as one abandoned by divine grace, bereaved of his mother's love, ignorant of Eros.

The lecturer in chemistry was a bushy young fellow, a kind of genius manqué. Praising the merits of the scientific discoverer, he would exclaim, "Perhaps here among us is the genius who is going to bring glory to Mexican science!" A thrill of excitement went through the benches full of students; we would have to make a great effort, the future was full of promise, and gratefully we thought, "Perhaps he himself is about to reveal some discovery of genius." The poor fellow was only a laboratory assistant, but we owed him moments of the purest and noblest illusions.

In the lecture hall, they systematically strangled our imaginations. "Don't give any credence to anything but the evidence of your senses; observation and experiment are the only valid sources of knowledge."

Our silly belief that we were in a new era, the snobbishness of a half-understood science prevented my recognizing that the marvelous calculation of the parallax and the amazing discovery of Neptune were only so many more cases of counting and recounting stars, the rise and fall of the waves . . . a human knowledge always limited by the bounds of mystery.

At the beginning of the century, I was installed in lodgings in a low house in the Callejón de Tepechichilco. A young poet from Jalisco, named Campos, visited us almost daily. He was taking law courses, writing verses, and getting drunk. We envied him. It was his idea to make a cooperative effort to publish a magazine. We did get out five or six numbers in small format. The heart of it was the poetry of Campos. In his undisputed role as editor, Campos assigned me my section of the review. Philosophy is what I had proposed; he corrected me: "Philosophy of art, that's what you're going to do."

After paying my last fees in the Preparatory, I had managed to enter Law School. It was important to do the year's work in the remaining six months. In the morning they gave us two or three hours of classes and the rest of the time we spent in conversation on the school benches.

Really, the best lesson is one we owed to Justo Sierra, years before Bernard Shaw said it: "Read Homer and Aeschylus, Plato, Virgil, Dante, Shakespeare, Goethe, and afterward read again Homer, Virgil, Dante, Shakespeare. Don't give much time to more or less illustrious second-raters; look to the heights!"

The whole approach of our teachers in the Preparatory School had been opposed to the play of abstractions. To free us from the vanity of such things, Bacon had invented the *Novum Organum,* the type of experiment which contains surprises, and can perhaps lead us to unravel the mystery. The Preparatory School of my day hesitated between the scientific hierarchy of Comte and the evolutionary doctrine of Spencer. Le Bon, Worms, Gumplowicz were beginning to be the leaders in sociology. From being positivists we went on to agnosticism, much to the alarm of the Comtian old guard.

I had matriculated in Law by a process of elimination. Having no aptitude for mathematics, I considered engineering forbidden me by my very nature. Having lived for considerable time with students of medicine, I had seen how they were expected to memorize the names of all the bones and joints. Lost in detail and embarked from the beginning on a career leading to specialization, the last thing they asked was the only one that interested me: the secret of thought processes, the theory of the will and the psychology of love. All that was rather to be found among the philosophers, and to study it there was no need to make myself resistant to iodoform. I should have liked to be officially and formally a philosopher, but under the new Comtian regime, philosophy was ruled out; in its place, sociology figured in the curriculum. Not even a course in the philosophy of history had been saved from the burning. They waged a war to the death against metaphysics. Logic was barely tolerated. On our own, and quite outside official courses, we had formed a group to study the philosophers. Antonio Caso, owner of a great library of his own, was reading away and preparing the weapons for his later work, the demolition of positivism. I was drawing up schemata of the separate periods of thought, from Thales to Spencer, relying on the histories of Fouillé, Weber, and Windelband.

The discipline of law was anything but attractive to me, but it had the advantage of assuring me a lucrative and easy profession. In the last analysis, it was my poverty that threw me into the practice of law. If I had been rich, I would have remained a laboratory assistant in physics or conducted surveys of general science. When I entered jurisprudence, I became aware of a kind of lowering of the standards of teaching. This was not science; at the most, it was applied logic and casuistry. The scientific reform had not touched law; it lacked a philosophic genius who would bring juridicial phenomena into the complex of natural phenomena.

Tired of eating badly in cheap restaurants and boarding houses, and also wanting more freedom, we decided to rent a complete apartment and do our own cooking. By eliminating the living room, the four of us were able to install ourselves in separate bedrooms and to have a dining room. An engineering student, Nacho Guzmán, acted as chief and treasurer. We handed over our share every month and he made the service arrangements. These consisted of an old woman servant who was mistress of the keys and cook, and her husky daughter. We occupied the inside of the third floor in a building with eight apartments. Those downstairs were very humble, occupied by workmen and laundresses. Those on the street front were inhabited by families that we scarcely ever saw, even on the stairs. Upstairs we were

lords of a flat roof, nice for studying in the evening, and for watching
sunsets, and neighboring roofs. At first everything was fine: we ate
well and chose the foods we hankered after.

I often cut classes and went with companions to medical clinics. I
came to know intimately all the rooms of the horrible Juárez Hospital,
which was at the same time an emergency hospital for victims of
crimes and all the excesses of the city and a general asylum for alco-
holics, liver cases, cancerous and rheumatic patients, venereal disease
and even leprosy. The quantity of horror you could see there in just
one morning exceeded anything the wildest literature can portray. A
female cadaver: the memory of it was sufficient to remove all possibility of voluptuous desires brought on by the temptations of the
flesh. The female cadaver: What good are such profound lessons to
youth crazy with the thirst for pleasure? So in spite of everything,
with our morning dose of corpses, at night we would chase any skirt.

The doctor, the high priest of science, penetrated with his ther-
mometer and his list of symptoms into the most secret parts of the laboratory of consciousness. Between the born criminal and the prophet,
there was only an accidental barrier. The mysticism of Saint Teresa
was a case of repressed eroticism. The charlatanism, half literature, of
glandular therapy and endocrine glands was about to start with Voro-
noff. The whole triumph of science, the triumph of the flesh, with its
rites of asepsis, sera, and bacilli trailed clouds of iodoform behind it.

It was better, with the madmen, to return to the world of abstract
ideas, in their home on the benches of the Law School.

My economic situation had not improved much, but that day I still
had a peso in my threadbare pocket, and I hesitated. I hesitated because in the bottom row of books there was a *Divine Comedy* for sale.
I don't know why my reading of such a famous book had been delayed. I was familiar enough with Shakespeare and the Odyssey, with
Goethe and even Milton, but first-hand knowledge of Dante had been
put off. True, it is hardly a book for the kindergarten, but my unlimited ambition had led me earlier to attempt more complicated reading.
I exclaimed to myself, "Happy and blessed! Happy to have been born
into a life that has also produced a Dante! Blessed by his love and his
flame!" How tiny my contemporaries seemed beside this great soul.
How astonishing, but how right is the self-assurance with which he
put himself among the six greatest: Homer, Virgil, Horace, Ovid,
Lucian. Strictly speaking, he should have listed three: Homer,
Aeschylus, Dante. The Romans can be left in limbo.

When I went back to textbooks in order not to flunk that year of study, the contrast was painful. Roman Law and Civil Law were circles of hell one had to cross without a Virgil or a Beatrice.

The date of the examinations was almost upon us, and quite aside from the little I had studied as a result of having cut sixty per cent of my classes, I was compelled to spend double time on the exam.

The rest of the curriculum—sociology, for instance—could be called literature; I had plenty of this from the days when I was killing myself studying in the Preparatory School.

My father had furthered my desire to get work; I would not have to interrupt my studies. His good friend, don Benigno Frías Camacho, District Judge in Juárez, would give me recommendations to his friends in Mexico City.

During the vacation, I spent the largest and best part of each day at home with my brothers and sisters. The youngest of the family, Chole, must have been twelve, and we spoiled her. I played with her, petted her, surrounded her with a tenderness that was almost paternal. The two brothers, Carlos and Samuel, spent most of their time in the patio with their animals; they had a playful little burro on whom they lavished their affection almost as if he were human. It was sweet to be at home again, where one could forget all anxiety, all the excitement of busy city life. With a lump in my throat and tears in my eyes, I tore myself away from this peaceful repose. It was the beginning of the school year; courses were starting; the winds of ambition and high destiny blew me once more to the capital.

To please my father I also presented a letter that I think came from some relative of my new stepmother. This missive got me into paying a call, always on Wednesday afternoon, at the salon of some French ladies who lived with their mother and a brother in what is now the Calle Uruguay. As far as always wearing mourning is concerned, they might as well have been Mexican, but otherwise they were the perfect type of blonde, gentle, delicate Frenchwoman, neither homely nor pretty, but perfect and hospitable in their manners. At tea time they served wonderful pastries, and I had learned enough of proper behavior to send a little bouquet of flowers on birthdays and holidays. I came to feel real affection and gratitude toward that family.

In general, my generation was skeptical and indifferent to religious questions. For myself, I adopted Comtism and the theory of evolution, and later Schopenhauer's voluntarism, as I did so many other stages of the long philosophical experiment that was to constitute my life. I accepted a mechanical cosmography, but not without a mysterious First Mover, and Spencer labored in vain to convince us that the appearance of Christ was an episode without major importance in the story of human development. What he could not forgive Christ was his not having been English.

What kept me from the Church was the intransigeance of its dogma. In this regard, Tolstoy was a great consolation to me. Following his way of thinking, I could once more regard myself as a faithful Christian. And I did not give up hope of solving the problem of the spirit, within the realm of the conscious, and without creating the dualisms that were attributed to certain Catholic savants—experimentation to arrive at reality, revelation to arrive at dogma. I longed for a monistic philosophy, a single coherent view of experience and insight into reality. In science itself I would find the path of the divine presence that sustains the world.

To arrive at God through experience. Not so much the mystical experience that William James taught in *The Varieties of Religious Experience,* as by the physico-chemical road that leads to the heart of the matter. I dreamed of making a series of advances up to the moment when reflection would cease to be reflection and would turn into the free act with a concrete goal, the pure activity of the spirit. This is what my whole life as a scholar was to be dedicated to. It was still on the level of schemes and plans. The time had not come to formulate conclusions, nor was my state of mind ready for plunging into the deep questions. I consoled myself by taking notes on the works that I would have to keep on reading, and beseeching my obscure destiny to provide the event which would lead to a vital change. I well knew what a disaster the actual use of my time was. Tentatively I made outlines, drew up schemata. In reality, my powerlessness overwhelmed me, although I sought excuses to which I could attribute it: that my style was confused and bad, and that it was not necessary to write, but only to live and think. Looking at the success of my comrades who were beginning to publish selected, polished works in prose, I yearned to have an easy, concise style that would lend itself to translation into all languages, and that would derive its value from its original and definitive content.

A message had arrived from Judge Uriarte. I had interviewed him, and he was sending me to a friend of his, a Notary Public who would pay me forty pesos a month. That very afternoon I was to begin work as a secretary. I ate in a hurry, brushed my clothes, and shined my shoes. The hour at which I was due at the office was close. Then

María Sarabia appeared at the open door of the room in which we were sitting. How eager I had been to find her! But it was just twenty minutes before my appointment. The surprise made me quite confused. She explained that she was just back from the country, had the afternoon free, and offered it to me. I kept looking at her and did not know what to answer. Contradictory desires pulled me in opposing directions. "I must keep my appointment! I'll leave you with my friends. Perhaps tonight?" I said. From that moment I was a marked man; I belonged with men of duty, not with pleasure-seekers.

When I returned home, the proper and careful Nacho broke out with, "How stupid you are! That woman came to give herself to you. You'll never see her again. She left in a huff."

That night my pillow received the first tears that were my tribute to the necessity of earning a livelihood.

The truth is that even then we students were noting the emptiness, the ideological poverty of the liberals and their European masters. Voltaire, Rousseau, Diderot—out of all the Encyclopedists you couldn't get a single real philosopher. The case of my employer was curious; he was the scion of a dyed-in-the-wool conservative, and was defeated. It seemed that a hopeless defeat had deprived him of his illusions while leaving him, in spite of everything, kindly and honest. He maintained a skeptical attitude in front of others, in contrast with his serene inner faith as a believer.

In spite of the friendly feeling I had for my employer, the routine of the work could not have been more painful. To have in your mind the ambition to write an essay on how Schopenhauer's will is transformed into aesthetic enjoyment, and in your hand a pen that is copying an inventory of furniture, is a refined and exhausting bit of torture. But not for a minute did I think of giving up the job; on the contrary, everyday I tried to become a little more satisfactory at it.

In reality I was far from having the strength of character or the love of learning which sets a man apart from idleness and the easy satisfactions of sensual life. In my student's room I would pass the early hours of the evening with my books, but the sound of a guitar strumming in the distance was enough to make the weight of the world descend on my shoulders. And I would abandon myself to the ocean of sterile daydreams—those terrible enemies of the soul, the wearing away of the imagination, mental masturbation. Desire would flame up. In the neighborhood to which we had moved, there were young neighbors who did not speak to us but did sing songs. The feminine voices conveyed an invitation. Often we went out to look for an opportunity, taking it if it was offered, stealing it if necessary, paying for it if we happened to be flush.

My stay with the Notary was short. The Judge assigned me a post in his court, the lowest on the ladder but well paid, thanks to the extras I picked up. These included honoraria for copying documents and for acting as an expert translator. At that time an infinite number of certificates, inventories, powers of attorney, etc., written in whole or in part in English, kept arriving from the United States. The lawyer presented them with his translation which was checked by an expert named by the judge. The judge habitually appointed the expert indicated by the client, but every time they left him free to do so, he named me. The new job took all morning; I had to miss certain classes. I was really overburdened with work. The hours at court were short but extremely wearing. And I was taking a double course in order to finish five years of law in three and a half, which I succeeded in doing.

It was said of our capital that it was a little Paris, but only because we copied the vices of Paris. There was nothing to recall the Paris of scientific discipline or of literary genius, much less the Paris of civil liberties!

Indeed, the capital of those days was not the cemetery into which later constant assassinations have converted it, but it contained the germs. The capital set no good example, and it did set the example of sordid pleasures, without the saving grace of irony and freedom. Every one of the little generals thriving under the protective shade of the Revolution heard tales of the vulgar orgies that went on in the underworld of the capital, and postponed the brutal satisfaction of his own desires until he arrived there. Their primitiveness did not allow them to give support to the values of metropolitan life: urbanity, culture, the love of music (which already maintained a symphony orchestra and a quartet), the good season of opera every year, the Italian theatre for drama and comedy.

Official action taken by Justo Sierra helped to develop the Mexican people's love of passionate, great art. The presence of important Latin artists brought life to our conservatory. Within the limits of its position in the new world, Mexico City was perhaps the only place to which artists flocked, not just for material rewards, but also for the applause of an interested audience with an ear for the finer things and a true love of beauty.

It was nothing but one of the many forms of sensuality that bound me to my fiancée. Looking at her attentively after several years of absence, I did not find in her that spiritual sympathy which makes love endure. The matters that concerned me, literary or ethical or philosophical, I could not begin to broach with her. During our conversations, if Aunt María was present, my fiancée kept quiet while I talked with my aunt. The silence which I took for agreement with my opinions was really nothing but indifference and lack of understanding. The discussions with my Aunt María were now reversed; she had been converted to the Church, and was so fervent a Catholic that she was about to become a nun. I was the Spencerian, arguing with the very woman who had first put a book of Spencer into my hands. We went together to hear the sermons of the Mexican Jesuit, Díaz Rayón, in the church of St. Francis. Díaz Rayón employed the rigorous argument of a skinny, strong, tough ascetic. At least, that is how it seemed to me in the only conversation which, thanks to María's insistence, we had. Perhaps I went ready to recognize the greatness of revelation and even to yield, if I could do so without being forced into it. What bothered me, I told him, was the Church's abuse of threats and anathema; I wanted works to justify, not faith. If a man was good he was saved, even if he was not a believer; if he was bad, he was condemned, even if he accepted the whole creed. I cannot accept, I told him, a God who is less merciful than I. I thought there was something inherently unfair in the theory of divine grace. The famous father had no time or sympathy for my doubts; he said I was full of vanity and pride, that all discussion was useless; and he dismissed me, much to the distress of my poor aunt. In reality, he drove me away from the Church for many years; I won't say whether it was his fault or mine, but it is a fact.

I say this without denying that my vanity was considerable and that it had led me to regard my own opinions as unique and wonderful novelties. . . . My Aunt María entered the Order of the Sacred Heart.

All my comrades produced writings full of citations and quotation marks. The books of Caso himself give evidence of this erudite tendency. The literati of my group could not, for example, make up their minds to write a novel; they spent themselves on commentaries and criticism of the work of others in the fashion of Henríquez

Ureña, who served as their mentor. Acting boldly on my own, I sought an analogy between juridical documents on the one hand, and the "voluntary act" of the psychologists, biological action, chemical process, and finally mechanics. Just as conflicts of force are resolved, so in a perfect society ought social conflicts to be resolved. I needed to discuss these matters, to talk out my ideas before writing them down. I began to talk to Caso about them, and he, with his savant's instincts and his clear vision, was very helpful. He did not agree with my approach; law for him was a social phenomenon; it did not appear where there was no coercion; it was not legitimate to think of law as a natural impulse, still less as a force.

When I showed my writing to Caso, before anyone else, he observed, "It is curious; you have written a lot of pages without citing anyone and without losing sight of your subject. It is rare to find anyone among us who is able to write this way. Altogether your work is original, and I congratulate you." His congratulations were sincere, for Caso, conscious of his own value, was above envy and by nature generous.

At home, my sisters Lola and Mela had for some time to put up with my abuse. Trying to immunize them against religious fanaticism, but with a cruelty and crudeness which it makes me ashamed to recall, I argued and contradicted them in matters of belief, and also on the fast days I had the maid serve me a plate of cold meat while they took codfish.

Another cause of disagreement was added to the religious issue. I learned from Grandmother that Mela was receiving the attentions of a suitor who dogged her steps in the street, a sort of village don Juan. Not very sensibly, but clearly and affectionately, I warned Mela about the dangers of these relationships. Both she and Lola made a lively defense of the fellow as a real gentleman and said they knew him better than I. Grandmother now warned me that Mela was talking with her *galant* on the balcony at midnight. . . . I broke in upon the lovers and gave the fellow a shove that landed him in the middle of the street. I kept clobbering him, not to lose advantage of my surprise attack. Although he was certainly the stronger, he put up no resistance. He tried to give explanations, to recall our schoolboy friendship. The next day the annoyance of my two sisters showed itself. "I was compromising them with this scandalous behavior; I had no right, etc." I pointed to my rights as the eldest, the fact that Mela was a minor, and peace was restored. The lover never showed up again!

A faithful memory could reconstruct the vision of the comings and goings of the person who worked in a little office beside the court-room, who looked upon the city as devastated and colorless; but what is hard to describe, or even to remember, is what was taking place inside that personality. To grasp the flow of inner life, diaries are written, but I never accustomed myself to keeping one. It always seemed useless to bother about the minutiae of the day. And when events were or seemed extraordinary, they were so out of the ordi-nary that there was no need to make note of them. Instead of a diary, I wrote in those days sketches for future books, notes about theses in philosophy and art with which I expected to shake the very bases of contemporary thought.

Apart from interest in my own fame, what moved me in those at-tempts was the necessity of finding a key, a formula explaining all life, a system coextensive with the universe. Finding this key was necessary not only for beginning a treatise on philosophy, but also in order for me to direct and organize my own inner life, so much in need of structuring. I suffered from the intoxication, the hypnotism of the Whole.

I penetrate with my loving vision into the heart of the object, and by conceiving of it in terms of beauty, I change its atomic bal-ance, I transform its mechanical balance until it becomes a joyful rhythm. All beauty bears the distinctive mark of a marching rhythm. Form has to leap over the boundary as the larva frees itself from the cocoon in order to become a butterfly. Without the miracle of rebirth there is no beauty. This does not imply a transition from one end to another, from a cause to a consequence, in the manner of physics, but a transmutation of dynamic values, above ends and causes, and directed toward the end of ends, the Absolute.

The characteristic of artistic intuition is thus an invention or dis-covery of those rhythms, which, departing from mechanics and the ordinary will, pursue the conquest of the Absolute.

Science discovers the laws of the movements of the concrete and relative. Aesthetics seeks the rhythm of that definitive goal which leads things and beings to reincarnation in the Divine.

These reflections may seem, may even be immature; but such a judgment does not detract from the great effort it cost me to arrive at them, as I lived the double life of a social slave earning his bread and a soul that must have leisure for the contemplative life which is es-sential to it. Or I should say a triple life, for not only does social con-tact demand our attention, the body, too, claims its part of happiness and ease; and everything has to emanate from a tiny spark of spir-

ituality which from time to time, little by little, may almost become
extinguished forever.

The social question was coming to the fore in Mexico; but in
Durango, an agricultural region, a strike was a rare and scandalous
thing. The two or three textile mills were used to treating their op-
erators like serfs who should be grateful for being exploited. The
official ideology, which looked down on the Indian, led some of us to
exaggerate in the opposite direction. We found in the Indian virtues which only needed an opportunity to be revealed. Within Durango and in the principal towns, the population is of European origin, almost white, but as soon as you leave town, you find the pure-
blooded Indian living under conditions that have changed little since
the time of the Aztecs. Through lack of courage and organized effort,
the Indian continues in his backward state, in spite of the revolutions
which from time to time raise him to power by way of the army and
its generals. In this way some emerge who immediately become
scourges of their own people, and the caste system remains untouched
because it is not enough to throw people out, to take vengeance as
revolutions do; we need to organize and to educate in statesmanlike
fashion. Although we did not suspect the tremendous upheaval of
classes—but not of values—soon to come about, even then wrath was
burning within us. In my own court I could take the pulse of tyranny.
Frequently, while passing judgment in cases of protection, although
I was a government inspector in the provinces, I found myself
recommending against the responsible authorities. They never
came down on me, probably because the errors that were of interest
to the government could be corrected in the Supreme Court. And
I must add that during the five months of my provincial activity,
there was no abuse serious enough to cause a scandal.

My heart beat wildly as I opened the telegram and read the conditions: "One hundred and fifty pesos and your professional independence; decide at once." I read it once more and reached for the
sheet of paper on which to write out my resignation. Liberty once
again! I left Durango, leaving there a piece of my heart, sadder than I
had arrived.

The Mexico City offices of Warner, Johnson, and Galston, New
York attorneys, are still intact on the sixth floor. On the corner is
a luxurious and airy room; that was Mr. Warner's office. The smallest
was assigned to me as an auxiliary lawyer. Without protest, I accepted
all the work that was dropped on my shoulders. It was laborious but

simple: legalization of contracts for the buying and selling of land or mines negotiated in the United States; organization of corporations; drawing up of contracts, collections, minor judgments.

My position in the office continued to be advantageous. Free from rivals but loaded with work, I consoled myself with the thought, "Give me five years of hard work, well-paid work, and I can retire from business to study and live."

So the time passed in law work and dreams of getting rich quick. My income increased, but so did my expenditures. Dissatisfaction with a job that was hateful and contrary to my tastes flooded over me every afternoon. In those melancholy hours, I bewailed the days that were going by without my filling them with a single illustrious action. My sisters were more or less arranging their own lives in suburban Tacubaya, and I was free to wander along the streets, to talk with friends on street corners, where fantastic propositions would end in some outlet for sensuality in hurried satisfaction that dulled the mind.

In the meantime, my old fiancée was in Oaxaca, but her brother Adolfo came to the capital frequently. One day he gave me a serious talking-to: he was displeased, I ought to put my relation with his sister on a more formal footing or break it off, I was making her waste her time for nothing. I expressed my intention of keeping my word and marrying her. I had not done so earlier and was in no hurry about it, in the first place because of the risk of children; I didn't want any chains, and perhaps I had some presentiment of the hazards that lay in wait for me; and secondly, I wanted first to put aside some savings to pay for the house before the wedding feast. I hated the idea of bringing children into the world without knowing where their food was to come from. What I did not say was that erotically speaking I liked change, revelations of new beauty. But my long-given promise was decisive. It would be a pleasant adventure, a clean love among so many filthy ones. One or two years together, then a divorce, American style, and each goes his own way.

For the nonce, instinct did its work well; I found my bride pretty. Right in Tacubaya we set up housekeeping with half a dozen pieces of furniture, several cases of fine wines and a jewel box for perfumes.

In preparation for the religious ceremony, I had had to go to confession. I was well recommended to the parish priest by the church activity of my sisters. I accused myself of all kinds of minor sins, no real exploits either of saintliness or criminality. I blushed with humiliation; in order not to risk losing the precious wedding certificate,

I did not dare, for instance, to say, "I don't believe in the resurrection of the body, nor do I desire it. I don't want to have to take baths for eternity, and I won't stop taking baths, for I have a nose. I am not Unamuno nor Swedenborg; I want a beyond with no sweat, so I will have to sacrifice my old hat to it!" I did not dare, and since I had not been entirely sincere, I did not take communion. This deprivation hurt me; it still does. Aside from questions of belief, I was restrained by the feeling of not being worthy, since I was guilty of the sins of appetite, of pride, of sensuality.

Like an outlaw I listened to the wedding mass, sorry I had not partaken of the wafer which is elevated during the mass. Perhaps it was to my own whole vocation that I was being unfaithful in undertaking pledges that were incompatible with my true nature as a solitary and a combatant. Without any doubt, half of the failure of all my subsequent career comes from that contradiction.

Doubts were put to sleep in the pseudo-philosophical discussions of our literary circle. Caso continued to be the axis of our group, but his apathetic and at times unsociable character would not have held us together without the collaboration of Henríquez Ureña. Brought up in schools of the old type, he was completely outside scientific theory and the movement of philosophical thought. In Caso's library or in the house of Alfonso Reyes, surrounded by books and celebrated prints, we talked nonsense on every subject in the world. We did undertake a careful reading of Kant. We got no further than the *Critique of Pure Reason* because we read it paragraph by paragraph, sometimes line by line. I brought to these meetings the sermons of the Buddha, in the English edition of Max Müller, which had recently been published. The powerful mysticism of the Orient opened higher paths to us than had scientific speculation. Our minds were broadened by that tradition, alien to our own, and vaster than the whole content of Greek thought. Descartes' *Discourse on Method*, the works of Zeller on Greek philosophy, and Windelband, Weber, Fouillé on modern philosophy, together with much Schopenhauer and Nietzsche on my part, and Hegel on the part of Caso—such were the subjects of our biweekly conversations.

My comrades were carried away by love of erudition. This was good, as the erudition of those days was dominated by the great figure of Menéndez y Pelayo. We all reread his *History of Aesthetic Ideas*. For myself, I never respected knowledge for the sake of knowledge. On the contrary: knowledge as a means to greater power, and in the last analysis, for salvation; to know as a means of reaching the essence;

morality as a ladder leading up to glory, without an empty Stoicism, such were my norms. Frankly, they were ways to happiness. No cult of that which is only the means or the intermediary; every effort bent on conquest of the essential, the Absolute!

In lightning flashes that caused me infinite delight, I captured concepts which I then set down in notes. My life now had an object since I had hit upon the theme needed to compose an endless series of variations, if not the complete symphony of a system. My notes of those days, incomplete, disorderly, unfit for publication, nevertheless contain the essence of what I have since developed.

I copy down one of the few notes that time has spared:

> The aesthetic sentiment is characterized by a reversion of the dynamic rhythm; instead of tending to constitute bodies, to integrate phenomena, the current of energy turns toward the pleasure of beauty and thus enters the realm of the divine. Aesthetics contains an effort which is just the inverse of ordinary effort. First, the labor of creation is accomplished, and in it our own spirit gains identity and a goal; then, with the personality secure, we begin with the aesthetic sentiment an overflowing and constructive stream, endowed with a goal. It does not keep on expanding indefinitely, but reverts to its source; it does not seek representation, but rather the absolute which begat and reabsorbs its creation. In all of this there are only different directions of the same energy, the same substance.

If the central thought of all my works was there from the beginning, this excerpt from my notes reveals what my memory also confirms, namely, that my ideas suffered from obscurity and a weak vocabulary, if not from lack of maturity. My body, worn out by the abuse of vulgar pleasures, was not capable of seconding the effort of my mind. There is good reason why the philosopher begins to produce after forty, when passion is spent, and not before.

The conviction of my failure caused long periods of sterility and hopelessness. Perhaps the best thing to do was to deaden oneself with work and to satiate oneself with small pleasures. But soon surfeit and the worm that ceaselessly gnaws within would again awaken my hope. It was important to work, to save, in order later to make the great withdrawal. For the present, social and family duty, and later, freedom for the cultivation of my soul, like the philosophers of all ages. Moments of solitude, of mystical exaltation would be succeeded by periods of hopeless struggle in the dark.

To utilize constant strength you did not know you had, and to clothe it with a sincere, serene human-heartedness. To combine thus greatness and tenderness. Such is my conception of genius.

The genius must carve himself like granite. He must be hard on himself in the first place, and toward others as demanding as the task necessitates. Circumstances and interests must all be for him a means to the conquest of that which must be, over that which is. For the finite, there is only one thing to do: cease to be "oneself" and move in the direction of the Infinite.

I now had two houses, that of my wife and that of my sisters. I was the sole support of the former and I helped my father maintain the second. In the latter house not all was peace and harmony. Little rivalries, arguments, and differences of opinion and taste often made life together bitter. Without any serious reason for hostility, the mere passage of time worked for disunity rather than for the disappearance of differences. My sisters suffered from the loss of close contact with me, and I could not be alone for a single instant. I kept hearing about their rights to my free person. I was continually reminded of what I ought to do, what I ought not to do.

Soon a new terror was added to the daily frictions. She had said to me, "Do you want children? Shall we have children?" And I had replied, "Why bring any more homely creatures into the world? Am I not enough?" But I was afraid; she was consulting doctors. Two years passed without any threat of offspring, but she did not accept this. In secret, she was plotting, seeking my destruction. There beside me, unpremeditated, was the danger, the threat, the enemy, although nothing of all this was put into words.

Meanwhile, there was a new loss in my sisters' house. Our Mela, our sweet, delicate Mela, the pride and joy of our broken home, fled to a convent. We could hardly believe it. We had opposed it. Our father, warned of the danger, had sent me a round, negative answer to her desire. She waited to reach twenty-one and on that very day she said goodbye, sent a letter to my father, sent me an embrace, and disappeared from our world forever. In the chapel of the convent, near our home in Tacubaya, the mass of death to the world was celebrated. My sisters and my wife were there. I stayed at home alone imagining every detail of that family disaster. The renunciation before the altar of all hope; the sacrifice of a happiness that was, if you like, false, but at least tangible. In my eyes, her step was a kind of suicide. With her departure, one more of the family was lost to happiness, abandoned to sadness.

Every time I returned with eagerness to the capital. Apart from the fascination of the country landscape, life in small towns always annoys me with its habits of playing pool and drinking alcoholic liquors. Return to the metropolis restores my peace of mind. Externally, the city is beautiful, splendid. The old architecture is noble, serene. The principal façades have lost their gray and are tinted rose or yellow. The sun never fails to bring out these tones. The air is transparent and the pleasant climate invites you to be in the street, to live out of doors. The sounds—the church bells, the melodious street cries, the noise of traffic, and the timbre of the voices—produce a symphony lacking any strident quality.

For some time I busied myself with the Hebrew cabalistic thesis, which sums up all knowledge in a single word. This it was necessary to find again, this magical, unique, single sign which would render quite useless all the pluralistic attempts to know through approximations.

It is clear that the gospels are the supreme model, but it is so far beyond and above literature that one cannot derive a school of writers from it. Better, to be sure, is the whole Bible. The immense literature of England has come from imitating it. But literature constantly debases its models. Philosophy has to be written in a sober, grandiose style.

Often, for a change, we went to the variety theatres. The audience was at the time divided into two groups, one composed of fans of a café singer of the Catalan school, Frenchified and bawdy; the other of followers of Amalia Molina, the Andalusian singer. I was crazy about the latter, and besides seeing her dance night after night, I sang her praises in our newspaper.

I owe to Menéndez y Pelayo the debt of having taught me who I am. When I discarded Catholicism, I did not replace it. All my immersion in Comtism did not make me an atheist. When I was a Spencerian, agnosticism meant to me an impersonal kind of theism, a kind of God-force that was infinitely conscious. But when I read Menéndez y Pelayo's book on the heterodox, I realized where I belonged. I was not an unbeliever, but a heretic. All religions seemed to me to possess some aspect of truth, but all the while I remained fundamentally a Christian and a believer. It was minor questions, really, that separated me from the Church. The Inquisition would have burned me, not for being impious, but for being a dissenter.

I have just referred to certain laudatory remarks about a dancer, which I made in *my paper*, and it is time now to tell how I came to be editor of a political weekly, without giving up my professional labors. The latent social distress of the country had at last taken definite form in the mind of a Mexican. His name was Francisco I. Madero; he was young and had resources and had just published a book: *La Sucesión Presidencial*. In this book he boldly analyzed the present and future of the country. I happened to be introduced to him in my own office, upstairs above the International Bank, in the street named for Isabel la Católica. Madero was passing through the capital and he preferred to look me up, in spite of the fact that I had manifested a desire to call on him at his hotel. Our first conversation was brief. He was looking for independent men, men of decision; he invited me to a meeting.

Our campaign plan, based on Madero's book, consisted of organizing the citizenry of the Republic so that, abandoning their thirty years of indifference, they would rush to the voting booths to elect the president of their choice. I chose the slogan which for so long remained official: "Effective suffrage, No Re-election!" Madero took no place on our committee because his mission was to tour the Republic organizing clubs, but before leaving he gave us two charges: to choose a man who would be willing to run for the Presidency against Porfírio Díaz, and to get out a periodical which would speak for the movement. I was one of those asked to visit the persons who might be called semi-independent. In every case we got a cold reception and met a skeptical attitude. Mexico had no hope; the ignorant rabble was an immovable rock. When Díaz disappeared on account of advanced age, he would be replaced by another dictator.

But in the meetings that we started to organize in the poor, congested districts, our success began to astonish us, and to alarm the government.

Collaborating with the intensive and very effective efforts of Madero himself, I took advantage of professional trips to organize clubs that then could function without me. The route of the Isthmus gave me fine opportunities: American capital was beginning to establish itself there in the fruit and sugar businesses.

The new United States ambassador was named Henry Lane Wilson, and we received him with enthusiasm on account of the speech in which he declared that any progress was ephemeral unless it rested on the solid rock of the Constitution. The phrase displeased the government, and was a windfall for the opposition. Besides, even

if we were not quite aware of it, the revolutionary ideology that permeated the country was a reflection of North American trade union-
ism. The doctrines that failed in the northern nation for lack of a
propitious environment found a better reception in oppressed and
desperate Mexico. North American leftist reviews and newspapers
that were free to print circulated in Mexico and spread stories of governmental outrages that we Mexicans could not speak about. The
dictator began to violate his own promise of freedom of the press during the election. One afternoon the police fell upon our paper. I took
refuge in San Luis Potosí.

There was an incident between Madero and me, by letter, which
arose from a certain weakness on my part. I explained to him that if
a rebellion was not prepared, I would leave the party, since I did not
wish to be the victim of a democratic movement directed against ruffians who would yield only to coercion and punishment. Madero replied without denying the rebellion and without pledging himself
to it. He warned me that my indecision would do me more harm
than it would the party. Finally, he took me back, sensible leader that
he was.

Anything rather than Mexico under Díaz—corrupt, militaristic,
murderous. Going home, I looked adoringly at my son, a few months
old, smiling and vigorous, and I thought, "I wish he might die if
this does not change."

For his part, Madero kept the faith. The enslaving power of
truth forced him to it. In his speeches he did nothing but talk to the
public just as he talked in private conversation. With one paragraph
of his Orizaba speech he wiped out royalism before the conscience of
the nation. This had been a party of the little people of the Díaz
regime. Jealous of the *científicos,* their rivals in administrative favor,
the royalists did not attack Porfírio Díaz nor his iniquitous methods
of government. They denounced getting rich under the protection of
power, but they sought the remedy in a change of underlings, and
they offered to work with the Caudillo. A large part of the lower bureaucratic strata was inclined to this kind of royalism. For lack of a
better flag to follow, public opinion hesitated an instant and began to
side with the royalists. Madero proclaimed that the evil was not in the
científicos nor the remedy with the royalists, whose leader had tyran-
nized over the people; the trouble was with Porfírio Díaz and his
methods. If Mexico wanted to achieve a place as a civilized nation,
she would have to get ready to condemn chronic despotism. A total
renovation of systems and of men was what was needed.

In private, Caso defended Porfírio Díaz to us, considered him the lesser evil for an ignorant people without hope. But ideologically, Caso continued to be the leader of a more important rebellion than that of Madero. The culture and talent of Caso, applied to education, avoided the return to the empty liberalism of the Jacobins. Although he founded no clubs, Caso's work was vastly more important than that of any militant politician.

The government had not underestimated the Madero campaign. It was not alarmed by the crowds that went to meetings, nor the flourishing of associations all over the country. But when Madero put his finger in the wound, when we dared to direct our fire at the very person of the dictator, open persecutions broke out. On the eve of the election, Madero, a candidate for the Presidency, was accused of insulting the President and was imprisoned in San Luis Potosí.

Frequently Warner sounded off in praise of his city. There was nothing like New York. What finally led me to accept his suggestion to go there suddenly was no desire to be served sugar in a silver spoon, but the hope of finding work that would enable me to continue to struggle without further sacrifice of my small savings while I waited for the revolution that would not be long in coming.

On changing trains in Texas my attention was attracted to the well-dressed people; they were carefree and quite different from our insecure, ragged humanity. Even as "greasers" we Mexicans enjoyed more human security than in the country of Santa Anna. We were no longer the prey of authority. The Yankee policeman smiled, joked with the passersby, and the few soldiers we saw did not feel obliged to put on the expression of Chinese torturers. In those days, we were really admitted through an open door to a "land of the free," the prototype of our dreams as democrats.

The train stopped for fourteen minutes in the Philadelphia station, and I was sad to be so near my brother Carlos. I had not notified him, partly because I did not know the timetable and partly because I expected to invite him to visit me in New York the next Sunday. Then we would have time to talk. For the present, it was better not to interrupt his night school classes. The Baldwin Locomotive Works occupied his days, and at night he went to a school for railway mechanics.

In those days the train went only as far as Jersey City. We crossed the river on a ferry boat. It must have been about eleven, and a fairyland illumination sketched the outline of the highest buildings on Manhattan and the banks of the Hudson. The line of the wharves stretched out interminably with the masts and stacks of the ships tied up at the piers. Everything one looked at seemed colossal. It was just an ordinary day, and yet the profusion of lights created an impression of a holiday. It would not have surprised us if suddenly the lights had all been extinguished, as happens when a fireworks display is over. But they shine this way every night. We were arriving at a city which had conquered darkness and where there were people on the move at all hours. The great metropolis is like a saloon whose owner took off the doors because business never stopped. The ferry left us at Twenty-third Street. A frightening metallic structure rattled away in the space above us—a kind of lighted dragon passed on wheels: the Elevated. I soon found the hotel that Madariaga had recommended: Mills Hotel. I have never forgotten it. They charged thirty-five cents. It was clean, thirty stories high, and it was inhabited by people midway between the tramp or vagabond and the gentleman fallen on evil days. A narrow but clean bed, in a tiny room with walls painted white, gave me, when I retired, the feeling that the whole trip had been a dream and that I was in a cell in the Mexican penitentiary. Besides, my body still felt the disagreeable sensation of a first meeting on Broadway. At nearly one o'clock, while I was wandering around taking in the high buildings, a lady of the night accosted me. It was in front of the Knickerbocker, famous for its suppers with marvelous women; but we took a mean side street; we went into an ignoble place, and all because my seductress was wearing a fur piece. After telling me she was Hungarian, she spoke only to collect her money.

Every night after bathing in the six-dollar-a-week boarding house, I had dinner in a popularly priced restaurant nearby. Always in a different one in order to find new dishes, although the type of food served was becoming pretty "standard." I would read in the local public library. There I began reading the Hindustanic books of Max Müller and Oldenberg, without omitting the theosophical chaos of Mrs. Blavatsky and Mrs. Besant. Their confusion gave me the idea of taking notes which later became my book, *Estudios Indostánicos,* meant to correct their distortions. They closed the library at eleven and I went back to my room and threw myself in bed, worn out but not sleepy.

I hated to return to my professional work. It was a nuisance to have so little money, but for a long time I enjoyed the complete solitude that an unknown person has among millions who are completely indifferent to him. It was a kind of monastic life dedicated to contemplation. Sundays I spent the whole day in the Metropolitan Museum. I studied methodically: Greek sculpture, with the help of the books of a Miss Johnson of the British Museum, plus Taine; Egyptian art I followed in the English summaries of Mommsen; for painting, Ruskin and Vasari. It was a delight to be able to consult in the library any book I desired. I could have gone on reading and thinking for years. And then, for relaxation, to look at some masterpieces of world art. At the time I cared little for the realism of Van Dyck and Velásquez and Rembrandt; I preferred the Italian paintings and the Ruisdaels of the New York museum. The incomparable rooms of oriental art with their collections of Persian lamps, Indian prints, Chinese polychrome statues, and pensive Buddhas did not yet exist. The Egyptian room was very fine. And the models of the Parthenon and of Notre Dame, the copies of Donatello and Phidias, the Roman heads, gave the beginner plenty to observe.

Everything would have been perfect without that headache and buzzing in the ears which bothered me, a consequence of lack of sleep, poor food, and accumulated fatigue.

Once or twice Warner wrote me; he advised me to return and offered to obtain a safe-conduct for me. I replied, thanking him for his friendship and explaining that our struggle against Díaz was one to the death. My fellow-fanatics also wrote. Madero, from prison, recommended that the struggle go on without faltering.

One day the mail brought me a terrible fright. My wife announced that she was getting ready to leave with our son to join me in New York. She was alone and I, meanwhile, was amusing myself in New York, and it just wasn't right. How could I explain to her what she ought to know? My situation, miserable enough for one, would be intolerable for two. What would we do if on the trip she used up the money set aside for food? I threatened her if she made the trip, but I felt better because I had been thoughtful enough not to give her a sum of money but only monthly checks that could not be cashed except as dated. I was confident that she would not find anyone to lend her money in my name, since I was an exile. I asked Warner not to advance her anything, which indeed he had never done for me either.

Mexico seemed now to be ready for an armed movement. The government, for its part, declared an amnesty. This, and the call of my party led to my decision to return. When my boss in New York learned that I had given notice, he came over to my desk and sat down beside me. I felt grateful to him and his staff. From the first they had shown me, with the frankness and generosity of the American of those days, their satisfaction with the way I did the work. I was a great translator, they asserted. He insisted, "Is it more salary you want? I'll pay you what you would get in Mexico. How much do you earn there? I'll pay you thirty dollars a week." Really, this was doubling my wage, but I answered, "The fact is, I earn a thousand pesos or five hundred dollars a month in Mexico." He stopped and looked at me and then as if he suddenly understood, slapped himself on the forehead, and exclaimed, "Oh, I get it; you're a refugee, a political refugee!" And he shook hands and wished me good luck.

A few days later I left New York on a Ward Line steamer, bound for Mexico by way of Cuba.

It was a pleasure to have money in your pocket and look forward to an afternoon and a night in Havana. Instinct guided us to the red lights. We spent the rest of the afternoon and part of the night there.

Back in Mexico City, I found little change; none in my family. We fellow believers held firm. Madero was preparing to flee. One lived in an atmosphere of conspiracy. In the office they gave me back my job. Loyally Warner admitted that they had not found any satisfactory substitute for me. Business was going badly, but Warner maintained that if power stayed intact and with the new re-election, peace would be sure and prosperity would come.

For all my idealism, my economic situation was not at all bad. I owed no man anything; I had not had to ask for a loan. The house was mine without any mortgage. When my son was born I had taken out a life insurance policy. If I were killed in the revolution, the insurance company would make a fuss about it. The main thing now was to gather together some cash for the next period of exile, which might be a long one.

The instructions they sent me were to be expected. As soon as the rebel groups grew stronger Madero would enter the country. At the same time, an Embassy of the revolution ought to be set up in Washington. Madero, knowing my experience in dealing with Yankees, had chosen me to be secretary there to Dr. Vázquez Gómez, who had already left Mexico and was in the North American capital. Diplomatic steps were even more urgent for border hostilities were beginning, with the Yankees stopping our traffic in arms and treating us as bandits with no program.

Within the United States both groups were active, carrying on dangerous tactics, sometimes leading to decisive results. Porfírio Díaz spent huge sums of money paying spies who betrayed the arms smugglers and tried in every way to have those of us who were working in the United States imprisoned. A brother of Elias Calles forged correspondence to make it appear that the laws of neutrality had been violated, and bribed railroad and telegraph employees. In Washington, Dr. Vázquez Gómez counteracted in every possible way the intrigues of the Díaz ambassador, who was trying to brand us as anarchists, demanding that we be expelled and handed over to Mexican authorities.

I stopped off half way, in New Orleans, to visit Pino Suárez, who had just fled from Yucatán. I found him steadfast, diligent, modest. I could not resist the charm of the place and stayed there two days. It was interesting at night when a fresh breeze blew and the pretty Creoles, a mixture of the French colonial and the Yankee, showed off their blonde coiffures, walking up and down the lighted streets. You could meet them, too, in the restaurants and theatre lobbies, daring and extravagantly adorned. Sensual women, brunettes, with very white skin and full figures. We are hardly men if we can see so much with no ambition to satisfy our appetites.

In the world of those days, New Orleans was listed among the capitals of sensuality and libertinism. At the far end of the gay district, there was the market place of Negro beauties with lots of white clients. A prejudice that I still could not overcome—a sort of pity, not really charity, but rather a childish repugnance—kept me away from the colored race and did not allow me to sympathize with the dances and shouts of the vaudeville Negro. The existence of those millions of human beings outside the range of our fellow feeling provoked in me a violent protest against what nature had done, against the unequal, stingy distribution of her gifts. Some got the power, the beauty and the glory, and others the physical curse of a subhuman face, and in their souls the ambition, the intelligence of the powerful and fortunate. It was only years later, in a trip through the Antilles, that I reached the point of genuine fellow feeling with the African. For the moment, at the time of which I speak, I left New Orleans with the stupid moral attitude of one who merely pities his brothers, the Negroes.

The first advice they gave me in Washington was to exchange my wide-brimmed hat for a new one. And as my expenses were charged to my own humble account, I lived in a room I got for six dollars a week. During the first day, I played the tourist, from the obelisk to the library and the ugly capitol. At night, in a luxurious hotel, I received the press at Captain Hopkins' table. Dr. Vázquez Gómez received me affably enough but gave me nothing to do. He kept to himself, and only once in a while invited us to dinner.

A series of beers or whiskey and sodas, shared with Central American diplomats, sustained us until midnight, the hour at which the correspondents came, giving us the news for the following morning and collecting whatever we had to give them. At two in the morning Hopkins, to counteract the effects of innumerable drinks, would order a Welsh rarebit. The necessity of somehow placating the gentlemen of the press—nice fellows and in many cases brilliant—helped me become accustomed to the whiskey which at first I hated. My great disappointment was the lack of feminine company at these alcoholic parties. Hopkins' son used to introduce us to marvelous women, but I didn't have money enough even for a taxi fare. Poverty, and not virtue, is responsible for my staying in my miserable rented room. Expenses kept going up and my funds were quickly exhausted.

There was no doubt that fame was beginning, and with my new post I would have to watch my clothes and my behavior, and the accursed necktie that was always sliding around. And a gringo friend had advised me to change my hairdo, which I wore brushed straight back, and to try parting it, and to shave off my beard. And indeed, the success that I symbolized in Washington (the capture of Juárez and its garrison by the patriots) was worthy of the enthusiasm it was calling forth. Once again, it was proved that murderers are never brave. The moral effect of the taking of Ciudad Juárez was great; it was only a matter of deriving from it all the profit that the precarious situation of our movement required. As soon as the customs house fell into the hands of the rebels, the diplomacy of Porfírio Díaz raised the question of closing the frontier. Our mission in Washington was to secure recognition of a state of belligerency and to reopen international trade. The Díaz Embassy won, the followers of Madero who had just conquered Ciudad Juárez could not import munitions and foodstuffs. The interests of Yankee businesses on the border were on our side. The policy of Taft, favoring Porfírio Díaz, condemned us.

Madero, then, patriotically, valiantly, without worrying about whether the people might return to him or whether he might be executed the next day, gave up his power, and from being a victorious general reverted to simple citizenship without privileges or command. The worth of Madero was his own outstanding personality. Those who did not follow his example did not survive for an hour the moment when they were despoiled of their command. Porfírio Díaz, also, with his resignation (as required by the treaty) became deserving of the respect of his enemies. The level of national politics temporarily reached a height that is most uncommon in our dark and lamentable history.

On the same day on which, as a result of the treaty between Díaz and the revolutionaries, our agency in Washington went out of existence, I left the Yankee capital without calling at the Mexican Legation. I was eager to get back to my profession and to strengthen my shaky economic position. During my absence I had had a daughter born to me. I had one more mouth to feed. By way of goodbye I sent Carlos a little money, telling him that I would soon send for him. One of the things I regret most in my conduct is not having taken him with me right then. We should have gone back together.

At the Convention of the Constitutional Progressivist Party when I loudly cast my almost decisive vote in favor of Pino Suárez for Vice-President, a shout went up amid the hisses of the opposition: "You got yourself a Ministry!" Such a stupid insult convinced me that our side was right, and to all who would listen I said, "I earn more in a month in my office than a Minister does in a year."

The only failure in the new policy glorifying the Spanish influence sprang from the first visit of Manuel Ugarte. When he stepped from the gang plank the malcontents trapped him, and the intellectuals of the old regime surrounded him. They fed him the line of the calumny that was being circulated: "Madero had conducted his revolution with Yankee money." Porfírio Díaz fell, they assured him, because he refused to give oil concessions to the Yankees. We hated to descend to the level of denying or discussing such nonsense. The trustworthy official registers of both governments prove to anyone who will take the trouble to consult them that all the oil concessions were given in the time of Porfírio Díaz. After his time there were no more concessions, and Madero never awarded a single one. About me, as one individual, the newspapers said that I would not attend functions in honor of Ugarte because I represented North American companies. It is a fact that at the time our relations with the Yankees were excellent, on account of the moral support they had often given us.

Public prosperity, stimulated by the influx of foreign capital, was on the increase; the foreign investors did not ask for special privileges and excessive gains, but only the security of a bloodless change-over from the dictatorial Díaz regime to one of democracy and culture. Everything pointed to a series of governmental leaders who would not be abortions from the barracks nor chiefs of roving bands, but university men with ideas, the same as in the rest of Spanish America, not to mention Europe and the United States. In my law office, I could easily see the effect of renewed confidence in our nation. The Light and Power Company was working on the extension of an electric line to Puebla, which, as Dr. Pearson claimed, would constitute one of the most daring routes across a splendid landscape, between peaks of volcanoes.

Dr. Pearson was one of the most extraordinary men of the day. His origin was lowly. As professor of mathematics in a New York school, he achieved fame by solving in public competition a problem for the New York Subway. He used the fifty thousand dollars he won in the purchase of a yacht, which carried him south in search of rest and sunshine. He stopped in Rio de Janeiro. Visiting the plateau near the coast, he saw at once the possibility of deriving electric power from the water which pours down to the coast, and conceived a brilliant plan for supplying light and power to the most beautiful bay in the world. He raised the capital, left the work under way, and set sail for Barcelona, where he worked out another vast plan for electrification. Moving to Mexico, he created the electric plant of Necaxa. When I became acquainted with him, he was dividing his time among his operations on three continents. In the railway car, he was accompanied by secretaries, typists, engineers, lawyers, and a trainful of helpers that his terrifically active brain kept busy. He would work until he became ill, and then after a rest start over again.

It fell to my lot to have an interview with Pearson about a vexatious problem. One of those bureaucratic engineers was objecting to approving his plans; he was refused the right to acquire land by right of eminent domain, thus leaving him at the mercy of landowners who were taking advantage of him. I don't remember the exact words, but he said to me with his usual vivacity, "Use twenty-five or fifty thousand pesos to overcome their resistance!" Quickly I explained to him what the Madero point of view was—it had been sold to him as a matter of sheer demagoguery—and how fatal it would be to us if we tried to pressure people with offers of money. In an instant he understood, begged my pardon, and agreed to go along with a change of plans which would have meant something enormous in world electric development if Madero had not fallen, and if later Carranza had not grabbed the company and milked it while the English were occupied with the war with Germany.

I never saw Dr. Pearson again, for he never stayed very long in any one place, but he left with me the impression of a man of genius. I saw in him a vague resemblance to Madero, in the quick way he got an idea and in the frankness and clarity of his thought. When he died in the torpedoing of the Lusitania I thought to myself, "The waters have swallowed up the magician who, while he lived, was their master."

On the night when the news of the election of deputies began to come in, I dined with Francisco Madero in his parents' home. Nothing was known of the results. After dinner we went to the theatre to wait for news, and in the presidential box Madero learned of the triumph of many friends, and not a few enemies. We all celebrated the contrast between a democratic President who learned the names of the elected Congressmen along with the public, and the old President, who made up the list of Congressmen months before the election.

Rumors and denunication began to pour into my office. Generally I paid no attention to them. The low-down, unscrupulous tone the struggle was assuming was disagreeable. Money kept coming into my strong box without my taking a peso from the government, but even this flow of gold saddened me. What I was doing was far from the meditation I thought was my destiny. I now owned lots of luxuriously bound books, but they were only a decoration for my library; I had no time to read them. Now that I could buy them, I could not read them.

At times, some piece of business that brought in little but involved a big idea pulled me out of the rut, arousing my enthusiasm at the prospect of doing something constructive. We were on the point of setting up an association which would have built a modern city facing Tampico, in the days immediately before the rise in prices caused by petroleum hitting its peak. My bank account really did increase. A good part of it was spent, but some still remained in the savings account. I well knew how to make a solid fortune without any kind of risk. Buy an apartment house, repaint it, and then raise the rents: make a sure thing out of human misery. The poorer the dwelling, the greater the profit of the speculator, but this kind of money made me sick. It was better to go on earning and spending.

He who has lived through hard times and suddenly becomes well off gets the itch for useless expenditures, wastes his money on meals in sumptuous restaurants, expensive cognac and exotic caviar. My nights in luxurious places reserved in advance proved to be very expensive. Mexico City in those days tried to be a little Paris. What with autos, champagne, sojourns of two or three days in nearby country hotels, life passed in delight. One day, going along the Esmeralda, I bought some diamonds for four or five thousand pesos.

Adolfo Valles was my confidant and friend. He had been since the dramatic days of the conspiracy against Díaz. Since law school days he had had a reputation for loyalty, elegance, and bravery. Tall, thin, with a narrow face and a big nose, gentle eyes, and elegant gestures, he was a kind of North Mexican musketeer. Fencer and orator, for many years he kept his place as sabre champion and President of the Debates of the People's Jury. His clear-headed talent, his tolerance, and his honesty made him an inimitable judge. It was our common love for walks in the woods that brought us together. In conversation, he was as sensible in dealing with philosophical themes as with matters of women and society. Early experience and a knowledge of good books had given him poise and benevolence. He lived a quiet life after having squandered first his father's, then his mother's fortune on a life of pleasure. A skeptic in politics, he discharged his duties in the government honorably, and was a good father to a family that grew larger every year. A shrewd judge of men, he had no illusions about the Republic. He served the Díaz regime loyally without being blind to its errors and without severing friendly relations like ours, which had soon become compromising. Almost always in our discussion, it was he who was right.

Early in the morning, on bicycles or horseback, he and I alone or with some other friend would traverse the beautiful roads of the park. On the terrace of the famous hotel we would have a breakfast of fruit, coffee and marmalade. If it was Sunday, the ride lasted all morning. Together we once saw the exciting silhouette of Adriana. She was wearing a tight-fitting black dress with a single flower on her breast. A dark lace hat brought out the paleness of her skin. Her haughty, distant look seemed unaware of the murmur awakened by her harmonious walk. From the opposite sidewalk we gazed at her, in a halo of light, until she disappeared among the crowd. And Valles said: "Good Lord, brother, this is a serious business; you turned pale just looking at her!"

Valles did not share my excited political passion, but he did not fail to give his frank opinion on the men who threatened the future of the Republic. His fair, balanced judgment left an impression that was noble and calming.

I was happy, with that happiness which surpasses thought, measure, or comparison. Happy in my flesh and bones as if a vigorous new body had by Divine Grace been conferred upon me. The vision of her eyes, half-closed in delight, followed me perpetually, in-toxicated me. Now my senses were of some use to me. Through every pore ran the same longing, and satisfied desire made a new man of me. Before, in other amorous adventures, right after the pleasure came satiety, if not disgust. Now the pleasure was so deep that to re-member it was to burn with a living flame. To drink and drink again and feel one's thirst grow! Bodies pressed together and joined with-out exhausting the soul's longing. Language does not encompass, nor any image sufficiently express the deep drama of that enjoyment which sets music vibrating and makes the soul long for union. Like one digging in a bottomless abyss, the sensation of the infinite grows, destiny itself yields. The whole universe seems to work toward a mys-terious consummation.

Now I felt the bitterness of lifting my little children in my arms to give them a warm kiss on the cheek, thinking at the same time of that other kiss I had just given as we were forced to part. I thrilled to think what life would have been together with my new beloved. My Only One!

The least important thing that happens in these cases is what was now taking place at home: discord even in small matters. Frequent annoyances, from how to make the bed to differences in matters of taste at the table. An indulgent attitude, growing out of guilt feelings, now characterized my behavior! The situation was aggravated by a flood of useless expenditures which would have exhausted the greatest wealth. I didn't have the courage to oppose the entry of guests and relatives. Besides, there were the stupid servants who didn't have sense enough to keep the coffee hot. Gradually, I had adopted the habit of eating most of my meals away from home; but when there was a guest, out came the fine wines, wasted and unappreciated among the ordinary drinks, consumed just to show off and do the expensive thing. If I made any objection, there was the immediate scorching reproach: "You spend more on your girl friends!" I felt remorse for being happy, crazily happy, and seeing discord at home. To relieve my own feelings, I opened my purse strings and money that might have been saved for a rainy day poured out uselessly.

Some laughed at the candor of Madero, and others showed irrita-tion because he did not commit brutalities, but very few understood his intention of establishing a precedent that would transform for-ever the shameful rhythm of our history. In Madero, as has often been said, the "apostle" prevailed over the "politician." But what good is a politician who has to descend to the level of the ruffians he is fighting? It was easy to censure Madero after his fall. Many, even among his best friends, said he had ruined the chances of Mexico by his blindness or by his faults. Nevertheless, now that we can see what he accomplished in better perspective, we reaffirm that he was the one who was right. For now we can see that it is not worth while to last a few years longer than Madero lasted, to fall as Carranza and Obregón also fell, not only having failed, but having lost the people's respect. How much better is a clean defeat in which the hero is still an example, an honor to a whole people, rather than the ignominious failure of those who go down after betraying their principles. If the saving impulse which Madero sought to impose upon the country did not find favorable circumstances, so much the worse for us, so much the greater his glory. When Mexico decides to rectify its frightful errors, it will have to take up the course of national regeneration where Madero left it.

I took advantage of an opportunity to talk at length with Madero during his morning ride in the Park. I tried to make him see the necessity of a reconciliation, and even the predisposition of Henry Lane Wilson, the new American Ambassador, to achieve it. "You can't imagine," Madero said, "the series of impertinences we have had to put up with; the other day they wanted me to raise my voice, but I wouldn't. Now they will find out what happened under Porfírio Díaz. Now the American Ambassador no longer runs the country. At least," Madero confided with a smile, "he hasn't much time left. In a few months Woodrow Wilson will become President of the United States, and he is my friend. The first thing I will ask him to do is to change Ambassadors. This Henry Lane Wilson is an alcoholic; he puts himself to sleep every night with champagne."

The Madero government appeared stable. Three rebellions had been put down with lightning speed. The mass of the population was contented and lived in freedom for the first time in its history. Prosperity was real. The railway workers were organized, the workmen of Orizaba growing in social and political power, the miners winning more security and better wages from the companies. Madero would never have fallen if treason had not defeated him. Even the strongest is helpless against that. You don't say Lincoln was no good because a madman shot him. It is as unjust to accuse Madero of falling because he was weak; he was much stronger than many who lasted longer. Madero humiliated his enemies on the field of battle and in the higher struggle of morality against crime.

Along with the moral transformation of its character, a transformation was taking place in the economic life of Mexico. From the pre-

Colombian era there had been civilizations on the plateau, but all were in ruins, and not comparable to European civilization. The economic reason for this inferiority was lack of fuel. The Díaz regime believed progress was achieved because an automobile reached Mexico City, but in the houses of Mexico City they were still cooking with charcoal as in the time of Montezuma. The first firm to bring gas to the city was organized under Madero; part of the pipe was laid, but then came Carranza who did away with it all. The work is still unfinished.

Dr. Pearson saw the opportunity which lay in the industrial use of the numerous waterfalls resulting from the uneven terrain. All that was needed was to add a little human ingenuity to what nature had already contributed. Mexico, without coal, could be the country of water power, and for this very reason predestined to ultra-modern industrial development.

I have always felt the need of being alone one or two hours a day. Perhaps this is only a remnant of the examination of conscience which our mother insisted on before we went to sleep. When I got home, I would shut myself in the library. After violent arguments, I had succeeded in keeping the servants and even my wife out of that room. Only my children played around me, broke things, pulled things apart—for children do not disturb thinking. (It is the cunning, inquisitive look that drives one crazy and prevents work.) Not even the noise children make is a distraction. I isolated myself again after a little supper. The soul finds its nourishment in hours of solitude. Not to spend a long while completely alone every day means, as it were, not to allow the soul to wake up. I had found one inconvenience in living with Adriana; the fatigue due to an unending dialogue.

We learned that Concha was returning to Mexico City after her novitiate in Chamartín. They were sending her to the college of the Sacred Heart in Guadalajara, and when she went through the capital we could see her. It was the first time I ever stuck my nose into the convent. My mind was tortured by a silent protest against the brutal injustice of fate which distributes happiness so unequally. I thought of what we had not said in her hours of doubt and anguish, and then of the way in which we accepted the inevitable. I had a violent pain in my throat. As we parted, I made an effort to keep back the tears. Barely had we gotten outdoors and into the auto when I burst out sobbing in broad daylight.

There was something worse: Concha was attached to a rich, active order; she traveled frequently, and her daily work as a teacher was a distraction. On the other hand, Mela, through humility, had chosen a contemplative order of the most modest kind and was shut up for life in a big old house in Tacubaya. It hurt me so to think of her that I did not want to see her. Periodically, I would send her some present: a cask of French wine, a phonograph, some provisions, sometimes money; but I was afraid of seeing with my own eyes what seemed to me intolerable suffering. When she heard that I had visited Concha, she sent word insisting I should see her too, which I finally did.

Madero never promised the impossible, no matter how much his enemies labeled him a demagogue. In his first speeches to the workers of Orizaba, he reminded them that the secret of prosperity lies in work, not in the trickery of systems which flatter one or another segment of the population. Without arousing the Indian against the white, he began the task of wakening the defeated race, without proclaiming himself a member of the right or of the left, he was ever thoughtful of the welfare of the lower classes, but never became involved in bitter hostility toward the exploiters.

His statesmanlike vision went beyond the economic sphere. During his term of office, public instruction got its first stimulus to expand. In the best days of the Díaz administration, the budget for education was never more than eight million pesos. Madero raised it to twelve, and with this increase he financed the first Federal schools in rural districts. He disapproved of the University because of its positivistic tendencies, which he wanted to see replaced by a more spiritual attitude. His efforts to spread education were related to his desire to strengthen democracy. From the beginning, our society has suffered periodic invasions of the barbarism of the countryside as it sweeps through the centers of culture formed in the cities. Every revolution has been a savage unleashing of forces which have swept away the transplanted values of Europe so laboriously cultivated by mestizos and native-born whites. Our cities are islands in a sea of ignorance.

From the days of the Missions, the difficulty of penetrating the Indian masses has explained the perilous position of the Christian idea, disseminated in an environment which deep down is still Aztec. The transformation of the underlying Aztec way of life is an indispensable condition for Mexico's securing a place among civilized nations. As long as the masses are not educated, the system of human sacrifices will continue, whether the Montezuma is called Victoriano Huerta or Plutarco Elías Calles. Madero felt all this boiling under the crust of the democracy he was implanting. The old blood-thirsty instinct was unappeased. To stamp it out, he trusted the power of his own example, and he trusted his schools. Given ten more years of Madero's schools, the Carranza movement would have been impossible; men like Orozco and Pancho Villa would never have appeared again in our history.

Only a few more weeks and the change of government in Washington would liberate us from our hated Ambassador. A little more diplomatic fencing and with Taft's going out of office, the notes would stop, the course of international affairs would change. However, the Ambassador was making similar calculations, and so were the traitors who hung around the foreign Embassy. With a shamelessness which seems incredible, they not only planned, but signed a document which they published when they triumphed: The Pact of the Citadel, a rascals' treaty, an agreement of matricides. In it the conspirators worked with the agent of Washington to destroy the only legitimate government in all Mexican history.

The telephone rang a few hours after dawn. Only my colleague in Tampico knew my hiding place, and his communication was the stunning news that the revolutionary, General Reyes, just after being freed, had been killed in combat. Madero was a prisoner in Chapultepec. Tampico was calm, and so was the rest of the country.

In fact, Victoriano Huerta was hastening to the Embassy to see the leaders who had risen in treasonous revolt.

The Ambassador was in a hurry. His tour of duty would end on the fourth of March, and it was already mid-February. The success of the anti-Madero rebels depended on having their coup d'état recognized by the American government.

Scarcely were the corpses collected, when Madero assembled the few who were with him and appeared on the balcony of the Palace, intending to call upon the people to aid him. Outside, totally deserted streets proved how careful Huerta had been to isolate his prisoner. In any case, the people had not wanted to rise. On an earlier day, after printing a proclamation calling the people together, we had driven in a government auto through the poorer districts where we had formerly been strong and had had friends. Everywhere we had gotten a cool reception. And they were right, for we had no arms to give them; the city did not belong to us. Within a week, the traitorous commandant, under the pretext of unifying his command, had dismissed the ministers and taken over all the government services. Anyway, it is much easier to arouse a people to overthrow a government than to defend it.

Retiring from the balcony, Madero understood that his only hope was to get out of the Palace alive. Outside he could find forces to support him. Going down by the private elevator, he found the anteroom below empty. But when he came out into the corridor, his progress was stopped by none less than General Blanquet at the head of his battalion of illiterates. With the rifles pointing at him, Madero faced the men, cried, "Halt!" and exclaimed, "I am the President of the Republic! Put down your arms!" There was an instant of hesitation, then Blanquet advanced, trembling, pistol in hand: "Surrender!" he stammered.

Everyone knows what happened later. The Chamber of Deputies could have saved Mexico if it had resisted the pressure of arms. But for the most part the chiefs of the groups on the government side failed. Not more than half a dozen deputies voted against accepting Madero's resignation.

It surprised some people that a man of Madero's caliber was willing to resign. He did it because he felt unsupported by the people, and because he was told that this was the way to save the lives of all his friends in prison.

There was another unspeakable resignation; that of Madero's Minister of Foreign Affairs, who according to the law, would immediately become President; he resigned on the instant, so that the Chamber could name Victoriano Huerta as Interim President. Some people who took part in these events excuse their cowardice on the pretext that by surrendering everything to the traitor, they saved the lives of President Madero and Vice President Pino Suárez. Paralyzed for the moment, the nation watched this downfall, fascinated by the final fate of the high who had fallen so low.

At the same time, the new government was receiving news that the public did not get. In various parts of the country there were uprisings following the flag of Madero. In the United States, there were meetings in various cities protesting the way the Ambassador had liquidated democracy in Mexico.

Arriving home, I was ashamed to embrace my children; I felt humiliated at the idea of passing on to them a country that had fallen so low. Our country was not worthy of Madero.

PART TWO

THE STORM

THE STORM

I review in these pages one of the most confused, perverse, and destructive periods in the life of our nation, and also the time in my own life that was most sinful and sterile, and during which my energies were most scattered.

A prophet, in the widest sense, is one who announces truth and justice to the people. And there are times when the prophet must keep quiet out of self-respect. For people who hear the truth and do not passionately follow it do not deserve prophets.

By my side, Adriana, with her fresh skin, her undulating walk, her amorous laughter, her voluptuous figure, moves closer or farther away, as if responding to the eternally contradictory desire of Adam that lives again in every man, and sometimes rejects, sometimes desires the contact of glorious Eve. At times she is the scourge, at times the most desirable treasure of creation!

Soon a modest but tasty dinner was ready. We had no more than touched it when loud knocks sounded on the wooden shutters. Pistol in hand I opened the shutters, but no one was visible in the street. Only some hours later, when I went to the streetcar stop on my way to Tacubaya, did I catch sight of two fellows with the characteristic appearance of spies, who were following me at a distance. In a few days we changed houses.

One morning when I came out to take the streetcar, Pancho Chávez appeared in one of the unpaved alley-ways crying, "This time, yes, Counselor! Three times and out! You are my prisoner, on orders from the top!"

Forcing a smile, I replied, "Congratulations on your success, but the fact is that today I have no reason to run away."

Jovially, Chávez began to recall the earlier times when I had escaped him, when he had arrested someone else, thinking it was I, when on the bank stairway, I told him, "He's upstairs there, your Counselor Vasconcelos," and left him outwitted.

Autos were scarce at the time, and even under Huerta there was not the official extravagance that came in with Carranza; so Chávez, in spite of his position as Chief of the Security Commission, didn't have his own car, and he and I and his agents simply took the trolley. On the way, he gallantly offered, "If you have any urgent business or want to make a call, we can go to your office; I'll give you half an hour to put your affairs in order, and then we'll go to the stationhouse."

From my office I talked on the phone to Adriana. She would be left more alone than anyone. My family would not lack relatives and friends; but she had left everyone to go with me. I told her, "Don't worry, I don't think this will last long, and above all, don't inquire for me, don't take any action, don't let anyone see you asking favors."

Afterward I telephoned to my home. It was the custom that the prisoner should have a bed and mattress brought to the prison. "As far as meals are concerned," I told them, "don't worry about that; they will send them in from the restaurant."

The meal arrived, well chosen and abundant, and with good wines. I made the mistake of gulping it down, which gave me a terrible headache in the afternoon. Experience allows me to pass on the advice that you should eat nothing the day you are arrested; the involuntary and unconscious flow of bile is so great that it leads to indigestion and trouble that you can easily avoid by fasting. As a matter of fact, this is the thing to do in case of any pain or serious trouble.

I spent the afternoon alone, but surrounded by the presents which friends began to send in: boxes of sweets, flowers, wines, even whole hams.

Insomnia bothered me for hours; the prison noises disturbed my calm. Before six, the service boys began to sweep; the sentinels changed guard. I got out of bed completely exhausted, and without the comfort of a bath, prepared to meet the confrontations and vexations of the day that was beginning.

Somebody sent in the morning papers. Every one of the vile sheets, which for generations have been poisoning the moral atmosphere of Mexico, dedicated to me the usual insulting, libelous statements: I was a dangerous fanatic and had benefitted by the fallen regime. With the protection of Gustavo Madero I had grown rich. The justice of General Huerta had at last caught up with me.

Do the exiles who talk about their troubles when they are abroad do any real harm to their country? What tyranny has not talked the same way since the days when the free souls of Greece rose against local tyrants? And could you call Huerta and the Huertistas the fatherland? They were not that, but if they had been, if they were, it would be the duty of a clean conscience to deny a fatherland which has become identified with criminals. To Hell with all the hypocrites who then and later blamed me for speaking ill of my country abroad! In every country the primary, urgent task that cannot be put off or excused is to repudiate regimes based on crime, hatred, repression, and murder.

My escape was abetted by a Yankee client who took me to have lunch at his house; then, in his car, with his wife, just as if we were going for a drive, he got me out of town and dropped me at a station platform. There I would wait for the railwayman who was going to accompany me. At four we would board the train for Puebla. We thought there was less watchfulness in that train than in the Vera Cruz express, which was loaded with spies. We were traveling without luggage. All my stuff would come after me, sent to a third party, who would see that it got on the ship. The spying conductor seemed satisfied. My friend gave him tickets for the bullfight. In Apizaco we got off, and after offering the spy a beer, we shut ourselves up in a little room at a second-class hotel. There I waited for the eleven o'clock train. The train arrived on time, and I went to bed in the berth my friend arranged for, after putting me in the care of the Pullman conductor, who was a friend of his.

I slept so well that they had to wake me when the train was near the end of the line. I had barely dressed when the Pullman conductor called me aside and, taking a list out of his pocket, pointed and asked, "This is you, isn't it?"

In about fifth place I saw my name, preceded by those of other politicians of the Madero party. Seeing that it would have been worse to try to deny it, I admitted it.

"The police gave us this list," explained the conductor, "with orders to let them know by telegraph if anyone on the list gets on. But in your case last night's recommendation by your friend is enough, although he didn't give me your name, and anyway I am a Madero follower, and I wish you lots of luck."

He instructed me not to get out at the station with the other travelers, because agents met all the trains. When we stopped, he locked me in the toilet. There I waited for his signal and then went to the street through the rear of the station. In full daylight I crossed the necessary streets to reach the home of the Fabera family. They received me with every kindness, and that same night got me on the Ward Line boat leaving for Havana the next day. I spent the morning shut up in my cabin, but when they were getting ready to sail, I decided to take a walk on deck. At the foot of the gangplank official agents and soldiers were examining the papers of those who were going and coming.

To celebrate the escape, we Madero people shut ourselves in the bar, over glasses of beer or cognac, the worst things in the world for seasickness. The next day the weather was bad and I didn't get up.

Finally, with the lack of discretion which is part of my make-up and was also appropriate to the circumstances, I confided my secret to my cabinmate Valenzuela. This was that Adriana certainly was sailing in the German ship that left Vera Cruz a few hours after ours and would reach Havana a little before ours. I sang the praises of Adriana. Prudently Valenzuela remarked, "In the long run, this is going to make difficulties for you."

But no warning makes any difference if the greatest happiness in the world is coming behind you on a first-class ship.

From Havana I wrote to Carranza. I put myself under his orders and informed him of the steps taken by the Huerta crowd to get a loan in Europe. If he wanted to make me his representative in New York, I could move on from there to London at my own expense.

The reply of Carranza reached me in Washington and was a disappointment. He sent me my credentials as Confidential Agent in England; I was to take the Plan of Guadalupe with me. This was a tasteless declaration by which Carranza named himself First Chief of the Constitutional Army, charged with Executive Power; all under the authority conferred by his own proclamation, with the signatures of half a dozen unknown and ignorant men.

In Washington, I talked to my old friend Hopkins; then I moved at once to New York. In both cities I managed to get the press to take my preparatory statements for the campaign I proposed to wage in London.

In Washington especially, opinion was on our side, as if President Wilson wished to undertake to repair the damage done his country by the disloyal activities of Henry Lane Wilson, the dismissed American Ambassador.

In New York I again joined Adriana, and together we took the steamer which in six days left us at Southampton. We spent the time of the crossing being seasick and reading guidebooks like Reinach's, which are good preparation for doing the museums.

We walked through the center of the city until we were tired; we went to inns, made an appearance in the lounges of the great hotels and at the night shows eager to get an impression of the whole of

London night life. You don't see much in these first glimpses into
the inner life of a great city, but there remains with you a confused
memory of a sea of humanity and of multiple mysteries that no
quieter vision can quite destroy or correct.

Worn out, our heads a bit giddy from the Port wine we had drunk,
we fell into the high bed of a German hotel I had chosen because of its
proximity to the British Museum. And the next morning, after a good
bath and better breakfasted than we could have been in New York, we
took to the street, ready to forget our own century, to abandon the
contemporary, in order to dedicate ourselves entirely to seeing and
worshiping the sculptures of Phidias, taken from the tympanum of
the Parthenon to the greater glory of the British Museum.

It was in the hall of Phidias, if I am not mistaken, that we noticed
a sign that told a lie and was insolent, to boot, toward everything
foreign. "These works," it said, "were rescued by Lord Elgin, who
brought them to England to save them from the neglect of the natives." Everything beautiful in the museums of London comes from
other lands. The British have created nothing in art. And unless you
have the tolerance to look at the Gainsborough ladies with their big
hats, and a few splashes of color by Turner, everything worth seeing is
the work of other civilizations, other peoples. Hence the impression
produced by these London treasures is that you are on a pirate island.
For two or three centuries, really, an imperialism characterized by
cupidity and tact has been accumulating riches, assimilating the re-
finements of creative countries like ancient Greece and the decadent
East. But the English are not brave conquistadores in the Spanish fashion, but claim to be liberators, and their very piracy is subordinated to
the complex that Bernard Shaw studies in *Arms and the Man*—the
necessity for giving a moral justification for one's actions. The in-
scription I have quoted is a typical case of insular ethics. On the one
hand, it defends Lord Elgin against the obvious charge of piracy, and
on the other, runs down the party that was robbed, declaring him to
be unworthy of keeping the stolen treasure.

There is, to be sure, the political aspect. Individual liberty is an
English or French, or better still a European advantage, and it is a
precious attainment of civilization; but even the conquest of a system of social institutions is reserved by the Englishman for his own
island, and he does not extend it to subject peoples, nor even stimulate
its development among friendly nations. They have been in Mexico
and in every country of America, always supporting the dictator who
gave them commercial advantages. Don't talk to me about the aid they
gave Bolívar, for that was the case in which their interest was the most

direct of all, a case of deceitful collaboration in a war in which all the advantages were with the English; and all of the evil consequence still weigh upon us, who from having been Spanish provinces have come to be nothing more than colonies, trading posts of the Anglo-Saxon.

My sharp critical judgments did not always find an echo in Adriana, who seemed to object: "That isn't in my books. Where did you get it?"

Since I thought of myself as an inventor of revolutionary points of view, I was discouraged by the fact that Adriana did not recognize in me what I thought was the best of myself—my spiritual call to define ideas, to coordinate doctrines. At the same time, my awareness of her ignorance converted my affection into something more human and profound, since it did not contain that element of admiration which creates distance, and which later on in life usually separates us from those we would like to win over by affection alone.

Without that devotion which the British Museum and the National Gallery call for, and only as a tourist's duty, we visited Westminster Abbey, Baedeker in hand. The history of England, summed up there in a series of mausoleums, did not deserve much more attention from us than it gets in a guidebook. The great men of England, with the exception of a few poets, do not attain the rank of universal men by a long shot; hence, the Abbey, which is the National Pantheon, impresses only the natives. The traveler knows that even from an architectural point of view he will find on the Continent many other structures more worthy of the limited time of a first probing of Europe.

By working on the lawyers furnished by my old friend Hopkins, I managed to get a specialized newspaper to publish my declaration that Carranza would refuse to recognize any treaty concluded with Victoriano Huerta, and then, on the advice of the same lawyers, I decided to transfer my headquarters to France, from which center it would be easier to work, and where, in the long run, the bonds that would be issued would have to be sold.

Before leaving, we again visited our favorite theatres. In one we had the luck to see one of the first performances of Shaw's *Caesar and Cleopatra;* in another we saw Molière's *Médecin,* given by a French company. Another time we listened to the London Symphony, and on our only night at Covent Garden we heard Caruso, the famous Metropolitan singer, who raised prices in Europe and filled the halls.

Suddenly, in one of the museums, I came upon the portrait of a well-known master, at least the official master of my generation, educated partly in the British tradition. I refer to Spencer. There he was, with his broad forehead, his squinty eyes. The only Englishman who had succeeded in formulating what today is called the "vision of the cosmos," but it had lasted so short a time that, as Frank Harris tells us, in his last years the philosopher of evolution stopped up his ears in order not to hear that socialism and not evolution was the doctrine of the immediate future. The portrait of Spencer recalled the thought of Darwin. It was said in those days that *The Origin of Species* was one of the supreme books. Very well, but today it is proved that evolution may affect species, but has no influence on the development of man and of cultural processes.

I concluded, then, by judging that we were leaving behind us two novelties that had just been mummified: Spencer and Darwin. They did not survive their own generation, and yet Spencer—the great pedant and master plagiarist—not only denied Kant and Nietzsche, he even allowed himself to look at human history without mentioning Christ, who, he said, had no influence on the evolutionary development of the species.

Along with the Nelson statue, there is one other impressive monument in London: the arch dedicated "To the English-Speaking Peoples of the World." An imperialism more widely extended than the Roman, and smaller only than the Spanish Empire of two centuries ago, it is curious to note that what the Anglo-Saxons practice is contrary to what they teach: racial and linguistic unity. And we, who think we are imitating them, divide Spanish America up into little countries! Imperial union based on language ought to be not just an ideal, but a tradition and the basis of patriotism. The restoration of the unity created by the Spanish monarchy, but in the modern form of a Society of Nations, a community of people of Spanish speech, including the Philippines: how many people in our continent have the brains to grasp this simple proposal? On the other hand, let anyone examine the teaching of those who have rated as our statesmen during the lamentable nineteenth century, and he will find only lackeys of English thought, lackeys who keep repeating the ostensible doctrines of "The English-Speaking Peoples of the World." And I refuse to make an exception, there is no reason for making an exception of the greatest: Juárez, Sarmiento, Alberdi. What would they have said, what would they say today if they came back and someone set them down in front of the London monument to the unity of race and language? Those who thought they were being modern by acting as detractors of that which is Spanish would tear their garments when they saw themselves reduced to what they were: mere agents of the cunning imperialism of the Anglo-Saxons.

For myself, I can say that I too was brought up in the hatred of our Spanish blood, combined with a doctrine which presents Juárez as a savior, a doctrine which did nothing but hand over the soul of our nation to the Yankees. Thus educated, and accustomed to speechifying against Spanish obscurantism and in favor of an abstract liberalism, there, in front of the monument I felt for the first time in all its profundity the bitterness of defeat at the hands of the invincible. For in the last analysis freedom is no use if it is won by complying with foreign enemies; this is the stain upon our Independence, this is the reason we have not succeeded in winning for ourselves true Liberty and Independence.

Paris: We were in France; soon we would be in Paris.

It was customary then for every person of quality, as he approached the Intellectual Capital of the World, to put himself in a worshipping attitude and exclaim: "Paris, Paris, at last Paris!"

One thing is sure: you enter it without any appreciation of the whole because of the flat terrain and the tunnels, and the first impression, even on that clear June day, was completely banal, to use a colorful Gallicism.

Endless lines of grey houses, neither high nor low, all alike with that insufferable mansard roof, and dark, narrow lobbies, with their dead façades, for the climate forces them to close the balconies. We got a room in a boarding house near the Grand Hotel, and immediately rushed out. There is nothing better than a carriage for seeing a city that has something to offer. The automobile is made for Yankee cities in which there is nothing to see twice. The Boulevard des Italiens was crowded with people, and was really inhabited by Italians with their stores and pastry shops. Paris in those days was cosmopolitan and authentically Parisian. After the war it became nationalistic, adopting uniformity of customs and driving out everything exotic. It is the exotic that gives life and interest to a great city. I would not exchange that old Paris for the Paris of today. Its air of distinguished antiquity and other respects made me think more of Mexico City than of New York.

Going down along the quais, beside that slow, illustrious river, we had spread before us the panorama of distinction and magnificence which we had sought in vain in the outskirts of the city, and which now fully justified the enthusiasm of the devotees of the great Latin city. In the background, on its island, Notre Dame; at the left, the Louvre; at the right the buildings of the Palais de Justice and the spire of the Sainte Chapelle; I don't know how many centuries of history, with an architecture perfect of its kind—the architecture of the Gothic Cathedral, expressed on a more modest scale in palaces and bridges. With the horizontality of a region without hills, it was inevitable that a desire for the vertical should arise, and this was expressed in the towers and spires of the Gothic style.

In London the excessive politeness, the constant changing of clothes by the men, the conversation always centering around income, had given me the impression of decadence, and I had even thought, "This empire is ripe for destruction." In prewar Paris, the impression of decadence took the form of unequivocal, dangerously exaggerated refinement and an excess of sensuality. The aura of voluptuous perfume that clung to the flesh of the women, the attention to cookery, a cuisine so delicious that it became a vice, facilities of every kind at the service of eroticism, the abundance of grey-haired men in the places that gave sensual shows: everything indicated a relaxation of public morals, the prelude to some necessary change—a war which would be a biological purifier.

While some lived a life of pleasure, there was freedom to work, and many of those who were amusing themselves had worked or would have to work. Material cruelty was unknown. Freedom could be seen in details such as free access to parks and gardens at all hours. It wasn't all a spree: behind the doors there was a hard-working Paris unknown to the simple tourist. Equality and freedom, in spite of the differences caused by capitalism, had never been so real in the world as in those prewar years. Personal dignity had never been so zealously and generally respected.

Lord, Thou hast created us: why must needs enjoyment be sin? Why, if there is to be copulation, should passion not lead the way? The flame of violent desire is purer than procreation out of a sense of duty. Hardly is consciousness born in the species than it deliberates before making the decision to beget offspring. In any case, love is more than duty, it is madness, uncontrolled impulse, infinite enjoyment; simple fecundation, so clean in the plant, is dirty in man.

What I know is that if I were to live again, and in the same conditions under which I have lived, I would certainly sin again, if the temptation were splendid.

The interview in the Treasury Department was solemn. We were introduced by the deputy Díaz Lombardo, who spoke for us. We asked that the French government withdraw its support for the bonds of the Huerta loan. Sánchez Azcona explained the details of the assassination of Madero. I spoke of the all-powerful oil companies on the other side of the Channel. Everyone told the truth without concealment. The deputy threatened a question in the Chamber if the government made common cause with the foreign businessmen who were supporting Victoriano Huerta. The Minister, serene, almost cold, listened, thought, and when it was his turn to answer, said, "Gentlemen, I would consider myself dishonored if in any way I helped to sponsor such atrocities as you relate to me. I will immediately give the order. The bonds of the Huerta loan will not appear on the official list of the Bourse."

It only remained to say thank you; we rose and left. In the corridor we all looked at one another in astonishment; someone embraced the deputy. Our group felt raised to the category of civilization by a few words from that Minister. It is hardly necessary to add that the public subscription was a failure, and that the agent of the Huerta government had to give up his loan.

I never left Adriana alone for many hours at a time, and I accepted only luncheon invitations so that the nights could go on being our own. Nevertheless, she began to worry about my absences. She was piqued for no reason when I gave her all the details about a meal in the house of a very lovely Mexican lady, in a light apartment adorned with flowers and objects of art. The beautiful lady had spent I don't know how many years in Paris, and she was interested in stories of the revolution in progress. She became enthusiastic when I told her Obregón had green eyes. With complete innocence I had asked Adriana to help me select for this Magdalene the vase of flowers that I was obliged to send her, especially because I was not going to see her again. Adriana went with me, but gradually she began to pick a quarrel. And one afternoon, when I came home after lunch with some friends, I didn't find her. I supposed that she had gone down to take a turn on the boulevard and I lay down, glad to get a chance for a little rest. She arrived a few minutes later and I asked for no explanations, but she made a point of them, which aroused my suspicions.

Instead of coming over as usual to greet me affectionately, she stretched out on a little sofa in her tight-fitting dress. She smiled enigmatically instead of answering the questions I began to ply her with, "Where did you go? Why were you late?"

"Do you think you are the only one who has friends?" she exclaimed at last.

And she gave me a story of friends from Texas whom she had run into quite by chance, who had invited her to take tea in a fashionable place and even to spend a while in the country. It was a question, she said, of a man she had known before, who was now accompanied by his family. At one time, yes, he had paid court to her, but now, naturally, she would not permit it; he was just showing a friendly interest. As she spoke I got more and more furious; pangs of jealousy even deprived me of speech. I had to fight back the desire to insult her. She looked so beautiful that I was in anguish at not making up my mind to kill her then and there. I ended by saying something foolish, "If you want to be free from me, we can divide the money and you can go with your friends."

"Don't bother! It will be easy for me to get to the United States with my friends."

And so, in an instant, without notice or reason, we were shooting to kill, and were creating a truly catastrophic situation. It was the first time that this had happened, and I felt something like terror as I thought of the immediate consequences. The remote ones worried me less, for I had the impression that a total separation between us was impossible, but a whim, the anger aroused by a hasty phrase, could unleash reactions which under the circumstances ought to be avoided. Our condition was doubly abnormal, because our love was illegitimate and because we were exiles and rebels. A break under these circumstances, quite apart from the sentimental pain of it, could lead to incalculable difficulties.

Crushed, I sat on the bed without speaking, and I don't know what would have happened had she not softened and come to put her arm around my neck. "I'll stay with you as long as you need me; don't worry."

After this, with joy in our souls, we went once more to see Paris by night. It was one of our last nights in France. On the banks of the Seine, late that night, we talked. The port of Matamoros had just fallen into the hands of the revolutionaries. My stay in Europe no longer had an object. It was important to appear in the field. My political future did not concern me, but I wanted to be in the front rank in a difficult period. And as she could not accompany me into rebel territory, there was no course open for her but to return to Mexico City. There had been as yet no case in which brothers of a political enemy had been bothered, much less the women of the family. She agreed to the rightness of these ideas, and then, to make up for our short stay in Europe, we decided that before embarking for America we would undertake a quick trip to Spain.

The revolution would be completed without us; we would get to

Mexico to work when I pleased, and nobody could demand that I render any accounting. What was the revolution without Madero? Intrigues and petty squabbles. Anyway, it would go on by itself. I couldn't do it. Not that I felt heroic. On the contrary, I felt enslaved. One's own will can be a terrible master. What I was going to do was barbarous. I would put her on a ship and send her off, perhaps into danger; and I would put myself on another, but take my part in civil hatred and slaughter. But the other choice was sensuality, and after some weeks it had become bitter to us. She herself never suggested a step back in the direction of sensual pleasure. What irritated her was my decision to send her back to the capital, when she wanted to take up life in San Antonio. But my idea was to enter Mexico and attach myself to the rebels, and I did not want to leave her in a foreign country.

Madrid is disconcerting, with its nineteenth-century architectural ugliness. They should have a Mexico City for a capital, we thought, and yet the old parts of town preserve a charm which you could see was the fountainhead of everything we had. The modern avenues are handsome because of their lighting and width and the way they accommodate people living in the street. In some provinces of Spain you feel a foreign atmosphere. In Castille we were in the home of our grandparents. Everything has distinction and grace. Just to hear people talk you would pay for the trip and prolong your stay.

"The trouble with you Americans," said the man in the hotel, "is that you come to Spain when you are all ready to sail home, after France has taken all your money and absorbed your attention."

And it was true. And right then I swore to be less foolish on future voyages.

Velásquez and Goya dominate the scene in Madrid. The dryness of the air and the diaphanous quality of the plateau lend the sharp edges of a drawing to all one sees. One can easily understand how great painters must emerge from such an environment. The gray of Paris disappears when you cross the Pyrenees, giving way to skies and valleys that recall the high country of Mexico. Clouds are few but have elegant shapes; the tone of the heavenly blue is light; there is color in the houses. Everyday the sun gilds the hair of women and the ochre of the façades.

"To go to Madrid is to go to the Prado," it is said, but this is foolish. For you cannot understand a canvas of Velásquez or a caricature of Goya if you have not seen the splendor of the distant sierra, if you have not taken part in the gaiety of a saint's festival.

We had a few days left to visit the most important of nearby places—Toledo.

Castille had taken solid form in those walls. Its speech and its soul had made their imprint on the Jew and the Muslim. The epic of America would not have existed without that indomitable blood. Christianity itself, and civilization, would not have continued to exist were it not for the heroic acts of the men who won, rebuilt, and then freed little Toledo, which, on the scales of human destiny, is a great city. The definition of dogma above commonplace heresies; the maintenance of human rights in the face of the menace of oriental despotism; the discovery and civilizing of America—all this had its cradle in Toledo of the Castillians, in Spanish Toledo.

[By way of Paris, London, and the United States, Vasconcelos returned to Mexico, and to two interviews with Obregón.] My visit took place in the afternoon, and was devoted to Obregón, the "rebel leader," as we affectionately called him. He had just been promoted to the rank of general. Surrounded by friends, stretched out on a canvas cot and wearing a simple linen undershirt, he received me with perfect cordiality. With a broad forehead, an intelligent look, light skin, robust constitution, tall rather than short, he immediately won the liking of his listeners by his conversational gifts.

Obregón invited me to follow him to the south, but before accepting any commission, I wanted to give an account of my activities and of myself to the chief of the movement, don Venustiano Carranza. And as his absence was prolonged and everything remained in a fluid state, I went to San Antonio to get settled. Seeing that the fight would inevitably be a long one, I decided to get Adriana as well as my family out of Mexico.

As a center of revolutionary information, San Antonio turned out to be unbeatable. As a place to live, it was a total loss. Neither body nor soul found complete satisfaction there. The food was enough to put an end to the gaiety of the world. A big beefsteak, plenty of it, but without condiments or salt; boiled potatoes and beside them a bottle of tomato sauce with a discouraging taste. And instead of wine, coffee with milk.

The only decent place to go was the public library. It had some ten thousand well chosen volumes, and the reading rooms were comfortable. There the hours slipped by uncounted. I read my Plato again and consulted Aristotle with a view to writing a study of Pythagoras which I had been planning for quite a while.

My family had arrived. My children were at the best age; my wife was in a good state of mind because she had with her a cousin who served as an inseparable servant. But I was going through a period of deep anxiety because Adriana was postponing leaving the capital. In a long letter that she wrote me on the boat that was taking her to Mexico, she gave me assurances of her sticking with me through thick and thin with a love that would be proof against every vicissitude. But now she seemed to be hunting for excuses to prolong her stay in Mexico City, and this caused me insufferable agony. I kept imagining inconstancy and betrayal on her part. I was so harassed that my wife, wondering, made a jealous scene of expostulation. Naïvely, I confessed what was going on. It wasn't anybody's fault; but I didn't love her, and I did need the other woman. For a long time we didn't renew the subject; we were further apart than ever.

A month or so later, Adriana arrived. She took a place on the other side of town where she had friends. We often took rides through a large woods of live oaks. After siesta, we read. As I would not give up my Greek philosophy, she too read several *Dialogues*. One evening we read *Werther* and I could not contain my sobs for the ideas of death and tenderness were two things I still associated with the death of my mother. When I went home, after leaving her at her place, I was torn to pieces by having her away from my side. I thought of the wisdom of the Muslim precept which is closer to nature and recognizes the fact that, as one goes through life, there is not one woman only whom one loves and it is possible for all to live in harmony. This is the proper way to avoid hypocrisy and deceit. The Yankee example of a peaceful divorce would also be a solution if it were not for the impossibility of agreeing about the custody of minor children. In short, because I knew that my children would need my personal influence and not merely my money, I kept up the miserable chain of deceits which in the long run benefitted no one.

"The revolution now has a man." The fact that I had pronounced this sentence in an interview after Villa's victories in the north of Chihuahua later enabled calumniators, interested in concealing their own weaknesses, to list me as a follower of Villa. I never was. In spite of the evident mistakes of Carranza, I was the most loyal of his followers until the day when Victoriano Huerta left Mexico City. After that, of course, I was not going to follow Carranza in his ambitions and evil-doing. But still less would I go along with Villa. Nevertheless, at that moment Villa did save the rebellion. It was a fact that wherever Carranza went, discord, hesitation, and slowness at once inhibited and dissolved the revolutionary movement. Obregón might have been the leading military figure from the beginning of the revolution, but if he were not, and if Villa instead came out in the lead, it is only because, from the day of Carranza's arrival in Sonora, the rebels did not fight. And instead of advancing toward the south, Obregón himself had to make repeated trips to the seat of government to defend his position as military chief. On the other hand, Francisco Villa, free from the tutelage of the First Chief, and master of the immense resources which he had conquered, little by little began to aim decisive blows at the structure of the Huerta power. From the first, Villa had proclaimed his adherence to Carranza, and it is clear that in the beginning he had not the slightest idea of independent action.

All of this did not prevent the international aspect of the Revolution from being a disaster. Unnecessarily so, for Wilson did everything possible to aid the rebels, but no steps had been taken to lift the arms embargo in favor of the revolutionaries and to impose it on Huerta or permit equal traffic for both. Through the stupidity of our agents in Washington, the Huerta party—in spite of Washington's disapproval of them—went on enjoying the benefits of free movement of goods, on the basis of being the duly constituted government. And we, as a result of the disorganized state of affairs that Carranza created, did not even attain the international category of a *de facto* government. If it had not been for the incompetence of Carranza, the revolution would have triumphed in three months instead of taking a year and half. There has never in all Mexican history been a more general uprising than the almost instantaneous one against Huerta.

I was present when Carranza entered Ciudad Juárez. In order not to feel later the remorse of one who has stayed abroad and done nothing, I went to see the First Chief, in spite of the fact that he had already politely turned me down once. I went to offer him my services again for whatever use he wished. We were with a group of friends, chatting on a corner crowded with people, waiting, along with thousands of curious camp-followers, for the First Chief to finish "shaving." Later it was revealed that the long delay was caused by Carranza's having halted on the outskirts of the town to call for a barber, a masseur, and a tailor to press his uniform. Finally the First Chief entered like Napoleon, with a warlike apparatus better suited for the battlefront, to take possession of a town that was already pacified and completely loyal.

It was not hard to have an interview with Carranza the next day. My stock was high at the time because of something I learned only later. It was noticed that although I had been with Madero and had once been rejected by Carranza, I was not in the south of Chihuahua with Villa, like so many other Madero followers, but had come to get my orders straight from Carranza.

In the last analysis, the person who deserves the blame for Villa's conduct was Carranza, who had the moral authority but did not know how to use it, and instead of being constructive, sowed discord. The very atrocities of Villa, his killing of prisoners, the raping and pillaging, weren't they the same things that went on elsewhere, only without the glory of victory? And slaughtering the defeated, wasn't that the result of the most infamous of all the Carranza decrees, the so-called "Law of Juárez" which required the shooting of prisoners?

From Ciudad Juárez they sent me with vague orders to New York and Canada. I was to pat on the back certain institutions and persons who were not very hostile to us, doubtless because they could see better than we that the so-called revolution had degenerated into bossism, disorder, arbitrary confiscation, and all kinds of excesses. I went about Toronto and Ottawa and Montreal interviewing businessmen and politicians, telling them about the certain approach of our victory, and assuring them—and this turned out to be untrue—that the First Chief was a statesman and not the leader of a gang of thieves.

The curious thing is that Obregón did not belong to the Sonora group either by direct connection or by belief. Obregón was not Yankeephile and had never even bothered to learn English. He brought up his children in Mexico and started them in life there. Nor can you say that the leader of this group was Calles, who because of his total insignificance was making no noise at all. The group was chaotic, but held together by a desire for a Mexico that belonged to their kind, the men of the North. On the other hand, they hated the men of Chihuahua. Behind the scenes, there was the doctrine that called for the downfall of the influence of Mexico City, the Latin influence, and the domination of Yankeeism, or, if you will, of a varnish of civilization—not true culture—which the Mexican was picking up in California, New Mexico, and Arizona. However it was, there was germinating among these folks the power which would create the regime of Calles: a hybrid mixture of ignorant and brutal bossism, confused thinking, and traitorous friendships in the fashion of Morrow. All this we shall call *Callismo* not because Calles had any idea of what it was all about, but because it used Calles as an instrument.

I never had any power in the Carranza movement; for that matter no cultured man had, unless he sold out to the First Chief. And although the First Chief was no Yankee-lover, he was deaf and blind, stupid and dumb, and so mad about commanding that he would listen to no advice. Anyway, the whole Yankee-inspired intrigue would have been avoided if Carranza had not turned out to be an evildoer; and it could have been crushed if Obregón had not taken it into his head to impose Calles on the country.

The North American correspondents who frequently went to Mexico had forebodings about the new war which would break out among the revolutionaries when Huerta fell. Not only were Villa and Carranza in irreconcilable camps, but Zapata in the south was also becoming dangerously independent. The Yankee writers were all on Zapata's side. They knew he was an Indian and they always cherished the hope that the Indian would revolt against the Spanish civilization of Mexico, which is such a thorn in the side of imperialism.

Often I stayed whole weeks in New York waiting for instructions that did not come. With Adriana, I had taken a couple of rooms with a bath and kitchen. Jealousy of each other was doing a lot of damage. Her past obsessed me, although many times she told me everything in detail in order to get it over and done with. And she, in turn, was not satisfied with the present. One afternoon we were taking our favorite ride uptown, the whole length of the Fifth Avenue bus line. In front, a young couple were talking happily.

"I want a man like that," she said, pointing to them, "a man who would be all mine." Nothing hurt me as much as these complaints of hers about a situation that had no remedy and that we had gone into with our eyes open.

On one or two occasions she had accompanied me to Washington. But she had an itch to show off. The feminism she absorbed from reading Ellen Key was beginning to infect her. Not only the men but she, too, was working for the revolution. One morning when she was walking around the Capitol, a rich and influential Senator invited her to visit the whole building, took her address, and sent her a great bouquet of flowers. I was in the hotel when the bouquet arrived, and without thinking, there in front of the messenger, I threw the bouquet out of the window and tore up the card. Her laughter completed my annoyance, and I threatened never to take her to Washington again.

The morning papers came out with an ill-timed picture of me and other revolutionaries and a long and infamous story. It was tough to be living with Adriana in a house that cost twelve dollars a week, keeping my family in a modest bungalow in San Antonio, and to see myself accused of betraying my country for two hundred thousand dollars. To a receipt for two hundred dollars, for the expense of a trip to London to obtain information, they had added three zeros!

We were in New York at the time of the occupation of Vera Cruz, and the impression there was in accord with the official version—that is, that without intending to invade Mexico, the soldiers and marines, who were blockading the port to prevent arms shipments meant for Huerta, had disembarked near the Customs House. Then the shooting started by the revolutionaries and a few marine cadets had forced the military to fight and take possession of the whole port, after many losses on both sides.

We sent a message to Carranza informing him that the whole press regretted the incident, that in spite of that he ought to publish the official protest of the government, and that he should use us in any way that seemed right. Carranza acted as well as possible in such an unhappy situation. By aiding a rebellion which in spite of its strength was endless, President Wilson put us in such a plight that the Huerta party, without waiting, accused us of betraying our country, and in spite of the timely and vigorous protest of Carranza, demanded immediate withdrawal from the port.

A few days later in the capital of Mexico, crowds of upper-class people, not commoners, were amassed in the squares, shouting against the revolutionaries who were endangering the country and demanding arms. Huerta's government gave some of them arms, not to send to recapture Vera Cruz, which the troops had abandoned, but to fight the revolutionaries. In the diabolical confusion thus created, there were people so simple-minded as to think that those (namely, Huerta) were patriots who had conspired in the Embassy of the United States to assassinate the President, while we were really the ones who "had sold out to the Yankees,"—we who were doing our best to give the country an honorable government, the only one fit to lead a country in a time of crisis.

The reactionary government party was losing ground and the decision was made to ditch the leader for the sake of safety. The scheme was to get Huerta to resign and at the same time to name a provisional President and appoint delegates to meet with the revolution. I owe Carranza the favor of having named me as one of the delegates of the revolution to this Niagara Falls conference.

To join my colleagues on the commission, I planned to go to Washington. Since I was going to be gone for some days, I thought it was better not to take Adriana. And she understood. We celebrated the day of my departure happily, moving out and taking a room in a central hotel so that I could get the Washington train while she went to the seashore where she was to wait for me. After dinner, we danced at a Broadway nightclub. It must have been about eleven, and my train left at midnight. I was sorry to leave her alone at the shore, but I did not want to cause a scandal in Washington. Our situation was delicate, and spies were all around. In recent days she had complained that she was a nuisance to me and that I was neglecting her. Now for some trivial reason, our conversation took a turn for the worse. She talked of not going to the shore, but to San Antonio with her friends, said that she would get a job, and seeing that the revolution was triumphant and I would be returning to Mexico City, she considered herself free to make a life for herself. I listened to this nonsense with bewilderment, walking from one end of the room to the other. And as I saw that the time for leaving was near and I suffer from a compulsion to do what is planned and decided on, I said, perhaps a little brusquely; "This is not the time to discuss these matters. In a week I'll be back and everything will be the same as before."

She was standing, combing her hair in front of the mirror, letting down her marvelous locks and knotting them gracefully. Suddenly, taking advantage of a moment when my back was turned, she cut it off mercilessly. Stretching out her hand, she said; "Take this," and she offered me the hair, "so that you will know it is not because I am thinking of anyone else, but just because I can't stand this life any longer, and it is better for me to go into a convent!"

I stood there silent and perplexed, as if she had committed suicide in front of me. The scene ended in tears. It was frightful not to be able to give her all the protection, all the warmth of affection that her extraordinary nature required. She softened and became infinitely resigned and sweet.

As if time had been suspended and the world outside ourselves counted for nothing, this night of suffering and sweetness was prolonged in a mysterious enchantment.

Naturally, I missed the train, but for things like this you would lose your soul. Together, like newlyweds, we took another train the next morning, and her first visit was to the hairdresser, who stuck the hair on with devilish cleverness; it looked beautiful when she wore it, and when she took it off there was the new attraction of her white neck and short hair.

In a word, the conflict was then between the Yankeephiles and liberals. And although you hated to admit that the party of old-fashioned liberalism had lost, you could not fail to realize that it deserved to. The liberals too had in their time gone abroad to ask for help, and had allowed themselves to be taken in about the purposes of that help. Now the imperialistic interests required more malleable men than the old liberals, and even less clever ones. It has been the misfortune of Mexico that it has always been subject to influences from the outside which have set the pattern for something that is decay rather than progress. The liberals did not have the sense to use their time of power to build a national policy and an independent economy. They could not, for they were founding the institutions of their country on alien doctrines, rather than basing their liberalism on the popular tradition of Castille, on that municipal freedom which Cortez himself taught the Indians. But it is also certain that the liberals were not the only guilty parties, but the whole nation which for thirty-five years had put up with the confusion, the ignorance, the contradictions of the Díaz regime. The difference between the old-fashioned liberals and, for example, Madero, was that Madero, for the first time in Mexican history, had given the Republic a program fitted to its needs and to the national character. Even in matters of religion, Madero wanted a change in the Reform Laws, that would leave the Catholic Church, which is Mexican, on an equal level with the Protestant Churches, which are foreign. Guilt is shared also by the Catholics who on the one hand, supported Díaz, and worse, Huerta, and on the other hand never understood Madero.

The revolution, demoralized by the incapacity of its Chief, had a military triumph, thanks to the energy of the Division created by Francisco Villa. Carranza took on the thankless task of the rearguard, behind the man who gave him the victory, and then abused the position that chance had given him, dishonoring his chieftainship with horrible intrigues and bloody errors.

It was certain that Carranza had failed in his duty. Functioning as absolute master of the national situation, he had at his disposal public funds and large new issues of currency, yet had no idea of rendering an accounting. Without a plan he headed a movement which everyone thought would emancipate but which slowly turned into a hecatomb. So low was the prestige of Carranza on the eve of his triumph that if Pancho Villa had not been the only other choice, no honorable person would have stayed with him. The terrible thing was that if Carranza had been eliminated by violence, it would have meant the leadership of Villa, who was an ignorant, ferocious type, already going crazy with the power of commanding, like a wild animal that gets its claws on machine guns and cannons. The thought of this danger kept me at the side of Carranza during the whole crisis, and until there was in the Convention a legitimate authority to which to attach oneself.

I was the more resolved to stick with Carranza, since Villa recommended me along with half a dozen others, as one of those who ought to have a portfolio in the new government which he was urging Carranza to form. Since I didn't even know Villa by sight, the suggestion about me came from the Madero supporters who were with him. I wanted to make my adherence to Carranza perfectly clear and absolutely independent of any ambition for a government post; and I wanted it known that I did not go along with the demands of Villa and his crowd, which seemed premature. Still, I was far from satisfied with Carranza, and I held myself in reserve for a later period of reorganization. I went back to New York, determined to return to Mexico on my own, without connection with the groups of either Carranza or Villa. Actually, I began to visit certain friends I thought might help me to set up my law office again.

But scarcely had I dreamed of this truce with politics, when difficulties arose which I could not so easily turn my back on as I did on the politicians. Everytime I had a misunderstanding with Adriana, the air became charged with electricity, and anything could happen.

"You go back; I'm going to stay!" she had said. She was taking up the piano at the time, and talked of not interrupting her "artistic career." If she had resolved firmly on this, I would not have opposed her, much as it hurt me, but quite aside from the fact that I could not see that she had any real talent, she kept changing, and next she would say that she would never leave me as long as she was alive, unless I drove her out. Some weeks passed in these temperamental ups and downs, and meanwhile the situation of Mexico became clearer, but only in the sense that it was more complicated. The fact is, no one wanted to enter Mexico City before Carranza, and Carranza never in his life knew what it was to hurry. Wherever he went, he amused himself with his secretaries, his weakness for women, his chef and his sommelier in charge of the wine cellar, for his lordship had gone in for drinking nothing but champagne at dinner.

In New York we did not drink champagne. My funds, always low, had diminished to practically nothing after all the long months of revolutionary activity, and the goings and comings. We sublet a modest room in the sordid Nineties. If only she and I had been truly united by mutual confidence; but we lived in a state of such excitement that once when she went out I took to searching her trunks, fearing, even desiring perhaps, to find some proof of her infidelity, some hints as to her plans, since it seemed to me impossible that I should not find something and that she was just talking nonsense to worry and confuse me. The search gave me no other satisfaction than that of caressing her lingerie that recalled past happiness. Not finding anything compromising made me regret my actions and predisposed me to a grateful reconciliation.

One morning as I was leaving for downtown, she asked if I would be back for lunch and I said she should have her lunch alone and not wait. I was in a hurry, preoccupied with a series of appointments, and perhaps I spoke impatiently; it is certain that I continued to worry, and since I could not help delaying my return until after lunch, I reached home eager to make excuses and to offer to make it up by taking her for a ride, when I found the place empty, a goodbye note on the table. The tone of the letter was ambiguous, almost irritating; she was leaving because she was in the way; she said not to look for her and wished me happiness.

I walked and walked, hoping the fatigue in my legs would make me forget the disturbance in my mind. I alternated between tender feelings and anger.

That night I took a late train to the south, stopping in Washington, since I wanted to say goodbye to Hopkins before going back to my country.

Washington, too, had become odious now that I traversed it with a feeling of abandonment. How unbearable was that monumental station! There is a big door which is opened only to receive Ambassadors, the sign said. Let a curse fall on me, I thought, if I ever come here as an Ambassador; I prefer obscurity to the glory of a colonial who has managed to become acceptable. The Capitol was there with its ridiculous dome. The tall obelisk, always being repainted, raised its point in the distance, conveying no meaning. I did have an affectionate thought, however, for the library off to the left.

As the train approached San Antonio, a vague hope buoyed me up; she might have sought refuge with a family of friends of whom she was always talking. In that case, she would have arrived only a few days before me.

On a sunny morning I reached my home, warmly caressed my children, embraced my wife; everything seemed quiet enough; we talked of preparations for our departure for Mexico City. But slowly, as soon as the surprise of the presents the traveler brings to the little ones had worn off, I found myself edging toward the telephone. The lady of the house herself answered and when she heard my name, she cried, "Oh, you don't know; such bad luck; I was hoping you would call! . . . I don't know your address, perhaps you can use your influence . . . imagine . . . Adriana has told us you are a great friend of hers, and now . . . I don't know what has come over her, she has gone crazy, she is in a convent . . . and she has cut off her hair!"

For American Protestants there could be nothing more absurd than this way of acting. But the sudden vision of her sacrifice, of her renunciation of the world when I was accusing her of sordid adventures, caused me such profound and upsetting pain that when the conversation—all in English—was over, I began to weep uncontrollably.

My wife came over, and without concealing anything I told her what was going on and that I had decided to go at once and get Adriana out of the convent. I would tell her she did not have to run away, that all was over between us if that was what she wanted, but that I could not allow her to make this sacrifice without thinking.

"Then I will go with you to see her," said my wife; and hours later we were in the railway which ran to the nearby town where the convent was located.

It was not hard to convince her to leave the place. "Really," Adriana confessed, as soon as we could talk together alone, "I wanted to leave; that's why I talked to the American lady in San Antonio, for I knew you would go to her asking for me; I wanted you to come and get me out . . . but why did you bring your wife?" As for the last question, I didn't know myself. It was a hideous mess.

By great good luck, it was a time of emergencies. Soon each of us went his own way; my wife returned to Mexico to set things in order in her house. Adriana stayed on as a guest in the house of the San Antonio family, and I went to Monterrey, at Governor Villarreal's invitation to enter Mexico through his region. The opportunity Villarreal offered me was magnificent, since I did not want to go through the zone occupied by the Villa troops, who invited me, nor through the Carranza territory, and Villarreal, an independent who was older in the revolutionary movement and a purer rebel than either Villa or Carranza, stood for the road of decency.

The known incapacity of Carranza made it easy to believe that he developed no agrarian policy because he never succeeded in understanding the problem or was afraid of it. The truth is that he operated deliberately. What was happening was exactly what he wanted to have happen. Zurbarán had told me earlier in Washington, "The Chief wants to destroy the enemy economically, and get a new agrarian aristocracy formed. His tactics are to create interests which will support him."

They had prepared lodgings for us in the best house in town. The best house in town is always at the disposal of the man who has just won.

Beside a running stream and in the shade of leafy trees they served us a meal. The good, hearty dishes of rice, Spanish style, salads and roasts, the whole manner of serving a good meal, are part of the Spanish heritage in that desolate area. The last thing a people loses as it degenerates is its cuisine. Even this becomes more debased every day by the inferior cooking that has been infiltrating from north to south for more than a century. In the north they rarely serve fried foods or kid in its blood; but they never fail to have some tasteless cake. And then there was beer. A little later, in the days of Ambassador Morrow, under the regency of Portes Gil, at Mexican banquets there would be toasts with ice water, they would eat lettuce without olive oil, they would celebrate the Festival of the Race, of exiles, with Pullman Negroes.

What claimed our attention most strongly in our hospitable entertainment, perhaps because we came from the North, was the softness of the voices in the choruses, the delicacy of the movements in the recitations. "Not a single rough gesture," as they say in North America, à propos of that harshness which is likely to make its appearance there, especially in intimate relations. Among Mexicans, on the contrary, courtesy springs from the blood, although in certain parts of the interior they exaggerate it unpleasantly. But from one end of our country to the other, the race we belong to possesses a decided inclination toward fine and noble forms. So that the humblest village dweller, as soon as he dresses up and learns a poem recites it with good taste, and if he sings or makes music at least you don't run the risk, so common among other peoples, of suffering in your very soul, as the body suffers when a pin scratches across a windowpane.

We had no inkling of what was in store for us; we were optimists, that is to say, idiots, and we were drunk, not with wine which when it is good does not intoxicate, but with the rhetoric of the speechmakers, with the habit of tyrannies, inherited from the Díaz days, of never making a frank analysis of a situation because of the risk of hurting the feelings of the powerful and of being content with phrases of some literary pretension that, having no other strength than petulance, immediately descend into banality.

Pride based solely on disdain for the alien is the worst type; it is expressed by those who have neither merit of their own nor the strength on which to build genuine self-confidence. And the arrogance of the capital's aristocratic caste which brought about the destruction of Madero was this kind. And they all fell ingloriously. Nor did the chief they had deified have the courage to face his enemies; he fled in disgrace as all despots do, and his gang, which originated in treason, could not attempt any worthy undertaking. We revolutionaries felt much bitterness against the well-to-do of the city, a representative sample of the well-to-do of the whole country that played so odious a role in collaborating with the crimes of Huerta. Even greater was our disgust with the hypocrisy of the last weeks of the spurious regime when people of all classes met in the squares to protest the occupation by the Yankees, and incidentally to praise the government, insulting the revolutionaries. As if anyone had a right to talk about loving his mother country who had stood by indifferently during the sacrifice of the President who was the incarnation of that mother country. Multitudes that had not thought of rising against Huerta had no right to pretend indignation because a port was occupied after being evacuated by the very man of whom they were asking arms and leadership in the struggle against the foreigner.

Our rich people—less diamonds in the rough perhaps than the cattlemen since they did not come from the ranch but from mining, which has become an industry, and from the old city which was a cultural center before Boston—were still far from being men of intelligence. Most of them went to Europe to spend time with the cocottes or to visit casinos, not for good music nor the theatre nor the lecture hall. Still, there must have been some good things in their collections, especially the painting and ceramics of the colonial period. All this was lost through the apathy and cowardice of Carranza. It would have been better to decree confiscation frankly and openly than to show the culpable indulgence which allowed the prolonged taking of all kinds of objects, which sold at ridiculous prices and ended by falling into the hands of foreign collectors. This is how not only family portraits but antique altarpieces from old churches went to end their days in rich men's houses in North America.

"Public education," the Yankee-loving faction began to say, "is a local function and does not belong to the central government; look at the United States, they don't have any Ministry of Education; therefore, a Ministry of Education in Mexico is superfluous." We listened to this propaganda by traitors and it was so infamous we could not believe our ears.

I received my appointment as Director of the Preparatory School and hastened to take up residence. It had been agreed that I should act with complete autonomy, and it was only on this condition that I accepted the post. I was Director for more or less a fortnight.

The outstanding occurrence during my brief tour of duty was the visit that some students paid me to ask for the reinstatement of the Professor of Ethics, who had been fired along with other followers of

Huerta. I replied, "How can a man teach Ethics or be a scholar who owes his position to Huerta and served Huerta? I thought you had come to congratulate me for getting rid of him."

The confiscations, practiced without any regulation at all, gave rise to injustices that cried to heaven. The word got around that we had saved a house, and people began to offer us houses by the dozen. Some well-to-do families had recourse to the expedient of lending their autos to friends in the new government in order to save them, since wherever a tire stuck out of a garage the policeman on the beat or the nearest lieutenant hurried around to take possession, always provided he did not run into the veto of a more powerful militiaman. I never wanted to ride in someone else's auto, but family obligations did induce me to accept the custody of a beautiful farm belonging to a son of don Porfírio Díaz, the Las Rosas ranch.

To all appearances life was agreeable in the mansion; in reality it turned out to be a lot of bother because all the time I had to be taking steps with the military authorities to throw out various military groups whose horses got in to eat the grain, the corn in the milpa, and to ruin the newly sown ground. And as the chaos grew and civil authority continued to be lacking, the insolence of the soldiers increased.

It was not the time to return to the Constitution; we were in a pre-constitutional period. On the scene, intimate with the men of the hour, was John Reed, and I don't know how many agents of imperialism, ultrasocialists and radicals, now in Nicaragua, now in Mexico, as suited the men of the North, but very cautious and even capitalistic when they were at home. And it was John Reed, buried years later with honor in the Kremlin, after taking part in the destruction of an alien country; it was Reed, or some comrade of his, who launched throughout the world the phrase, "Dictatorship of the Proletariat." The farces of the dictatorship of the proletariats served to conceal from world public opinion all the iniquities, all the robbery and destruction of the Carranza regime.

In this way the Carranza period marked a new era in the history of our political breakdown; you not only saw the domestic brand of petti-fogger accompanying the ignorant chieftain to give legal form to his excesses and to justify his crimes, but above and beyond the domestic adviser, the foreign agent set the tone, put the stamp of international socialism on the old outrageous acts of a revolutionary movement that had neither ideals nor effective leadership. At the side of Villa—in addition to the pseudo-cabinet of Mexican civilians and, above them, one Carothers as counselor, the agent of the Department of State in Washington,—there was also a cloud of pseudo-radical reporters who applauded the destruction, the pillage of Mexican property, although in their own country they would not have tolerated the killing of a single cow.

We did not want to believe the evidence of our own eyes in those days, the irresponsibility and evil of the extravagance. A little later, in the hour of his triumph, instead of honoring his own signature, Carranza was to disown the already depreciated, already valueless spawn of his printing presses, in order to issue another lot without backing or limit, which he called the "unfalsifiable." And for a second time he robbed the Mexican people, the most resigned of all who inhabit the earth. Not only were our people resigned, but they put up with six years of the government of Carranza with its endless robbery. They supported it as they always support success, without worrying about how legitimate it is. And Carranza fell, not as he should have, and not as we his enemies wanted, wiped out by means of a national protest and swept away by a popular uprising. He fell betrayed by his own gang. And naturally they never talked about the robbery by inflation in which they participated; on the contrary, they held up the catastrophic administration of the First Chief as a model of honesty. The only thing they held against him was that he did not get out in time to leave for them the enjoyment of despotism and the possibility of new money issues, actually carried out by Calles.

In those days, however, we had no idea of the depth of the abyss into which the nation was falling.

Voluntarily cut off from direct political activities, I worked to build up my professional life again, confident that sooner or later, as almost always happens, everything would be straightened out and I should be able to work in peace. Personally, I had not a single enemy; indeed, the people who surrounded Carranza showed some liking for me. They did not see in me a competitor for public office, and they all were forced to recognize that my dossier of services to the revolution was impeccable.

I received an official paper notifying me that I was dismissed as Director of the Preparatory School. When I left the directorship, I scribbled a message in pencil: "I make you a present of my salary for the days I worked here."

And I did not go to the Villa party as some suspicious people imagined; I neither communicated with the opposition nor left the capital. They began to torment me with officious warnings that I would be arrested, that I had better go into hiding.

"I will not hide, and you will do me a favor if you arrest me," I replied. "The government of Carranza is on its last legs, and tomorrow we, the enemies, will be the heroes!"

And I went to my office regularly and appeared everywhere.

Not all the Carranza crowd were disloyal; the First Chief had made us, had bestowed gifts upon us. He had never given me anything; on the contrary, he owed me something for the revolutionary services which I rendered, nearly always without payment, while Carranza himself had not merely a salary, but the whole public treasury. But some dogs have a very odd concept of loyalty. Loyalty becomes pestilential when we use it to conceal slavish complicity, or notorious dishonesty, simply because an evil leader gives us money or position or honors. In brief, loyalty to a tyrant is complicity in crime, not chivalry nor characteristic of a gentleman. The gentleman owes allegiance to his conscience and to his honor rather than to any human power whatsoever. If this is not chivalry, so much the worse for chivalry! I am sure that it is Christianity, for Christianity has in its moral law an object more worthy of loyalty than any fatherland that history has made or race engendered. The fatherland has no right to demand vile actions of us, much less right has the chieftain of a war-band.

The constables arrested me in the street with less consideration than the police of Victoriano Huerta had shown, and took me to police headquarters in the same building in which Huerta had held me prisoner. Now, however, I knew them all, from the Chief of Police to the lowest officer, and they said they were sorry to have to hold me. They shut me up with more than a dozen political prisoners, mostly ex-Huerta men. I had a hard time communicating with the outside to let my family know.

The order for my arrest read: "At the disposition of the First Chief." So I was a high-ranking prisoner!

Practically the whole population, except, of course, the foreigners, was at the mercy of a disorderly, voracious pretorianism. And this is the vilest of the Santa Anna types of policy we suffer from: the servility with which we crawl before the North American, and the contempt with which we treat our fellow countryman who happens to have been defeated.

I got in touch with Adriana through an intermediary and she informed me that a certain former fellow student with me, married to a friend of hers, had offered to hide me in his house if I succeeded in escaping from captivity. This finally caused me to decide to attempt it.

In public law sovereignty is understood as the right of the people to govern themselves according to their own will. The people is sovereign, with the power to give itself a government. In exercising this sovereignty, it gives itself the government which seems best to it according to its own judgment. In Mexico the only sovereign is the people. In normal times, the sovereignty of the people is exercised through a popularly elected government, divided into three independent powers according to function: Executive, Legislative, and Judicial.

Once elected, the First Chief don Venustiano Carranza was the representative and continued to represent legality in the country, but he held this position as Chief of the Constitutional Army, since the true sovereignty resides and since February 1913, has always resided in the Constitutional Army, which is the army of the sovereign people.

The Military Convention of Aguascalientes assembled to deal with the threatening chaos is the only sovereign power which can exist in the country under the political conditions of the time and in accordance with our laws.

A revolution is a violent transformation of an order of things recognized as oppressive and unjust. Ideas take definite form in people's minds; anxiety and hope ferment in their hearts; then on one great day, first the man, the precursor, the leader, and then the whole people rise in their divine wrath, raise their arms in the gesture of a man breaking his chains, tear down and demolish institutions and monuments, idols and laws. Their destructive instinct seizes them and sweeps all before it. As if these very things were enemies and obstacles, the movement goes against all that has represented their infinite longing—the longing, imperious and triumphant, which every being carries in his heart. For this reason revolution is the antithesis of a Constitution. The Constitution epitomizes the practices, laws, and usages established by man so that he may live in a society. The revolution aims to reform and to reconstitute all those practices, usages, and principles.

Almost all revolutions can be classified according to their essential aims as either political or economic. The revolution of 1910 had both characteristics. It was political in that it protested against the fraud committed in the general elections by the dictator Díaz and in that it sought the civil liberties that had been repressed for so many years by the same despot. It was economic in that it promised a remedy for the precarious condition of the rural class and the workers. When the revolution was consummated, the government of Madero granted all kinds of freedom, but it either forgot or did not have time to carry out the economic reforms.

The revolution has the right to forget the Constitution as long as it prevents the carrying out of revolutionary reforms; but as soon as a government is organized in a region the revolution must respect and enforce the Constitution in every respect which does not run counter to the new principles which the revolution is implanting.

Separate commissions were named to publish the double agreement that Generals Carranza, Villa, and Zapata no longer be recognized and withdraw from their commands and that Eulalio Gutiérrez be elected President. Obregón, Villarreal, and Lucio Blanco undertook to present the agreement to Carranza. It fell to my lot, along with Generals José Isabel Robles and Raúl Madero, to inform General Francisco Villa.

"You do the talking," said his two generals when we were at the door of the private car of the train in which Villa transacted business. As soon as he had us sit down and was waiting expectantly, I said without any preamble, "As you must already know, General, this afternoon the Convention agreed to thank you and Generals Carranza and Zapata for your very important services to the revolution, and to ask you to give up the command of your troops, putting them under the orders of Provisional President Eulalio Gutiérrez.

The General's eyes rapidly became bloodshot as they had told me was habitual with him when he was in a homicidal fury, but he got control of himself. "Very good," he said after a long pause. "Very good . . . tell them that Pancho Villa is going . . . I leave everything to them."

I thought with distress of the confusion of our people, those right there in Querétaro, those who ought to have understood, ought to have taken the lead, but had fallen into a decadence which made a mere rite, rather than charity of religion; an affair of scapularies, rather than heroic deeds. Doubtless these fine people lamented from the bottom of their hearts the failure of Victoriano Huerta; doubtless it was also lamented by the hacienda owners, the bosses of the ill-fed, badly clothed, workers, who, before they could draw their wages, were forced to show a slip proving that they had gone to confession. This was the aristocracy of the Republic. And the rest, the group that went along with us, consisted of strong, ambitious mestizos, the mixed-bloods who had denied Cortéz and the plantation owners of a century ago, but now bowed low in submission to the present foreign influence which was much more oppressive than the old regime.

All over the country the Carranza crowd was in flight. The First Chief took off for Vera Cruz. In the North, Villa had his district; Zapata ruled the South, and in Sonora there was Obregón with no army. While the leading figures of the column of the West argued in the Convention or met in the capital, Plutarco Elías Calles, always in the rear guard, had remained master of Sonora, there to confiscate and shoot to his heart's content. But as soon as the moral support of Carranza was withdrawn, the civil chief, the ex-governor Maytorena, who seemed beneath contempt from a military point of view, defeated Calles and took the whole state from him.

As a matter of fact, the Zapata movement never was anything but a lower-class movement, although the agents of foreign penetration and their unconscious dupes, the so-called intellectuals of Zapata, did work out a thesis that was apparently contrary to the Texan and Yankee-imitating thesis introduced by the northerners. Contrary in appearance, I say, but in reality in agreement as far as working for the destruction of Mexico was concerned. The hidden doctrine of the school of Zapata was the return of Mexico to the primitivism of Montezuma. This return was preached by European creoles like Díaz Soto and by Yankee newspapermen; the aristocrats of the capital, taking part in the movement in a kind of defensive mimicry, practiced the doctrine in the form of dress they wore. And if it went no further than costumes and barbarism, if, for instance, it did not also reject the Spanish language, it is only because the masses of aborigines knew no other language than Spanish which could serve as a foundation for an Aztec revival. Cultural elements for a viable Aztec society—they simply do not exist. The form of Aztec tradition that periodically raises its head is the element of cruelty which four centuries of Christian teaching by the Spaniards have not been able to eradicate. The *teocalli* of human sacrifices is the only Aztec institution that survives. The followers of Zapata perfected it with machine guns and automatics.

"What do these Indian followers of Zapata believe?" asked the soldiers of Villa, sons of the border steppes, in whose blood the Spanish element predominated, even though from their lips, poisoned by foreign propaganda, there burst out abuse of those who were their ancestors. "Do these Indians think we are going to put on huaraches?" (the sandals made of coarse leather that the Indian wears). "Let them wear shoes like us and dress like decent people."

And so the footwear of the North and the khaki uniform the Carranza forces brought from Texas saved the Republic from returning to the rough mantle of the Aztecs, saved us from the return to primitivism.

Only on a few occasions did we go to the Palace, for example on the day of the swearing in of the Ministers, when the cabinet was formed, with Lucio Blanco in Administration, Miguel Alessio Robles in Justice, Valentín Gama in Development, Felicitos Villarreal in the Treasury, and the writer, in Public Instruction. It was the first time in Mexico that the inauguration ceremony had been conducted without evening dress and with an almost rustic simplicity. The cabinet was warmly applauded by the audience which filled the ambassadorial hall; there always seems to be an audience ready to serve as a chorus whenever it is a question of the assumption of office by thieves like those who formed the cabinets of Calles. At the time, however, I was young enough so that it seemed to me that the applause was the natural echo of honorable conduct, the reward of merit. Little did I know the baseness of the crowd. As a matter of fact, Eulalio had assembled the best men of the revolution.

Without loss of time, I went to see Eulalio, supposing he would give me orders to turn over to a Judge accused persons held by the revolutionary general. But Eulalio, who was always so deferential in every matter connected with me, this time was not to be moved.

"You know," he explained, "the state of our relations with Villa; I can't order him to hand over prisoners, for if he refuses it will cause a real conflict, and I don't want the break to come because of a mere secondary incident. And I won't ask him anything as a favor. You go and ask him; perhaps he will pay some attention to you . . ."

"It is important that I see General Villa."

"Sorry, Counselor," said the officer, "but I have orders not to wake him; he went to bed very late last night. What can I do for you? Tell me, and perhaps I can handle it."

I explained; at that very minute they were executing men among whom there were certainly innocent ones; I asked for an immediate suspension of the shooting.

"What the devil, Counselor!" cried a chorus of two or three fellows with pistols who were never far from the side of the guerrilla chieftain. "This seems important to you? That a few more or less should die? After all, this is a revolution. A lot more will die before it is over, including ourselves, today or tomorrow perhaps." And while they were talking, I could hear the shots.

"There, you see, it's no use, it's all over."

And so, terrified by what was going on, I left without saying goodbye to that gang. It was as if the shots had been fired at my own chest.

In the taxi, I told Adriana: "Even if I had arrived in time, I could not have saved them. These men are beasts, not human beings. Tell your friend Encarnación to forgive me if she can; I can't forgive myself for running with this kind of people." I cursed Villa and swore to hate him forever!

From Zapata I received proofs of his appreciation and requests for modest jobs for protégés of his, which I took care of at once. But ambition and envy blinded the pettifoggers of the South, they aroused the most ignorant generals against me, accusing me of being a friend of Madero and of working against the thing they dreamed about, namely spreading Zapata's control all over the Republic. In truth, the enemy of the spread of Zapata's rule was the Villa party that was saving itself for the future when it should have gotten rid of Eulalio. And because of my loyalty to Eulalio, the Villa men were beginning to direct their fire at me.

To my mind, the whole revolution had turned into a nightmare of cannibals. In every officer of the new army I saw a villain. And I was not so wrong, for night after night the Villa soldiers kidnapped well-to-do people and shot dozens of peaceful citizens who were total strangers to them. And it was well known that every morning in Villa's own railway car the favorites divided up the rings and watches and wallets of the people shot the night before.

To destroy Villa and Zapata after having destroyed Carranza: this was our mission, and to accomplish it we would seek the aid of all good Mexicans.

I took just one officer and two soldiers to constitute a daytime bodyguard, and the rest of the troop I divided into two groups that took turns in accompanying me home and guarding the house while I slept. Soon, however, bored with having to depend so much on others, I had recourse to a trick. I placed the escort at the Las Rosas ranch, where I had my official residence and where my family spent the nights, and I went to sleep in the houses of relatives or friends, constantly changing from one place to another. The higher government functionaries of the period frequently did this kind of thing. Only your intimate friends knew where you spent the night, and you went to your own house to sleep only once in a while.

"I have orders to ask you for data on your biography," a reporter said to me one morning. I replied, "I am too busy living it just now."

One afternoon I took Adriana to show her the inside of the building, and made her a present of one of my few thefts from the treasury, a handsome volume devoted to Rubens, with illustrations and text, thinking, "Who knows who will come along next? It is better that this should be saved from the fate that will soon befall it." And those who came first were the Zapata group, and then the Carranza crowd. Not content with pillaging all the furniture, the latter even suppressed the Ministry.

What we feared came to pass: Villa suddenly turned up in Mexico City and we had to make room for him at the official New Year's table; and with Villa present, it was obligatory to invite Zapata. The diplomats with their wives were already in the Palace when we remembered one hitch. Both Villa and Zapata, doubtless because of the number of perfidious assassinations they had committed, were in the habit of never being separated from their bodyguards, not even for meals, and it would be horrible to have a score or more of soldiers with fixed bayonets entering a room in which we were greeting the ladies. "See what you can do about it, now that we have gotten into this fix," said Eulalio.

I took up my stand in the anteroom. Villa arrived, clicking his spurs, arrogant in a blue military uniform but without ridiculous braid. I asked him to leave his escort at the door and he agreed. Tinoco then took him into the dining room, followed only by Fierro and one other gunman who stood all through the meal, covering his back. But when I made the same request of Zapata, who arrived a few minutes later, practically without replying to me, the southerner told his soldiers, "Go ahead in, boys!" and he lined them up against the wall of the banquet chamber. I must say that the diplomats and their ladies were brave and took it very well; they appeared to pay no attention to the military apparatus, and soon the good wine and conversation lent a joyful note to these scenes that might have come from a tragic operetta. It fell to me to sit beside Villa. Opposite us, Mrs. Ayguesparsse tried to make conversation with him. A photograph of the banquet has been reproduced in which I appear sucking a stalk of asparagus while Villa is gnawing on a chicken leg, and this document has been used to insinuate that I was a partisan of Villa. The certain thing is that at the meal Villa and Zapata occupied an official position that was lower than mine, since I was a Minister and they were only generals commanding troops. A little distance from my chair, at Eulalio's left, Zapata ate without saying a word. In contrast with the simplicity of Villa's costume, Zapata had dolled himself up in what bullfight fans call a gala costume. Indeed, he did remind you of a picador, what with his jaundiced complexion, African rather than Indian in character, and in his short jacket, covered with beadwork and gold.

The meal was excellent, with first-class French wines, and finally champagne, but they avoided making any toasts. When Eulalio gave the signal to rise from the table after the coffee, cognac, and cigars, Villa, who had been most correct, felt obliged to say something: "All right, gentlemen! Meal's over! Break it up!"

After that famous banquet I never saw either Villa or Zapata again, but I retained an amusing mental picture of how the latter looked at the moment when he was disobeying my order to leave his escort at the dining room door, and I thought to myself, "This man is scared."

Among Eulalio's constitutional powers was that of dismissing without explanation the man who was commanding the government forces, but he knew very well that Villa's answer would be to send soldiers to arrest and execute him. What was needed, therefore, was to be all ready to carry out the arrest of Villa or to defeat him the minute he rebelled. Eulalio could count on sufficient support to make himself respected in this way. The forces of Lucio Blanco amounted to ten thousand. In San Luís there was Adrian Aguirre Benavides, who informed us that we could rely on his nine thousand soldiers. In the capital (controlled by the Zapatistas to the number of about eight thousand and by more than five thousand Villistas), we could count on our side only one or two regiments attached to José Isabel Robles, and no more than five hundred directly under Eulalio. The plan called, therefore, for evacuating the capital to join the Blanco forces in Bajío and presenting a united front to the attack which Villa would unleash upon us from the North.

Adriana listened to me but did not share my optimism, and finally gave her opinion: "What you ought to do is to get out of politics; I don't think things are going the way you say they are; you ought to come to terms with Villa and not fight him."

For her part, she did not want to get involved in any more adventures. What hurt me was not the skepticism of her opinions so much as the contempt with which Adriana treated obligations which I thought were as clear as day and as noble as man's highest calling.

During my absence unbelievable things had happened such as the assault Villa made on the very house in which Eulalio was living, surrounding it with his cavalry to demand that he should not resign.

The Villistas understood that without the moral backing of Eulalio, who, quite apart from his personality, stood for the will of the Convention, they would have nothing to rely on except their military strength, and that they would be without prestige and quite outside the law. At the same time, they could not make up their minds to obey the government, but wanted to manipulate us all by terror.

With unparalleled boldness Eulalio had said to Villa, who, accompanied as always by his hired assassins, was pointing his pistol at him: "I have no intention of resigning; what I want is to get rid of your influence."

And Villa, disarmed by such frankness, almost wept, protesting his loyalty and promising improvement.

You could see in everyone the decisiveness, the enthusiasm for action that would free us from the shame of working with Villa.

I had everything ready, including my little suitcase which was already in Eulalio's house; downstairs, in an auto, Adriana was waiting. I went down to tell her the latest news, and then took her to a hotel in the vicinity to spend the night. It was agreed that the next day she should take a passenger train for Texas. Our farewells were tender and anxious, as we were not sure of ever meeting again.

From the *Manifesto* of President Gutiérrez

Generals Francisco Villa and Zapata have not only been disturbing elements within the social order, they have systematically prevented the government from doing its job in the most important branches of Administration. In the South, they have claimed that the government has no right to appoint the Postal and Telegraph employees. During the long period when that State was under the rule of General Zapata, not a single social reform was effected. A ferocious military dictatorship was the only kind of government. There were no elections, no civil liberties, and—the main thing—the solution of the agrarian problem had been forgotten, since instead of distributing the dispossessed lands and breaking up the huge estates, they had followed the system of giving guarantees and protection to large landholders in exchange for monthly payments made by the latter to General Zapata, who did what he pleased with the money. This is contrary to the public interest, for the only justification of forced loans or other attacks on property is that the money so obtained should be invested in public works, after having been deposited in the National Treasury and distributed according to statutes passed for the purpose.

All these facts clearly contradict whatever just and honorable elements there were in the Morelos Revolution. The Government gave sincere recognition to how much good there was in the movement in the South, how legitimate and idealistic it was, how closely connected with the broad purposes of the Revolution, but once and for all the Nation needed to see the difference between the deep-lying causes of the Revolution of Morelos and the Zapatista bossism which was taking advantage of them.

Worse, if that is possible, was the administrative behavior of General Villa. For long months he had been exploiting the National Railway Lines, burdening the Nation indefinitely with the costs it would some day have to pay for his pillage. Ever since I began my labors as President, I have proposed to take the necessary steps to put an end to the military administration of the railways and hand them over to a company that would run them, but in which the Government would have its representation. Nothing of this has proved possible, in spite of all our efforts, for every effort has met with opposition from General Villa, who exploits and runs the railways as he wishes. The same applies to the Postal and Telegraph Service. Another of the serious questions which concerns the government and the public is the problem of our paper currency; up to this day the government I am charged with conducting does not know how many millions of pesos have been issued by the State of Chihuahua, nor what limit is put on the issue, nor what use is made of the money.

Without consulting me, General Villa appoints governors and military commanders in the states he passes through, thus usurping the functions of the Secretary of Administration.

In the highly important branch of our international relations, General Villa also intervenes; in his constant press conferences with American newsmen and personalities of the government of that nation, he makes declarations, offers, and promises which are improper on the part of a General who ought to limit himself to his duties as a soldier.

Since General Villa returned to this city, I have become aware that kidnapping and assassination are repeatedly taking place. Daily, homes are violated, attacks are made on life and property, sowing fear and alarm in Mexican society. With shame and indignation I have had to be a spectator of all this infamy.

In these last months the revolution has encountered such difficult going and has achieved so little because of its division into factions, and because it has degenerated into personal rivalries. Those who follow Zapata, Villa, and Carranza are bad revolutionaries; so is anyone who fights for persons rather than principles, and at this time of grave peril for the Nation, it is necessary that all good Mexicans should stand united for the defense of principles.

I have hesitated for a long time before reaching this decision, which may have grave consequences and may lead to much bloodshed, for those who have not had the decency to respect the government they themselves helped to call into existence have the material power on their side.

I. General Francisco Villa is relieved of his command of the Division of the North.

II. General Emiliano Zapata is relieved of the command of the forces under his orders.

III. The government will continue to require the unconditional resignation of Carranza and will accept the cooperation of military leaders who have been supporting him if they desist from so doing.

Given at the National Palace, the 13th of January, 1915.

Eulalio Gutiérrez, Provisional President of the Republic . . . Counselor José Vasconcelos.

For their part, the Carranza group gave out our Manifesto from Vera Cruz, suppressing the charges against Carranza and offering it as proof that the Villa party was going to pieces. Obviously, we were the destroyers of the Villa party. Without our sacrifices, the cannibalism of Zapata and Villa would have lasted longer, and it was not our fault that the Carranza gang returned, but the fault of the clumsiness and cowardice of public opinion, which did nothing to help us, although it welcomed us enthusiastically when we entered the towns. Anyway, the battle of Celaya would not have taken place, and the Carrancistas would have been pushed into the sea if we had not dissolved the Divison of the North. And what is more important, we created the moral atmosphere in which battles are decided, even in the absence of public opinion. The loss of prestige we inflicted on Villa was such that afterward even a sergeant could have defeated him.

And I was overcome by the painful thought of the years that pass in futility for the impotent soul that cannot sing, nor paint, nor make music, and is incapable of any kind of lyrical response to the serene mystery of nature.

But perhaps I, myself, still had the resource of writing prose. Ruskin had found words to express the charm and, as it were, the musical delight of a landscape. Perhaps some day, when I had quite forgotten all the current of stupid events which was sweeping me along, I could tell the story, not of the vicissitudes of the politician, which are minor circumstances, but of the perplexity of the soul which discovers not only the many forms, but also the under-lying harmony of beauty; the order in things, which they must possess to achieve beauty. An infinite number of observations popped into my mind, almost making my head explode and leaving me in a state of depression because I thought, "I'll forget all I'm thinking, and it won't come back to me when the time comes to write my *Aesthetics*."

Poor America, you sad continent; with your second-class races always following the same course that we were following: man-hunting! Curses on the Villistas, fanatical followers of a criminal! And what dogs the Carrancistas were, with their fangs ready, and the Zapatistas worse than savages, "liquidating" lives with their machine guns, like their forebears in the old days with their obsidian axes.

Why shouldn't the Anglo-Saxons rule us? But this thought increases our sadness; for there is nothing more painful than to be obliged to recognize that our salvation lies in the hands of a people inferior to what we once were, a people incapable of rising to what we might attain.

Perhaps there exists a future for a race that will put to use the alluvial lands of the tropics, but the high country is, and will remain, a graveyard. With its mountains, it resembles the fleshless skeleton of a monster that perished millennia ago. "Earthy souls," Count Keyserling was to call us a few years later, speaking of the natives. And "the continent of the third day of creation."

In any case, we will never be a major country, with our body eaten into by the deserts of the North, with the poverty of the center, the interlaced line of the harsh bulk of the cordillera. The rains rush down the slopes, and the soil which sustains vegetable life is washed away, dissolved in alluvium, and earth that could have saved the plain is swallowed by the sea that hugs our coast. Not even in the golden age of the tropics shall we attain the power of Colombia or Brazil.

The strong whom we were displacing, the heirs of the colonial period, had made up an autonomous, powerful, and respected empire. The bands that we now led were incapable of consistency or even of conscience. They grabbed the land, but they repeated the lesson of socialism absorbed from the foreigner. Instead of replacing the owners and achieving a fair distribution of land areas, the present revolution, poisoned by the Yankee influence of Texas, would lead to handing the land over temporarily to the rebel steward, and then, without transition, through the hands of the demagogue and the petty politician to the Yankee trust and the Northern proprietor.

Here was a whole culture which in the midst of general apathy and incurable ignorance was melting away in our hands. Perhaps this is why, when we saw wine, the symbol of the civilization of our fathers, we set about drinking it in a kind of farewell rite. Those who came after us were whiskey and tequila men, addicted to the harsh drinks of savages, dull races that must feel the brutal blow of alcohol.

Aguirre Benavides arrived with six hundred selected men; but, after all, that was a sad contingent compared to the division of nine thousand for which we had been hoping since we started the movement in the capital. He arrived in a state of deep disappointment, saddened by the desertion of many in whom he had believed. We were defeated.

With our column we moved inland through the north of Guanajuato. One of the first marches was extraordinarily cruel. It was a winter night on the plateau; I kept my body well covered, but my knees and especially my feet, at the point where they came out of the stirrups, froze until I felt shooting pains in them. You wanted to stretch out in the road so as to protect your stiff limbs. At three in the morning we halted at an abandoned farm. We rested for some hours, warming ourselves with brandy.

The earth was hard and our blankets did not keep us warm; still, we dozed, and at dawn I dreamed: We were again in the capital under a brilliant sun. A gaily decked crowd surrounded a new building decorated with pennants. And I was making a speech: I was Minister of Education; I was inaugurating a new era for the country. I woke up with a rock hurting my ribs. The desolation around me, the memory of the last few days, the melancholy sight of the horses nodding their heads about us produced a contrast of such cruel irony that it made me reject the prophecy of my dream.

Nevertheless, I had glimpsed for a moment my future line of action. Presentiment does not reveal the approximate date of the event; but it does, at times, point toward it and in our imagination illumine the future.

It is clear that the danger is not that Mexico may return to primitivism: the Indian does not have the strength for that. The danger and the scheme are that a Spanish Mexico should give place to a Texan Mexico with the Anglo-Saxon acting as owner and builder, and the Indian as roadmender, peasant, and fellah, in "Mexican towns" such as you see from Chicago to New Mexico, more miserable than the medieval ghetto, but without the genius which suddenly blossoms and lifts the Jew above his oppressors.

It was then that Eulalio insisted on sending me to Washington to inform the outside world about our aims and activities. Also, in case it proved feasible, I was to go to Sonora to make certain of the cooperation of Governor Maytorena.

Manuel Rivas opposed my leaving, saying, "If you go, the Carranza group will put pressure on Eulalio through his brother Luis, to get him to surrender to Carranza and give up the fight."

Brother Luis was in command in the north of Cuahuila and had already threatened to defeat us if we did not go back to the ranks of don Venustiano.

"Don't you believe it," I replied to Rivas. "Remember that Eulalio has been the most determined in facing all factions."

For his part, Eulalio told me on the eve of my journey, "While you are in the United States, if a rumor gets around that I have surrendered, deny it. I am resolved to stand alone rather than do that."

When we were all on horseback, about four o'clock on an afternoon in March, 1915, we went to Eulalio's Headquarters to bid him farewell. There the majority of the chiefs were waiting, and one by one I walked around embracing them. Among us there was a mutual appreciation that had been put to the test by experience. And perhaps we had a presentiment that once the dispersal that was beginning with my departure was completed, most of us would never again see each other, united or separated. Almanza was one of the first to fall, while fighting Villa. His mutilated body was subjected to brutal torture. And it was actually, by some strange instinct, that I said the most effusive goodbye to Almanza. I opened my arms to him and he folded me tight in his.

"Believe me when I tell you I love you," he said.

"And I, too, have learned to hold you in high esteem."

I said nothing when I embraced the others, for one's voice is the first thing to break down under these circumstances.

In San Antonio, we only changed stations. There was no reason for stopping in that stronghold of vulgarity. The little newspapers published in Spanish represented various factions of low standing: followers of Huerta, Carranza, Villa. No decent public opinion existed and this led me to make the observation which they published: "I would boast if there were anyone worth boasting to, that I had been persecuted by all the tyrants of Mexico, from Díaz to Villa and Carranza." The phrase met the fortune of all pearls thrown before swine, literally and figuratively: nobody got the idea.

Picking up one of the papers, I read something that made me angry and I refused to admit that it might be a prophecy. Some hack, eager to ingratiate himself with the Carranza outfit, wrote, "Separated from Vasconcelos, General Gutiérrez will listen to reason and return to his allegiance to the First Chief." I was the plotter and schemer, the ambitious fellow who had led Gutiérrez into an impossible adventure. This made me sick.

The first day's stop we made was in New Orleans, to buy clothes and give ourselves a civilized rest. The next jump was to New York. There I found Adriana transformed. A few visits to a beauty salon were enough to have brought back the milky smoothness of her skin, that softness which is common among Parisian beauties. A few inexpensive dresses restored to her all the glorious freshness of youth. In the furnished apartment we rented in the Seventies, we began to receive friends from the Spanish American colony. Our eagerness to have some pleasure after the months spent in rough campaign life led us to attend a concert in the afternoon, the opera at night. On one of those nights we attended a performance of *Siegfried,* and when we came to the scene in which the bandits kill the parents and abscond with the child, it was impossible for me to hold back my tears, for with communication with Mexico cut off by the civil war, I had not been able to get any word about my children and I imagined the possibility that they might have been the victims of vengeance by the forces of Villa.

My brother Samuel was travelling with us, and through him I met a North American lawyer, Mr. Hall. With Hall I went to Philadelphia. There he introduced me to a colleague who was friendly with Bryan, the ex-candidate on the Democratic ticket, who was Secretary of State in Washington. The Philadelphian was a dry and pallid blonde, English by blood and North American by temperament— kind, frank, religious, and cordial. The first thing he did was to invite me to dinner at his home in the suburbs.

As it happened, the Philadelphia papers had published my picture the day before and had recalled my escape between the Mexican soldiers and the rangers of the Bravo River with the caption, "Mexican Rebel."

One of the regrets I felt as a result of the total defeat which followed was that I was in no position to repay generously this Philadelphia friend who made a trip to Washington to deliver the memorandum in which we members of the Convention pleaded for nonintervention in Mexican affairs and nonrecognition of Carranza and Villa, or indeed of any government until elections—the only way to create a legitimate government—were held throughout the whole country.

Our request was received respectfully but relegated to oblivion because we never reached the point of having enough military victories and were not sufficiently flexible to gain protection in exchange for tacit concessions.

Lack of funds forced me to live in seclusion in New York while the Carranza men were spending literally millions of pesos to achieve what they got a little later—exclusive recognition of their faction, in spite of the earlier public promise of President Wilson that he would recognize no government that was not based on general elections.

Always accompanied by Adriana, I began to frequent the Fifth Avenue Library. By giving her Plato to read, I could keep her entertained for a long time while I poked into the patristics and the gnostics of Alexandria.

"I will recognize none of the factions as a government," President Wilson had declared, and he suggested that they should all come to an agreement to elect a chief who would then call for elections. Before Wilson made this announcement, from the time of the Convention onward, we had been demanding the same thing; so the logical step would have been to give us moral support in order that our country could organize itself around the principles that our government incarnated. But you cannot expect logic or justice in the relations of the powerful with the weak. The one who always triumphs in these cases is the highest bidder. And we did not even get into the game of offering shreds of sovereignty in exchange for victory over our rival.

We did not enter the evil contest that was going on in Washington nor worry about it, because we were confident that the good sense and patriotism of our nation would throw out any deals and would discredit any faction that founded its future on the support of the North American government.

But I cannot deny that the sudden decision to support Carranza caused us naïve surprise, precisely because it was the leader of this faction who had seemed the most distrustful of Yankee policy, the most openly nationalistic and independent. The effects of Wilson's decision were not long in making themselves felt. With the arms traffic closed to Villa's faction, he could no longer put up a resistance to the forces of Carranza. With the discouragement of some of those around Eulalio, and with the preference shown to Carranza, there arose one of those surges of public opinion which, debased as they are, can be decisive. And the very people who had fought with the battle-cry, "Down with Carranza!" began to change flags.

It was not many days later that the papers gave us more bad news, almost incredible news. Eulalio Gutiérrez, the Provisional President elected by the Convention, was resigning and handing over to the First Chief, Carranza, his troops and the territory that we had won with so much blood.

Not for an instant did I fail to recognize the difference between going down to defeat because others are in the right, and being defeated in spite of the fact that one is right. The first sort of defeat is humiliating and poisons the mind. I have never experienced this. The second sort saddens one because of the dishonor of those who win, who in the last analysis are men like ourselves, and in this case were also Mexicans. A triumph like Carranza's was a national disgrace. This is how one's soul grows sick with contempt for the multitude of one's contemporaries who thus give in to ignominy, and even call it victory and celebrate it by ringing bells and shooting off rockets. This is how the Old Man went about, traversing half-destroyed towns and forcing the schoolmasters to line up the sons of the victims every time he thought a parade was a good idea, feeling that he was another Benito Juárez. One more agent of North American imperialism!

Nobody remembered the Convention; those who betrayed it were not even disgraced. It is wrong to expect that the future will remedy evils which only the human will of those who commit them can set straight. Peoples do not recover from their errors and crimes; they pay for them. Had it not been for the failure of the Convention, the revolution would not have ended as it did, in sheer confusion and piracy. Victory of the foreigner and decadence of everything Mexican. Triumph of the wicked, the imbeciles, and humiliation and sacrifice of the patriots and useful citizens.

We were all traitors, all of us who were beaten by Carranza, all of us who hoped to free the country from dictatorships and the cannibalistic practices that stain its history. Nobody would have imagined that it would be the loyal ones themselves, the followers, and not we, the traitors, who would bring down Carranza, and not only that, but kill him. But before the final disgrace of the regime, the country which did not have the sense to avoid it had to suffer through it. The followers of Carranza had to suffer in the flesh the humiliation of a victory which made them the lackeys of one man. The first who was thus marked was Obregón. Three circumstances had given Carranza a triumph which had come to seem impossible even to him: the com-

placency of Washington and the promises he secured there, the dis-
owning of Villa by Eulalio's government, and the military victories of
Obregón. To only one of the three factions that created him was
Carranza loyal: to Washington, which won't stand for deceit. He re-
paid us men of the Convention with exile, humiliation, and cruelty,
and the reward of Obregón was sharp sarcasm. Obregón did not lose
countenance. On the contrary, in front of the public and the troops
he gave the First Chief an embrace.

Exiled from my country by the bullets of Carranza and by my own
disgust with the situation, I shut myself up in the New York Public
Library and there found my true spiritual home in Greek philosophy.
Whatever was translated into French or English passed under my
eyes, and in addition, the commentaries of Zeller which I leisurely reviewed once more. As much to clarify my ideas as to give myself an
occupation that would last, I set myself the job of translating some
chapters of Plotinus in the University of Mexico classics series. I also
translated Porphyry's *Life of Plotinus* and had the idea of translating
Iamblichus in order to publish it some day. What a marvelous world
unfolded before my eyes every time an Alexandrian revealed his
thinking to me through the magic of the printed word! What did the
Mexican revolution and all its wickedness matter in comparison with
that immortal work of the spirit?

Everything would have been happy and peaceful had it not been
for the fact that so often an inner stab tore my breast at the remem-
brance of my children who were growing up far from their father's
care, and that I also felt remorse about a happiness in which my wife
had no part, but from which I could not entirely exclude thoughts of
her.

Adriana, less suited to solitude than I was, began to make con-
tacts which I never wanted to share. At first it was with people in the
neighborhood, mostly Jews, the only race that gets along well with
foreigners, perhaps because they are always strangers in a strange
land.

I soon tired of simple reading and note-taking, and started writing.
I spent several mornings at the typewriter. It was like the case of the
musician who remembers his themes but has lost the composition, and
produces different variations.

Now and then, as an exercise, she played on the piano Mozart's
Turkish March; her sinuous body, clad in a light dress brilliantly illuminated by the summer sun coming through the windows, moved

with the rhythm. What I was organizing under the name of Pythagoras was precisely a new theory of rhythm; an idea which was the
basis of a whole system of philosophy, and I came up with that page
which gave me ingenuous delight every time I repeated it to myself:
Pythagoras is meditating on the nature of things, and near his re-
treat an artisan is working on iron; his blows can be heard from a distance, sometimes dull and sometimes clear and loud, as the hammer
falls on the anvil. The intermittent sound of the beaten metal
awakens strange echoes in the mind of the philosopher. It seems as if
the soul resounds every time the iron imparts its vibrant clamor to
the air, as the string of the lyre vibrates sympathetically every time a
note is struck on the next string. The philosopher must have asked
himself over and over: "What is the essence of sound? Matter possesses a voice that reechoes in the souls of men; its mysterious expression is not always mute; it can sing in unison with the spirit. What is
the order that sound must have if it is to awaken this echo in us?"

The problem had now been stated which was to occupy me during years and years of reflection. It did not matter that the future was
full of menace.

According to my calculations, my wife, who was about to arrive
with the children, could hardly scrape together more than a thousand
dollars, even by selling some pieces of furniture, by sacrificing jewels
and savings; this would not last many months in New York. After a
lot of difficulty I found a new cheap apartment in the Two Hundreds. I felt grateful that my wife was bringing my children in spite
of knowing about my absorption in Adriana. This generosity of hers led
me to love her anew, in a fashion that had nothing to do with the
body, but in a brotherly way. I would see to it that they got around and
saw everything, even if afterward we had to go back to Mexico and
live on half rations. I would not look for work until the last possible
minute; I needed some months more in the library to finish taking
notes for the Hindustanic book which would pull together my re-
searches of many years. The chaos which prevailed in the matter of
occultism, New Thought, Yoga, and Theosophy impelled me to write
a book in which the extremely rich material of Indian philosophy
would be methodically set forth.

And my children arrived when winter was beginning.

My bank balance at the end of the year gave me the shivers. I went
downtown to the office of an old Yankee friend, an ex-client from
Mexico, whom I asked to help me find work. I suspected that he himself would offer me something, since he still had important interests
in our country. I was not counting on the fact that a rebel against

tyranny becomes a real bearer of the plague. Not even jokingly did my friend offer me anything in connection with his Mexican affairs, but he did give me a piece of advice: "Get out of this country, my friend. You are a Latin, you always will be; this is an Anglo-Saxon country, you have fewer and fewer prospects of a future here; you could at the most earn a bare livelihood, like so many others, and only in a subordinate position."

I had indeed been thinking just that.

I got the *Revista de Habana* to publish my *Pythagoras* in two installments. At the same time, they would permit me to publish the printed material in book form at my own expense. I could not fail to be distressed by the late date at which my first book came out, when all my comrades had already published something. It consoled me somewhat to learn the age at which philosophers begin to publish. In general, production of the kind of work to which only maturity can give exact form comes late in life. The more so, as every philosophical system is a kind of story of explorations in thought. It was not that I lacked subject matter. The very excess of ideas which I considered novel stood in the way of my giving them concrete form, and I ended by telling myself, "Later, when you have read what has already been done on the subject!" I did not understand the method of limiting oneself to a specialty like those who study nothing but logic, or read and reread a single philosopher. My job was not to be a professor, but an inventor. Whatever I read was material for future use. A great memory for ideas made up for my absolute lack of verbal memory, so notorious that I could never commit to memory even a short poem. On the other hand, a theory, an idea—those did not escape me. But for all that, I was not merely an ideologue. My ambition was greater; I sought a kind of synthesis for which I needed literature and the arts rather than abstractions and scholasticism.

When a new theme came to me, as, for example that of the symphony as a literary form, I became drunk with enthusiasm; I walked the streets in a kind of delirium, imagining chapter after chapter of books which could be written, whose development seemed to me an inspiration from heaven, making up for the havoc of an emotional life that had gone bankrupt. In general, my nature was better fitted for hymns and praise than for reflection. For this reason I rarely felt that I was a philosopher; what philosophized in me was not ratiocination so much as the ambition to grasp everything in all directions—thought, emotion, and action. That is why I have always ended up in the field of religious thought.

There is, it would appear, not sufficient stuff in man to create a whole personality for himself under the circumstances of our living, and what was torment yesterday, today is matter for laughter, and it all ends in mystery: the incomprehensible reality that eludes our grasp.

An urgent message—fate is always in a hurry in modern times— called me downtown. They offered me the Lima agency of International Schools. Two hundred dollars a month, plus possible commissions. Need I say that I accepted on the spot? It was immediately agreed that in a few days I would leave for Schenectady with Mr. Parsons, the head of the business, to get my briefing on the Institution. Unfortunately, I told my family and Adriana the news of the imminent journey. This new separation from my children was cruel, in view of how far I would be moving and the uncertainty about my return. Only the fall of Carranza could speedily free me from my commitment to Lima, and for the nonce this was premature. Adriana also showed no enthusiasm, but made up her mind to leave.

"Your job," they told me in Schenectady, "will be to increase the number of courses subscribed for in Peru." The subjects were mathematics, draftsmanship, motors, railways, mechanics, and electricity. The function of these courses, they informed me, was not to take the place of a university, but to help the young workers, the students who cannot afford to attend a University.

Schenectady, and its impeccable manager, left me with an impression of horror, but I did not hesitate before the challenge.

By the Ward Line I made the voyage as far as Havana with my wife and children. The hours during which the ship stayed in port we spent visiting the most important spots by car. Havana was beginning to beautify itself with the Malecón and the splendid parks along the Vedado. After so many months of listening to nothing but English in the staccato tones of New York, it was a pleasure to hear the Andalusian Spanish of Cuba. And extensive as the Americanization of the city was in its bars and de luxe hotels, the savor of Spain was too strong to be overcome. Our approaching separation embittered our last hours. There is nothing more desolating than the absence of one's children.

Havana had not yet been contaminated by the influence of Venezuela and Mexico, that is to say, by Gómez and Calles, which later would produce the tyranny of Machado. Still, there was plenty of corruption among government personnel, and along the sumptuous avenues they showed you the palaces of people who made their money in politics. But there was liberty, the full liberty of Latin countries

which includes not only the exercise of civil rights but also the full
flowering of the personality.

I spent the three days of waiting for the ship that was bringing
Adriana and would then take us together to the Panama Canal, in
dinner parties, visits, and long conversations on matters of culture.
Soon we were sailing toward the Caribbean. We had blue seas and a
clear sky for the voyage, and a clean ship with impeccable service,
with corners of the stern that were like palm gardens. One afternoon,
through the warm mists, enchanting islands appeared. The novelty of
the voyage had restored our confidence in the future and the joy of
being together. In Colón we found a growing city, active, modern,
with asphalt streets and signs in English, trying to be like Yankee
cities. In the traffic there were people of all nations, and Negroes, who
seem to be taking possession of the tropics which for other races are
places to pass through or suffer in. Among the passengers on board,
almost all Yankees, the only topic of conversation had been the engineering works of the canal and the spirit of enterprise in North
America. With all the pride of conquistadores, far superior to the rest
of the passengers, with their immaculately clean white clothes the
Anglo-Saxons passed through the lands which a century before had
seen the triumphs of Spain in the commerce of sailing ships and the
fairs of Cartagena. Not even the Spaniards, who were numerous
enough in the modern city, remembered the times of their ancestors
any longer, and everything tended toward serving the new masters.
It was instead the Yankees themselves who insisted on recalling
Balboa and the early civilizers of those regions.

The railway took us to Lima. We left our bags in a hotel recommended by another traveler, and set out. At last we were breathing
the legend-laden air of Lima. There were the famous arcades and
jalousies. In the plaza were porticos of Italian style like those of
Mexico, and the Cathedral that cannot be compared to ours but is not
without a certain charm. Stands of sweets were numerous around the
supporting columns, and in this respect it was easy to see that Lima
was our superior. The pastries and fruit tarts were what they must
have been like in Mexico before the suppression of the convents—an
absolute delight. In the center of the plaza there were palm trees
covered with dust. The street that was pointed out as the main avenue
seemed at first rather lifeless and without many shops. Still, the show
windows gave evidence of selectivity and good taste. Advertising was
neat and not garish as it is in North America. "Something of old
Paris," were the words of the guidebook, and we also found much

resemblance to old Mexico, without the elaborateness of our architecture. But the melancholy of the surrounding was in strong contrast to the lively, jovial air of the people. Nothing of that tragic expression which marks Mexican faces. In place of a barracks-room atmosphere, there was a free and easy feeling and an affability that were altogether captivating.

The Agency, situated in the Calle de Espaderos, was turned over to me by a very nice North American who had paid no attention to it; he had other fish to fry. At the end of a few weeks I had put things to rights and the business began to yield enough for my salary, which I never had to turn in to the main office.

There was mail from the North three times a month, and the first to arrive brought me the details of Villa's attack on Columbus and the beginning of the Pershing expedition. When we saw that Carranza had decided to work with the foreigners in persecuting his rival, Villa, we thought that our exile would soon come to an end, because the country, even if it had to put up with the North American troops that Villa had provoked into an invasion, was not going to forgive the man who by his ambition and stupidity had gotten into a worse fix than Santa Anna. I did not know then the unlimited passivity, the sheep-like patience, the criminal tolerance of our people in dealing with all dictators who do not hesitate to use terror.

With much less reason, famous Presidents in countries like Colombia were resigning; only among us does it not occur to anyone that one should impeach and get rid of a President who does not have the sense to avoid hopeless situations. The consequence is that for a long time now our country has not known the honor of giving itself a government, much less of getting rid of one. We have grown accustomed to putting up with things, with tolerating them, with no other outlet for our feelings than grumbling, cruel, abject jokes and underhanded sarcasm—purely verbal protests. Next comes the reconciliation of brothers in shame as together they drink nasty, coarse, brutalizing tequila.

It was not true that the North Americans were really to blame for all this. Imperialism took advantage of the brutality of the savages, but did not cause it. Often colonies remain colonies and even bless imperialism, just because submission to the outsider usually frees them from their own native ferocity. In history, we find that the only peoples who can preserve their sovereignty are those who know how to give themselves a decent internal order. It was distressing to think of what was going on in my country, and I continued to look into Peruvian history, thinking, "If these people who are, after all, of the same blood as ourselves, have been able to live according to truly human norms, why don't we make an effort to clean up Mexico and rid it of its criminal dregs and Aztec leadership?"

Riva Agüero, my rich, aristocratic, historian friend, could not be called blind merely because he did not see the terrible problem of all Hispanic American nations, victims of a new conquest achieved under the guise of the heroic legend of Independence, an independence which England paid for and from which the United States has derived the profit. In Peru, too, the oil already belonged to Standard Oil and the mines to the Guggenheims. A country that does not develop its own resources loses them, and nowhere do you see a spirit of enterprise.

In the United States the plutocracy has created a great gulf between rich and poor, a sharper separation than exists in Europe, at least in nations like Spain and France, which have an innate feeling for democracy; but the United States is so populous that rich and poor do not know each other, have nothing to do with each other. In Lima, on the other hand, the different social classes jostle each other and spend their time in mutual insults, distrust, and ridicule. Whereas in Mexico before the revolution, the caste of the rich laid claim to a superiority that was not merely economic, but almost biological.

I concluded, "This aristocrat is still in the period before running water, when for lack of showers and bathtubs you had a basin brought to the bedroom for a sit down bath. Even among us, in Mexico, railways and Yankee industry had popularized hygienic facilities, and you no longer established social distinctions by having your shirt ironed. For that matter, the question of cleanliness is not a matter of class, nor even of education, but of money. In the poor section of New York, baths are not abundant, and although the Yankees as a nation are the cleanest on earth, it is not unusual in the upper gallery of the theater or in church crowds to notice the odor of seldom washed women's heads.

In Mexico, the revolution, if it had fallen into less ignorant hands, might have put in command the more or less professional class which throughout history has been the repository of culture, the creator of values. But among us the situation was the opposite of that in South America. In South America, from one end to the other, the rich class runs things, the caste of the plantation owner, the boss with some claim to aristocracy in Chile and Peru, with the pomp of plutocracy in Argentina. Countries like this do not make progress. But in Mexico a catastrophe occurred that is perhaps worse, since with the upper class ruined, those in the middle have still not succeeded in winning. The

guidance of public affairs has fallen into the hands of the most un-
couth ignorance, by way of an army that is no true army, since it is
untrained and is recruited from the uneducated countryside. And
this army rests, not upon a citizenry that volunteers military service,
as in Argentina, but upon mercenaries recruited from among the Indians who are capable of nothing better than tramping upon values,
confusing goals, bastardizing ideals.

France since her revolution, Spain in the great days of the poverty-
stricken nobles, the United States in its triumphant development before the time of capitalistic stagnation, have been peoples governed
by the middle class which has won the highest position in politics,
business, and professional life. This is not exactly a bourgeoisie; it is
the victory of intelligence resting on a foundation of virtue. Virtue I
understand in the classical sense of rigor in behavior and sobriety in
manners, all improved by the egalitarian and libertarian feeling of the
Christian. The bourgeoisie is the corruption of all this and the rule
of the businessman's avarice, the seed of capitalism which tends to do
away with the middle class and make it into a proletariat. The main
reason for the backwardness of Spanish America is that a cultivated
middle class has never dominated a single one of our nations.

In Peru, as in Mexico, mines, oil, even the great transportation
enterprises and the export crops were in the hands of foreigners.
The foreigner brings in his own employees and leaves only menial
jobs to the native. The nationalization of wealth ought, therefore, to
be the beginning of every social program in countries like ours that
have allowed their patrimony to be lost. This is more urgent and more
effective than going about mouthing theories like fascism or communism which are also foreign.

The social problem, the problem of the industrial proletariat, is not
going to be solved by any specific doctrines such as Fascism or Marxism. The problem of the wage earner is going to be solved by the very
technique that created it. It will be solved with the disappearance of
the big factory and the methods of mass production. Correctly seen,
these methods follow from the imperfection of the machinery. As
long as the use of coal prevailed, machinery was expensive, huge,
and difficult to handle; you need a lot of capital to produce goods that
will pay for themselves. But the electric machine promises to be so
perfect that a single one, of low cost, will come to produce what today
requires a factory. So, necessarily and fortunately, we will go back to
the private workshop. The workman will own his own means of production and will not fail to fix prices and organize markets.

To conclude, let the economic system deal with economics; the economic system has nothing to do with the other problems, the really important problems of morality, pleasure, virtue, happiness, freedom.

Capitalism is bound to disappear because it is the betrayer of freedom, but Marxism and the base ambitions of the totalitarian states must also fail, for man must constantly rise above his works.

I stayed overnight at Riva Agüero's house because the next day we were to get up early for a trip on horseback to Pachacamac and the Inca ruins.

"There was the place of worship," explained my guide.

"A pretty place for religious meditation," I commented, "but what did those barbarous, stupid Incas know about the things of the spirit? A mechanized race, bowing down in droves before the Son of the Sun, the Inca. I despise them! . . . I know you are interested in Inca archaeology: the well-ordered State. You dyed-in-the-wool conservative!" I spoke half in jest. "You are like the Yankee archaeologists who spend their lives and their money around here and in all the ruins of America. They make Indians fashionable, the better to bury the Spanish sediment which the colony bequeathed us. And then, after getting rid of us mestizos and creoles by means of successive rebellions of Indians, the Yankees will occupy the position once held by the Spaniards of the colony, for it is obvious that the Indian by himself and cut off from the Spanish tradition, will remain what he is in Texas, a fellah and a pariah. This is why the Yankee universities spend so many millions of dollars in excavations in Pachacamac and in every site in Mexico where a piece of crude pottery turns up. You must realize that the archaeologists are the advance guard. They take white Mexicans and creoles at an early age, give them scholarships to study archaeology, train them in the Smithsonian, and then twenty years after the scholarship a book appears full of learned apparatus, in which over a signature of Spanish origin, it is asserted that the indigenous civilization was wonderful when it was destroyed by the Spanish. We have lots of riffraff of that kind in Mexico already."

"Flanagan is considering a plan for building a railway to Iquitos," I explained to Adriana. "If they give him the contract he will take a trip with the engineers who are to study the line, and he has invited me to go along. Imagine penetrating the Amazon wilderness! I'll bring you jaguar skins!"

Giving me a cold look, she asked, "And in the meantime, where do I stay? Or shall I wait for you in New York?"

Frankly, I had not thought about what she would do meanwhile, and to that extent her complaint was justified, but the veiled threat in her talk of New York startled me.

And we sank into vulgar recrimination, "I was an egoist; I never thought about anybody but myself. Well, I was right, she was a mill-stone around my neck, but it was my fault: I had taken her away from New York where she had a future. Soon, perhaps, when I got bored with her, I would leave her abandoned there."

"Look," I said without thinking, but feeling that I was pronouncing terrible words, "If you want to, go to New York."

"All right, I will, by the first boat."

Then, really irritated, with an air of mutual defiance, we started hunting in the paper for the date of the next sailing toward the North.

We did not talk about the matter any more and it even seemed as if we had both forgotten our quarrel. On one of the following nights I wrote the story, *The Tragic Hunting Party*, in retaliation for the trip I did not take, for I did not even see Flanagan again; but soon, à propos of some other bitter dispute, the subject of the trip was remembered and she settled on a date; I offered to have the ticket money ready.

In reality, her going frightened me, for I had a presentiment that it would be permanent. "Go to Mexico City, to your own folks," I had said, "and I won't oppose you; we'll separate temporarily and perfectly peacefully, but bound together forever. But don't go and stay in New York, because I'll never look for you again. I know all too well the kind of life you will have to live there."

That irritated her; my doubt appeared insulting to her. "So you think I'm common, do you?" And she coined a phrase: "You love me, but you don't respect me! And I need to be respected!"

It was ten days before the date I feared, and the hours became one long agony. It was frightful to let her go. And yet, at the back of my mind, deep down, two or three levels down, a malicious voice whispered, "Since she wants to, let her go. She will make her own life. She'll be happy and you'll be free."

It was beginning to be the style to wear short skirts, and in New York they carried the style to extremes. I thought and then said, "You are getting ready to go there and show off your legs."

She whirled around as if I had struck her; then, laughing angrily, she cried, "I'll do more than that; you'll see. I'll marry a gringo; Latins don't know how to treat a woman."

From that night on we didn't speak. Two days later she sailed.

The best chronicler of Lima began flattering me.

"Do you know what I like about your *Pythagoras?* The style."

"What?" I laughed in amazement. "Style? It is not a book with a style; it claims to have ideas."

"All right, all right; but your style, my friend, reminds me of Oscar Wilde. You know the test to which I put a style? I set about trying to change the words the author has used; if my substitution is better, the style is bad; if I can't find a more exact word, the style is good. Now, your style is clear and precise."

I stopped working and resorted to reading. In the National Library, González Prada was the Director. I had been introduced to him and he had given me a warm welcome. I found him, as he was said to be, upright, intransigent, a fine type of white man, ruddy in complexion and quite white-haired. In any case I enjoyed free entry into all parts of the library, but I was not in search of rare manuscripts and have never cared for incunabula. All that is fine for those who appreciate books for their covers. There are others who seek their substance.

One Sunday I happened to go to the house of don Ricardo Palma. His son, Clemente, always treated me with kindness in his paper, and the great old man was a patriarch of letters, always good tempered, interested in all questions related to America right up to the end of his long life. Listening to him talk, I learned details of the history of Mexico in its relations with Peru, of which I had had no idea. Generally speaking, in my time we scorned the history of our own country.

At midnight I put the letters in the mailbox; then I said to myself, "Seeing that she is amusing herself, I'll do the same." And calling a coachman I asked him to show me the best places for a gay evening. It had been years since I had gone to houses like this. Those of Lima reminded me of the ones of my student days in Mexico City, perhaps with some superiority in the available personnel, for the Peruvian race is on the average very beautiful, with a slim waist, long legs, fine features, nice to deal with. However, I experienced what I had read about in a certain French novel: a deserted husband who never succeeded in arousing any enthusiasm with another woman, ended by forgiving his wife. What I would do was not to pardon the fault, but make a resolution of chastity and renounce all women!

About this time Villarreal wrote me. In his opinion, it was a good time for me to come to Mexico. He was writing from New York. There were three kinds of exiles, as they said in those days: the rich exiles, connected with the Díaz regime, were in Paris; the middle-class exiles, from the defeated revolutionary factions, were in New York, where it was possible to find work; the lowest class of exiles stayed, *faute de mieux,* in San Antonio. Someone added, "And those who stayed in Europe because they couldn't raise the money for passage home." The fact is that no Mexican dictator threw more people out of the country than Carranza. It was because he was afraid. The illegality of his behavior was apparent.

Chance helped me to get out of my commitment with the company: some honorable compatriots, exiles belonging to the Zapata faction, were passing through Lima. I proposed to one of them that he take my place. The branch office was informed, and I soon received the acceptance of my resignation and of the new appointment.

Before sailing, I had a chance to accompany Riva Agüero on one of his political trips to the high Sierra region.

The telluric feeling of races that have gone back to the animal level. You cannot find in the peoples of history any that are more limited in the power to change and progress than the aboriginal races of the two Americas. Human activity was on the wane when the Spaniards arrived and continued so for centuries afterward—imagine what our peoples would turn into if suddenly they were pried loose from their European cultural matrix. Not even the United States would escape the retrogression of the Red Skin! But it is clear that the real danger is not this; but lies rather in the decay that is making way for the new conquest. The Yankee knows it; we are not primitive men, but decadents. It is not a ferment that is working among us, but a disease. In any case, the Yankees are right when they say: "Old Mexico." Youth would be the new cosmic race which we could forge; but Indianism means going back for millennia.

When I took the boat, Luis, the proprietor of the pension, said, "Well, I hope when you come back the bay will be full of flags flying to welcome you."

He undoubtedly thought I would return some day as Ambassador. I did not feel that way, not because the prospect displeased me, but rather, as I watched a beloved coast disappear, I felt the melancholy of one who knows he will not return.

Talking to Emilio Madero on the boat, I insisted, "We men of the Convention and friends of Gutiérrez have not failed. What failed was the country, which was not wise enough to support us. The crude pseudo-revolutionary crowd of bandits that today thinks it runs the country, knows booty but no victory."

Emilio urged me to go with him to New Orleans, but New York drew me with cords of steel. I had been in Lima for nine months, and I was bringing back no more than two hundred dollars and some sketches for feeble essays, *Aesthetic Monism* and others. But nothing of this mattered; what concerned me, what obsessed me no matter how I tried to fight it off, was the problem of Adriana. For almost three months I had not received a single word from her. Would I find her in New York? How? What I sought in Adriana was her unique, irreplaceable quality of being for all eternity a part of my destiny. My story with Adriana was the adventure, the miracle, the experiencing of the infinite through the meeting of two temperaments. To such an extent, I thought, suddenly moved to tenderness, that I would go to the house of the other man and abduct her with my fists, and whatever she did, I would not break with her unless she deliberately and coldly broke the vows that bound us.

But at once the flesh spoke; the wounded male bellowed, "If I could, I would open her bare belly with a sharp blade!" or with a trick I would get her to Harlem and pay a dozen Negroes to violate her before my eyes!

In a comforting half-dream, as soon as my head touched the pillow, I saw our Lord Jesus Christ with his luminous tunic, and I ran with all my strength to kiss its border. My eyes filled with pure tears and the infinite joy of his grace rang in my ears. The God of all mercy had passed by me, and when I was fully awake, I felt my mind at peace. I had, as it were, the feeling that nothing that happens to us is definitive except the conquest of the light of the Lord.

A certain brand of psychology calls this conversion, and the Yankees call it being "twice-born." In my case it was not conversion but a return to my faith. I don't want to deceive the reader by saying that I made an immediate resolution to turn over a new leaf. No, the Lord did not talk to me about that. I did not see him as a dominie, as a theologian, nor as an irate confessor who denies absolution. I saw him as he is, all Compassion. The gift he bestowed on me was salvation, not a sudden undeserved conquest of virtue.

To put down something of all that was whirling in my brain, I traced the letters of that poor essay in the volume entitled *Aesthetic Monism*, which presents our Lord Jesus Christ, not only as the figure foretold by the Hebrew prophets, but also as prefigured in Hindustanic ideology, as Buddha, the all-merciful, the final revelation of eternal wisdom.

Piety and goodness: this is what the world lacks, and it is well that we should recognize these values as the supreme ones, at least in the deity, since it is so difficult to put them into execution in the world.

A North American salesman, an acquaintance from the ship, accompanied me on my visit to Kingston. Architecturally, the city is inferior to the others of the Antilles. What Kingston needed was more time under the Spaniards, to acquire a square with arcades, forts like those of San Juan of Havana, palaces and walls like those of Cartagena, a cathedral like that of Santo Domingo. The inferiority of the English colonial system can be seen also in the distance separating the classes; the Negro does not joke with the white man as he does in Cuba or throughout the Caribbean. It was a misfortune that Jamaica fell into the power of the English. If it had remained Spanish, it would be today a nation like Cuba, like Santo Domingo or like Mexico. It became English and was turned into a trading post.

Don't tell me that there has not been a mixture of races. There are in fact lots of mulattoes with dark skins and curly red hair. But their position is not recognized, they are denied and ignored. In the United States the same thing happens: the mulatto tends to draw closer to the Negro, for the other path is closed to him by custom.

It did not cross our minds to look more closely at the temptresses, but a little later, in the port area, some music attracted us. Penetrating through a narrow alley, we came out into one of those sailors' havens, a narrow hall, dimly lighted with couples dancing veiled in tobacco smoke. The women were of the black race and the clients white. Leaving one group, a free and easy young woman, slight and with a good figure, took my arm to dance. She had a sweet voice and the hard elastic flesh of her people. And in her whole person there was a gentle rhythm like that of the Cuban Negress, the rhythm of the Antilles which is so different from the harsh, angular gestures of the Negro women of North America. Many men have relations with Negro girls out of a desire for the unusual and without conquering their physical repugnance, which naturally is reciprocated. In the state of mind in which I found myself, I do not know whether any other woman could have produced the same impression of humble, human sympathy. Her vigorous black body was throbbing, and I thought, "This is love! Why take it seriously? Why make a tragedy out of it, if it is a matter of instinct, and instinct is innocent?" There was a human soul within that beautiful body, however much prejudice might deny it, and one must love it or leave it. She did not deserve that mere chance copulation which commercialism makes still more deplorable. Looking around I could see that I was not the only promiscuous one. I stayed three or four days in Jamaica, always in the company of my Negro friend.

From Panama I had written to Rigoletto, announcing my arrival in New York. On account of a mix-up in Jamaica, I telegraphed him of my changed plan to sail from Santiago. I asked him to notify Villarreal and my other friends. I had no idea he was in touch with Adriana. The reply to my last message reached me on board two nights before our arrival at New York. It was laconic: "Adriana and I together wait for you on the wharf."

"What happened to Adriana? Your telegram said she would come to meet me."

"She is at home," he replied. "She is expecting you; she sent me to meet you and wants us to go to see her right away, to have a talk."

"And what are we to talk about?"

"Well, she wants to tell you that she has fallen in love with me and begs you to let her alone. Your letters have hurt her deeply. She has shown them to me. What do you expect me to say? It's a terrible business. I'm the first to regret it, but we love each other."

He began to tell me details of his own intimacy with her, and he repeated, "The best thing you can do is to leave New York without seeing her."

"No!" I cried. "You go and tell her for me that she's a whore, and come back and tell me how she takes it! And you know another thing; if you don't do it, you and I will kill each other!"

We left the bar and I waited half a block from the house. I was amazed at his docility, and half believed he would fool me, that he would give her some excuse or other and come and tell me whatever was necessary to calm me down. It was a regular farce. In ten minutes he was back; he clutched my shoulder, weeping.

"She threw me out, she threw me out of the house; she said I was a coward. 'So that's the kind of friend you turned out to be!' she cried when I tried to explain. 'You know what you are; you're a coward. Get out!' And that's all she said."

The first evening I looked up Villarreal. I found him feeling fine because the impending downfall of Carranza was obvious; still, no one could imagine when or how he would fall. Of all the solutions, the worst was to wait for the elections, which Obregón would certainly win, for that would be a kind of legitimization of the whole regime. That which had been created by force and not votes had no right to create a legitimate successor for itself; it ought to suffer the punishment of all usurpations of power.

Obregón, after having resigned the Secretaryship of War, alleging that he "didn't want to dirty his hands with it," had taken refuge in his State, making preparations for the future, but without clarifying his general policy either for or against Carranza, whom he still continued to call "the Chief," and from whom he accepted favors and permission for some lucrative pieces of business.

The worst thing about the situation, Villarreal and I agreed, was that Villa kept out of sight. He was still marauding in Chihuahua and Coahuila, wearing a sort of halo as a result of the failure of Pershing's expedition. And as long as the opposition was affiliated with Villa, the natural thing was for the mass of the country to support Carranza as the lesser evil. Consistently in recent times, the governments had been bad, but the opposition still worse. This happens in countries in which there is no solid mass of citizenry, but only factions, differing in their personnel, but alike in their savage methods and their selfish aims.

Of every barbarian among those who govern us, who kill, rob, destroy, and leave scorched earth behind them, it is said later by the historians of our obscure subhistory that they meant well and that the only thing wrong with them was that they were not surrounded by good men. As if a man without culture, without civilization, could surround himself with others who are not like himself! As if true ability, in any part of the world, would be willing to subordinate itself to the judgment of a ruffian!

She entered without warning, going around by the corridor and gliding into the room in which I was walking up and down talking to my brother. He left, making the excuse of some business he had outside, and so we remained alone together, and I said, "Do sit down!"

And she replied, "How pale you are! I wanted to see you so badly!" And then, "You are very generous. I got your letter, but I don't need anything. I managed to get them to send me money from Mexico, and I am going into renting furnished rooms. You'll see."

Her act in rushing to my house, her incredible presence, had disarmed me. Without doubt, if I had had any warning, I would have been ready to throw her out, but this way, her coming unexpectedly and with that humble attitude in the face of disaster, and having made up her mind to start working so as not to be dependent on anybody, made me feel as though it were someone in the family coming to consult me after one of those tragedies which transforms one's whole way of living. I stood there just looking at her, and I saw that she, too, was pale, had gotten a little thinner, and that her face showed traces of worry. And I objected that she might lose the money, that she would be better off with her own folks, and she kept explaining her plans, how sure she was that she would make out all right.

She avoided talking about what had just happened, and after a few minutes she said, "I only wanted to see you; now I'll go; I don't have far to go; my house is very near by."

Since it was already evening and she was walking alone, I had an instinctive feeling that I ought to see her home. She agreed readily and when we reached the door of her place, as I was saying goodbye with my hat off, she said, "Come in. Why shouldn't you call on me as a friend, now that all that is over between us?"

I had a quick vision of the scene that after all that had happened would certainly take place: blows, ferocity, and then the satiation of lust. I don't know where I got the strength of will to avoid it. I put on my hat and left.

But the poison had taken. I lived through days of trying to shake it off.

At five o'clock one Saturday I knocked at her door.

She was not surprised to see me. She even asserted, "I had a feeling this morning that you were coming. I was expecting you." And a long, dangerous, roundabout conversation began; we tried to avoid the serious topic, but kept falling into it. She did the talking; I watched her. It was getting late, and she remarked, "I haven't anything in the house to give you for dinner, but if you like, we can go out."

I agreed, and she went to change. I stayed in my chair beside the window, but she called, "Look here, don't you think I've gotten thinner?"

Once more I resisted temptation. She put on her makeup and jewelry, and we went out. In a restaurant with the inevitable orchestra, we made a pretense of gaiety. It grew late; I walked her home, went into her room, and this time did not leave. That night I saw her weep real tears, not hypocritical ones, but sincere and bitter.

About ten on Sunday, we were again walking the streets together.

A cold wind was blowing. Her gloves were well worn. It made me sad to see them; I looked for a Jewish shop, one of those that never closed, and bought her a new pair. She put them on, deeply moved. It would have been better if we had never known each other!

I had been drawn to San Antonio in the hope of joining one of the armed movements that were being prepared to attack Carranza. The same purpose was in the minds of all us exiles, and there was discontent to spare, and opportunity, but what was missing was organized effort. While I was waiting for things to shape up, I devoted myself to the business of selling some clothes I had acquired in New York; Villarreal had helped me with this transaction by furnishing part of the capital. And as there was no immediate solution for the political situation, I decided to send for my family, who reached San Antonio without difficulty. I spent some months working and observing my children, whom I took to school and cared for personally, the way one cares for a treasure which is a living, changing miracle. The press, the accomplice of all those unspeakable regimes, still, twenty years later, continues to distort the truth, deny charges, throw the blame on "our reality," and above all to present as paranoid whoever dares to tackle the task of putting a little common sense into decisions, of requiring a little decency from public officers, some modicum of virility in public opinion. And this is not all, for as everyone knows and as will become clearer later on, it was not a matter of passing censure on a policy, but of condemning a betrayal. To shrug your shoulders in the face of these facts is to be completely lacking in the qualities of an honest man.

Let anyone begin leafing through the press of the United States in the Carranza period, the years 1914 to 1917. At the beginning, Carranza is attacked and censured. But once Wilson grants him recognition as Supreme Chief of the Mexicans, there is a complete about face. In the United States, the press is well disciplined in foreign affairs. It requires only a hint from Washington to make all the parties and groups—which in this respect do not differ—subordinate their private judgment to the order from above. Hardly had Washington smiled on Carranza when the press of all shades began to chant his praises.

The Saturday Evening Post went over to Carranza, and later followed Calles just as loyally.

The first condition involved in the recognition of Carranza was breaking the European Bank for the sake of the Yankees and placing the monetary policy in the hands of the American Treasury.

In Public Education, naturally, the so-called "Plan" had to show itself in cruel exultation. The Ministry of don Justo Sierra, the pride of Mexican civilization, was killed off by Plagianini. The Plan cannot endure seeing Education possess the kind of unity which would create a national conscience. The states-rights theory of Carranza, improvised on an occasional trip to San Antonio, declared that the schools ought to be run by the municipalities "as in the United States." This phrase, "as in the United States," has been the letter of marque for all kinds of nonsense among us. They did not even notice that since townships in Mexico do not have independence nor any important source of tax funds, it is impossible to hand the schools over to their tender care. But the law was carried out, for the First Chief never reversed himself: he issued decrees, and a decree is not subject to discussion, it is carried out; and so, in the capital itself you could see school buildings like the one in the Plaza de Carmen, being turned into offices for the administrative bureaucracy; others went back to being barracks.

While Carranza was President and Dictator, he allowed himself to be given a sumptuous house near the Paseo de la Reforma. The cost, not less than four hundred thousand pesos, was paid by favorites recognized as exploiters of the regime and generally hated. If there is anyone who judges that accepting gifts of this kind is honorable, I will wait confidently for a time when new generations or new races people the land of Mexico: then the historian who reviews the archives of this rotten period will have to proclaim that Carranza was a thief.

I never went in for political leadership because I have always reserved my participation for mental work which investigates the whole length and breadth of the world. The politician has to limit himself to a reduced area. But I have always thought it was a man's patriotic duty, and more than that, the duty of man as man, to do his part to make the environment in which his life is spent cease to be that of a cannibal tribe and to convert it to the purposes of civilization, of at least a lowly civilization.

So it is that in those days I would have followed any honest man who raised the flag of regeneration. But the Mexican intellectual lives a cramped life. Long years under the rule of brutality have reduced our class to a servile condition, good enough for the pettifogging bullies who draw up the legal papers after the assassination has been consummated. The inferiority complex thus becomes contagious, and so we get the unique case of Spanish America, in which the college and university man feels unfit for command, is sure that these posts belong by right to the worst ruffians, provided they are ignorant enough. And it was definitely in order to break with this pattern that I decided to accept responsibility if my turn should come.

The situation of the country was terrible in 1917, pregnant as it was with all the foetuses which would soon be born monsters. This obvious situation and the conviction that my destiny was, in essence, connected with things of the spirit, made me concentrate once more on writing.

My *Monism* was published, and it sold.

One morning I went to the post office. Among the letters was a fancy white one. It was hardly necessary to tear it open; it was an announcement that said in plain printed letters: "So and so (a Yankee name) and Adriana X, announce their marriage, which took place on such and such a day in Brooklyn, New York."

The first effect was as if, when I put my hand into a box, a spider or scorpion had bitten me. I started and said to myself with a smile, "Well, now I am free!" But I did not feel like staying alone, and went to see some friends. At dinner time, I went home and was gay with my wife and the children. It was an almost unrestrained gaiety!

But as soon as night fell and I was alone in the room where I was in the habit of reading or working, what a frightful, savage struggle burst out in my heart!

She had carried out her threat. Now I should carry out mine, as if someone else were holding my hand and moving my pen, I wrote an insulting letter, a despicable one. "I left an old pipe and some slippers there; be careful to save them." And I ended by challenging him to a duel.

The thing about the pipe was true enough, but not the slippers; I have never been one for slippers. I put on my shoes in the morning and take them off to go to bed. Slippers are something for a too-domestic type—and I have spent half my life traveling—or else they are for people who have uncomfortable shoes.

Then, as if it would do any good, in a burst of madness, I added some lines for her. "If you married out of spite, leave that gringo and come south; I am waiting for you."

The last thing that passed through my mind, only to be dismissed, was the possibility that they might decide to turn my letters over to a judge, to accuse me of libel. But it seemed to me offending her to suppose that she was capable of having united her life with the sort of a fellow who could behave in such a crude way.

The farm hands of our friend Watkins were almost pure-blooded Mexican Indians, and they were well treated and well paid, or at least better off than in our country, their own country; otherwise, they would not have moved North . . . but they were fellahs, they were prisoners of a situation which is the natural result of every conquest. Since Texas became an Anglo-Saxon country, since the war with Mexico, the Mexican has been looked down upon there, as has the Spaniard. "Down with the conquered!" who are now a plebeian class, the same in free America as in the ancient country of all tyrannies, Africa.

Identical with the situation in Texas would be the situation in all of Mexico if the Plan triumphed, if the Carranza party remained in power. The Texanizing of Mexico—how many have desired it without suspecting in their imbecility the kind of future they were preparing for their children!

It is not that Mexico lacks prophets. The trouble is, it doesn't listen to them. Worried as I was then by a thousand distractions that prevent one's thought from taking form, I still contributed to clearing up the existing situation by continuing my polemical writing with *Crater,* the defender of the Indian, in which, without ceasing to defend him, I pointed out the dangers of the anti-Spanish policy, which is the basis of the Plan, as well as the dangers of the evil deeds which Carranza was committing at that moment. And Caso, in the same period, was writing distinguished books which brought him fame, but which won for him no government post through which he could carry out his ideas.

In a ridiculous situation I stayed in Laredo for more than a week, hiding in the house of a poor but generous friend until a small loan reached me, which allowed me to move to New Orleans, there to wait for the boat for Cuba.

I had spent two or three hours in my chair in the library when I felt a hand on my shoulder and saw above me the kindly face of my friend, Cepeda Winfield. "I've been looking for you since noon, why didn't you think of giving me your address? I said to myself, 'Where can he possibly be? Surely, in the public library?' And I was quite right. This is urgent; Hopkins wants to see you! See him right away at the St. Charles. I think that you can't go to Havana now."

Hopkins' argument was, "Come on, Pepe, make up your mind; you won't be sorry. Tomorrow at ten o'clock we'll leave for Los Angeles."

Up to that moment he had not even told me where he was inviting me to go.

Los Angeles, a new city, with buildings that are not very tall, but all brand new, with sun and a blue sky, low green hills in the peaceful distance, and the wide Pacific; and along it, enchanting beaches. Some corners sheltered flower stands, as in the capital of Mexico. There was freshness and cleanliness in the atmosphere. The air and the mountains were still Mexican; only the modern houses and the people were foreigners. That is to say, they seemed so to me, if I imagined myself back to the California we had lost. Some of Mexico remains, my friends admitted it, and they praised it courteously.

The Yankees have made good human use of California, not only because they have built cities and parks, monuments and roads, but also—and this is the main thing—because for a long time they have brought about the co-existence there of races from all over the planet, Chinese and Mexicans, Italians and Frenchmen, Indians and Negroes. And the average wage has become the highest in the world. Life there is free and genuinely human, and throughout the territory there extend like a smile on the face of nature, orchards and gardens thick as a jungle. Christian life, fair and hard working, produced a kind of benediction, and we arrived just at the time of a turning in the road. Liberty was quashed, social demands were repressed, under pretext of war and for the sake of the plutocracy which had been turning California into its garden, with a loss of the human quality of its civilization.

It was the old round of Bacchus, carried out in automobiles, and in a vast area of mansions and palaces—with greater wealth than the Greeks ever had, but without any spiritual tone. We called all that "fast life." It was a continual round of drinking and smoking. I suppose that among them, behind the scenes, there must have been a lot of affairs, but of that I cannot speak with certainty, considering how reserved the Anglo-Saxons are in such matters. Everyone of the members of the group knew he was risking a nervous breakdown, which would be followed by a rest cure in a de luxe sanitarium. It was the custom to end the round of cocktails with an improvised meal on the beach at nightfall. They undressed there, in the cabins of some club, men and women alike; after cooling themselves in the surf, and still dripping with sea water, they sat around campfires eating sandwiches and sausages. Under these circumstances, to be sure, it frequently happened that couples, under the pretext of walking off their supper, would get lost in the shade of the cliffs, but as the slogan of their English forebears has it: "Honi soit qui mal y pense." And that discretion was a good lesson for me, since the worst thing among us is usually not the sin, but the gossiping that accompanies it.

Undressing to go ascetically to bed, I thought, "What great guys these modern Yankees are!" A while back, traversing a California highway with magnificent views, I had commented on how I disliked the advertisements of industrial products and the story of the guide who points out monuments and palaces dedicated to the man who invented the safety razor or who is in the chewing gum business.

"Why don't you ever remember Emerson and Poe?" I asked Sears.

"Because," he said, "this is a stupid country. You ought to know that by this time, Pepe."

Self-criticism, I reflected, is an advantage that new countries have over old ones.

Among themselves, the Yankees call us renegades, because of the indifference with which we look upon the stupendous work of Spain in the colonies. In the official literature it is not uncommon to find the imperialist praising the type of Mexican like Benito Juárez. In his heart, the Yankee looks down upon or ignores those who were simple instruments of peaceful conquest. On the other hand, there is no Anglo-Saxon who does not venerate Hernán Cortés. We cannot pardon him for having given us, with less blood than any caudillo has shed, frontiers that extend from Alaska on the north to the Isthmus of Panama on the south! The Yankees of California and the south feel that they are continuing the civilizing work of Hernán Cortés.

San Francisco is one of the few cities of the New World that possesses an aura of mystery and legend, because of the Chinese, because of the Spaniards who won it and could not keep it, because of the pirates and the gamblers of the Golden Age. The Chinese quarter of San Francisco provided the literary material for a generation, and even in 1918 the laws excluding yellow people had not completely destroyed the Asiatic population and the atmosphere in the restricted zone which was set aside for them.

Los Angeles possesses all the attractiveness of a city of parks; on all sides one's view is refreshed by brilliant scenes, and at every step, along streets and parks, are spread carpets of lawn and flowers, fountains and pools of water lilies and iris. People seem to be dressed in new clothes and the houses are all freshly painted. The main body of the city could not be more beautiful nor better cared for, spotless, one might almost say manicured. But I defy anyone to find in it the slightest trace of a soul.

In talking to the girls who go to the cabarets to dance and drink, I found some of them hopeful of making Hollywood, others with no interest in the screen; you would find in all of them the same standard uniformity which pursues the traveler from one end of Yankeeland to the other. The favorite pastime of every one of them was figuring out the salaries paid by the movies. The news of the day, a stereotyped comment on the war and its leading personages, the hygiene of dress and food, and a certain concern with science, such is the mental baggage of blondes and brunettes, young or not so young. It reached such a point that when any one of them began to talk, you had the impression of a scratched record, so exactly alike did they sound, from the Atlantic to the Pacific.

Our immigrants to Yankeeland lose their civilization, for all the refinement they may have acquired in cultivated cities like Guadalajara or Mexico City is exchanged for jazz rhythms and negroid dance movements as soon as they have spent a couple of months in the dance halls of California.

What betrays the barbarian is the ease with which he imitates the civilized man in all that is related to the use, consumption, and waste of wealth, and his incapacity to create and replace what is spent. The sense of responsibility which obliges us to budget our expenditures, first making sure of the indispensable, a house in which to live, a stable business, and only after these needs are met, seeking luxury and pleasure, is something the immigrant absolutely lacks.

On the office table they left a telegram for me, containing the totally unexpected news of the death of my father. He died before reaching sixty, though his robust constitution had promised long, untroubled years. He had no other vices than those of the table, which are often dangerous, and were pampered by the culinary skill of Antonieta. The news stupefied me. I didn't ordinarily give much thought to my father, because I knew he was happy in his modest post, his enjoyment of which my worst enemies would not think of disturbing. But slowly, and as if from a depth hidden by several levels of superficial concerns, there came to the surface an affection so deep and full of feeling that it astonished me. I was experiencing a cruel pain. I began to feel irritation and despair, rebelling against an ill fortune which had deprived me of the consolation of seeing him in his last days. Finally, the tenderness associated with so many deep, pious memories made me burst into tears.

The conviction that I had often been lacking in affection toward him, and at times unjust, at least in my thoughts, caused me real pain. There appeared before my eyes that countenance, the only one on earth that looks at us, as it were, with ecstacy, the face of our father, the image of God.

The Old Man would fall soon, swept away by hatred, punished by the avenging rebellion. Not many months earlier, the dishonest regime had refused to give a general unconditional amnesty to all exiles. Now the amnesty would not be needed, and it would not fall to the lot of one who was guilty of crimes against the country to grant it.

We had reached the time for regicide, tyrannicide—the only case in which homicide is heroic, and not a crime. On the other hand, the vilest of crimes is killing for supposed reasons of State: homicide committed by the tyrant.

It was the first time that I had made a nonstop trip from New York to Los Angeles. Nowadays you make it by plane in a few hours, but then five days by train was considered remarkable. I spent the last day of the trip with no food except a banana. That is how close it was after paying for a farewell supper and my last small expenses. My bank account in San Diego was already much reduced, but I had made up my mind. I would not even look for work. Before that I would finish my Hindustanic book. I would shut myself up for several months to write. All that treasury of profound thought was analyzed in my notes, and it was only necessary to put it together into a volume —to make the paragraphs turn out right.

Sad as it is to admit, I did not feel like a homebody and was not alarmed by the idea of the anxieties and solitude of old age. Medieval couples, when they became convinced of the uselessness of living, went their separate ways to the convent to learn how to die. That is a beautiful way to grow old. As for myself, I wanted long, wild years, like those of the ancient prophets, devoted to sleepless meditation, laden with experience, rent by profound visions, years of bold clamoring for Justice and Mercy!

It was necessary to reduce expenses to the minimum. Butter was dear, and I proposed to eliminate it from our table. My little daughter, who was beginning to repeat phrases and even to put them together in the English she learned in kindergarten, made an innocent, really unconscious and rather funny protest, in which she showed her excellent English: "I can't stand without butter!"

I must have stuck to my typewriter for two or three months, ten or twelve hours a day, with only the interruptions necessary to check up on data in the local library. Taking the writing of a book seriously seemed so strange in that environment of businessmen, gamblers, and politicians, that I practically had to hide out to avoid explanations and serious questions. And even my wife, perhaps bored at seeing me chained all day to my typewriter, remarked as she watched me work, "Well, so it's that easy to write books! Nothing but copying from other people!" Indeed my *Hindustanic Manual* has lots of quotations; it is a systematic summary of traditional doctrines.

How full my head was of philosophical ambitions! One idea after another went through my mind, ideas which needed a book for their full development, but which were frequently reduced to a miserable article.

New York was the rather unpleasant sewer of refugees from all the dictatorships of America, and among us we cherished a common ideal and a vague hope of getting the advanced groups in every country to work together on the common task of emancipation.

What we hoped would occur openly, by direct rebellion, was not possible. The opposition, badly led, divided, and incoherent, could accomplish nothing against Carranza, and this in spite of their being in theory the whole Nation, and in spite of the fact that Carranza, up to the last moment of his activity, was still ignorant of the most elementary principles of morality and political skill. The worst infirmity of people is the one that attacks majority opinion, attacks opposition movements whether organized or unorganized, movements doomed because they lack a credo and a Chief. For that reason, because properly speaking it did not have a definite opinion, the sheeplike mass that tolerated Carranza began to take the side of the Obregón adventure, which essentially meant disloyalty. Then they would present themselves in the role of reformers and purifiers, those very same people who had brought on the Carranza plague.

We decided for Obregón, in spite of the unsavory character of his candidacy. It was not, properly speaking, a candidacy, nor would his be an election, since he would not have a rival and his only competition would come from the official side; but in the uncontainable struggle of power against power, the triumph of Obregón, who represented at least a vague hope, was better for the country than the triumph of Carranza, who already stood for evil.

Obregón, then, promised something, and no serious personal obstacle separated us from him. On the other hand, Carranza had created an abyss between himself and honorable men.

I never accepted more than a part of the creed of the Industrial Workers of the World, which, in a word, is the one that has permeated the Mexican Revolution—our poor revolution without a creed of its own—because it believed that an illiterate Zapata, a Calles, a candidate for a village schoolmastership, can by means of a few assassinations be turned into a scholar and reformer.

I read Henry George again in those days. He was to be found in all the people's libraries and he is easy, pleasant, impressive reading. A great but incomplete talent; a man who discovered a vein of economics and was skillful enough to follow it to its end, to extract everything possible from it.

I read Marx, too, at the time. *Das Kapital,* in three volumes, was passing from hand to hand among the readers in our "Circulante" group. They found it very obscure, those people who did not understand a word of the strange Hegelian philosophy. In reality, it is not obscure, but it is behind the times. It is based on two worn-out philosophies: Hegel's and Comte's.

In cafés and cheap restaurants we spent long hours discussing the methods of Lenin and the new principles of education introduced by Lunacharsky. One of them I copied when I came to direct the education of Mexico: the publication of the classics, for which certain writers of purely local fame have criticized me on the ground that it was an aristocratic measure. Humbly I confess where I got the idea for this edition which, among all the fine things that the Ministry of Education produced in my time, is what gives me most pride and joy. Incidentally, my edition of the classics was also the best propaganda for Mexico in all its years of existence. There is nothing like it in Spanish and there never has been, and no Spanish-speaking person of any cultivation has failed to admire the collection, and to bless it for the good it has done for humble readers, for the honor it brings to the country which the enemies of this publication have dishonored. Amen.

One or two months before the democratic campaign began, Obregón was in Los Angeles and spoke to us.

I asked Obregón just one question before offering him my support.

"Will you go on to the end, like Madero, or accept an unworthy defeat out of loyalty to the First Chief? We don't want any repetition of the business of the Aguascalientes, you know." In Aguascalientes, as you remember, Obregón promised to bring down Carranza; afterward he became his right hand man.

Obregón was very pleasant to deal with, very intelligent; when he came to power, he always behaved correctly. He made no *mea culpa,* nor did he become arrogant; with his natural talent he got out of the difficult corner into which my question put him, asked as it was in front of six or more people, and replied, "Look, Counselor; we are going to forget the past. Now I promise all of you," he added, looking around the group, "that we will do things well; you will not be dissatisfied!"

He said no more, and nothing else interested us. And temperamentally, he was the antithesis of what we had been calling *pocho* and *pochismo* [Yankee-loving, Yankophilism]. Of pure Spanish blood (although in his desire to follow the style, he claimed to be Indian) and brought up in a decent home, in the old-fashioned atmosphere which you can still find in Sonora as in few parts of the country, Obregón had the real Mexican mentality.

In the newspaper of the Obregonists in the capital, they published regularly the articles that Villarreal and I sent. It is easy to see why, in a campaign against Carranza, what the old lackeys of that regime said was of no use. They had to lay hands on the exiles who had suffered persecution for the sake of justice. And we began to serve as the clean, severe mask of justice, behind which the traitors hid to launch their darts at the former protector and chief.

The great papers had ridiculed Madero, considering him weak, and they deserted Obregón when he represented the highest interests of the country. Afterward, when he went over to the Plan, and served as a gendarme to Calles, they fawned upon him to the point of masochism.

Unexpectedly, Calles offered his resignation from the Carranza cabinet and left for Sonora. One or two months after his entry into the State, all the local forces had risen against Carranza, and Calles came to be in command of the troops, Military Commandant, or what have you, of the whole region.

To me they later gave a Ministry, or in better words, allowed me to violate the Constitution of Querétaro in order to create a Ministry of Education which was the only glory of the Revolution, but which Calles destroyed with fury and handed over to pickpockets; this story does not belong in the present volume, but it is not superfluous to call attention to it. I have few pages left in which to complete the present volume, and I shall limit myself to what I have planned; I shall tell how my return to Mexico and my entry into the new government were accomplished.

The friendly presence of Antonio Villarreal woke me one morning. "This money," he said, "is from the treasury of the State of Sonora, and it is to help you join the movement."

I pocketed the money and said jokingly to Villarreal, "Tell them that they still have to give me public satisfaction and a special car to take me from the border to the capital."

A few days later I received a telegram; they asked urgently for a proclamation drawn up and signed by me, to distribute among the troops in Sonora for the purpose of explaining the change of front to them and justifying it. I drew it up and sent it by telegraph. It was reproduced all over the State. Poor fellows, they had to use an exile in order to speak to their own people, since what they had to tell them was the opposite of what they had been preaching during the six miserable years of Carranza rule! Discredited before the bar of public opinion by their servile attitude toward Carranza, the Obregonists relied on the word of revolutionary veterans like us, provisionally and until they could give us a kick and go back to their old tricks, that is, to despotism, political assassination, abuse, theft, and submission to the Plan.

A few weeks later, when Villarreal and I reached Mexico City by way of Monterrey, General Obregón was waiting for us in the station. And it was that very morning, in the special car that brought us to the capital, that we learned of the assassination of Carranza.

Adolfo de la Huerta arrived. With his habitual generosity he opened his arms to me, gave me a place at the table of Chapultepec, took me hither and yon with him on official visits. Always with him was Miguel Alessio, who now began to act as Private Secretary to the President. And it was Miguel who reminded him in my presence, "Well, why don't you sign it and give Vasco an office, so he can take charge of the University?" Turning to me, he added, "Adolfo agrees that the Ministry of Education ought to be reestablished."

I was obsessed with the idea of the University as a base on which to create the Ministry which would perhaps transform the soul of Mexico.

De la Huerta sent for me. "Pepe, I didn't know you were a Catholic!" he said.

"Well, now you know it; but Catholic or not, if I am to carry on in

Education, the Protestants have got to get out of there, for they have carried out a foreign policy; but since this is making difficulties for you, I have come to give you my resignation."

De la Huerta then conducted himself with perfect loyalty as a friend and with firmness as an official. "Don't ever tell me that again! Go and do what you like!"

In the various schools of the University, even if it meant sacrificing old fellow students and friends, I tried to appoint as Directors men who would know how to demand something of professors and students. I persecuted and tried to exile the type of Director they had had in the chaotic periods: the director who is always smiling at the students, flattering them, raising their grades, so that the poor kids won't lose a year's work. In the case of the "poor kids" who don't deserve to pass because of their incompetence or laziness, you are doing them a real favor if you drop them from the rolls so that they can quickly get to work, according to their aptitudes. And incidentally the level of the school rises too.

While we were still discussing in the Rectory of the University a law that would create a Federal Ministry, we were already beginning as a Ministry. I invited many exiles and absent scholars, from the United States and Europe, capable of making an important contribution to the great impetus that the work had gained. With complete impartiality we opened the doors to merit, and he was my best friend who worked hardest at the common task.

Soon you could feel that something serious was beginning in the country. There were some who compared our pulse to that of a vibrating dynamo, from which energy pours. Since then many a fool has called himself "dynamic"; the adjective made a hit; but it is not enough to move; you must know where you are going. It is not the aim of this book to tell the often repeated story of that fiasco.

PART THREE

THE DISASTER

THE DISASTER

At that moment, by the irony of circumstance, I was the government as far as education was concerned. And to make the change more apparent and more productive, I decided to overstep the narrow limits of the old Ministry of Justo Sierra, who had jurisdiction only in the Federal District and two deserted territories, by making the projected Institution once and for all a broad Ministry, whose functions would cover the whole country, and then extend, as to a certain degree they came to do, to all Spanish-speaking countries. We could, of course, count on the warm cooperation of interim President don Adolfo de la Huerta and the promised support of President-Elect Obregón.

The truth is that even under the series of barbarous administrations from which we habitually suffer, there had always been in every State a self-sacrificing group of lovers of knowledge who, considering the miserable resources they had at their disposal, accomplished real miracles. The great brief intellectual flowering which we succeeded in creating would not otherwise have been possible, for the hardest thing to improvise is culture. Everywhere we found intelligent men of good will who in the midst of indifference and skepticism were almost heroic.

I had my Law outlined in my mind. I had had it from the time of my exile in Los Angeles, before I dreamed of being Minister of Education, when I read what Lunacharsky was doing in Russia. I owe my plan to him more than to any other outsider. But I think my plan turned out to be simpler and better organized—simple in structure, but vast and complicated in its realization, a plan which managed to attack every problem. I drew it up in a few hours and corrected it several times, but the complete outline appeared to me in a single instant, like a flash of lightning which illuminates a design that is already there.

In a word, my plan set up a Ministry with branches all over the country, divided functionally into three great Departments: Schools, Libraries, and Fine Arts. Under the heading of Schools come all scientific and technical instruction in its various branches, theoretical as well as practical. The creation of a special Department of Libraries was a permanent necessity, for the country was struggling along without serving the reader, and only the State can create and maintain such services, which are complementary to the school, the adult school, and schools for youths who cannot matriculate in secondary or professional schools. The Department of Fine Arts took under its wing—starting with the teaching of singing, drawing, and physical education in all the schools—all the institutes for more advanced work in the arts, such as the old Academy of Fine Arts, the National Museum, and the Conservatories of Music. From the very beginning in the primary school the three Departments worked together, each charged with its proper function: the sciences taught by the school itself; physical education, singing, and drawing under the direction of specialists rather than the regular classroom teacher, and the Library serving them all with its various sections: children's, technical, literary, etc.

I also set up auxiliary and provisional departments, to supervise teachers who would follow closely the methods of the Catholic missionaries of the Colony among Indians who still do not know Spanish, and to attack illiteracy in densely populated Spanish-speaking areas. Deliberately, I insisted that the Indian Department should have no other purpose than to prepare the native to enter the common school by giving him the fundamental tools in Spanish, since I proposed to go contrary to the North American Protestant practice of approaching the problem of teaching the native as something special and separate from the rest of the population.

Scarcely had I left the Ministry when the above mentioned Institute of Indigenous Education was started, but it was a copy of the Indian policy of the United States; the anthropology of the Smithsonian won out; and consequently the Yankee influence was imposed on all the rest of the program. We left to the States, generally speaking, the business of looking after urban schools. In townships which already had a school, we did not open a new one but gave our support to the existing one. In general, the Federation took upon itself the heavier burden of rural education. We left private persons quite free to maintain schools, which in many cases we encouraged. And to get official recognition we required only that the private schools should adopt a minimum part of the official study program. What the Ministry spent, it administered itself.

On the day of the inauguration of General Obregón, I was in the Palace with the various groups assembled there, when they called upon me to speak to the crowd from the balcony. I promised that the educational work would go forward. When the ceremony of swearing in the Ministers was over, Obregón called me aside and said, "I was sorry that you, who do more work and earn less than anyone else in the government, could not take your seat in the capacity of Secretary."

I thanked him for the thought, and replied, "The existence of the Ministry will only be a matter of two or three months, if you give us your support in the University."

Obregón did give us that support unreservedly. Of his own volition, he authorized me to ask Congress for a big budget for the first year of work, an appropriation, if I am not mistaken, of twenty-five million pesos; a ridiculous amount for a serious task, but double what had been assigned to education by the Madero government and three times what Justo Sierra had had to work with in the time of Díaz.

With the object of pushing through the educational reforms and preparing the ground for the large expenditures our program demanded, I had taken advantage of every opportunity to reach the public through statements in the press and speeches. From one end of the country to the other came expressions of support and congratulations. The most remote towns were aroused by the assurance that they would soon get a teacher, or at least a package of books from the new circulating libraries. Every holiday was the occasion of new efforts to get the whole people interested in the work of the University and to secure their cooperation in it.

A brother of Blanco Fombona, the novelist, who had escaped from Santo Domingo after resisting the Yankee occupation, was with us, teaching the recently established course in the history of Spanish America. I had set up this chair in anger, calling attention to the fact that a course of this kind existed in every Yankee university. But we had never bestowed on anyone the honor of a special chair devoted to our common struggle, and to the parallel existence of twenty sister nations bound together by language, religion, race, and culture. Hispanic-Americanism was launched, and October 12 was the day!

As luck would have it, we had already established the rule of having short programs. The condition I made for presiding at ceremonies was that they should not last more than an hour and a half. At the end of the programs I waited for the customary shouts: "We want the Rector!" I pretended to be distracted; they shouted again: "We want the Rector! We want the Rector!" I left my chair. A strange force seemed to take possession of me.

"As far as possible, I will step out of my role as a functionary of an administration which has friendly relations with all established governments, and I will, instead, fulfill my duty as a counselor of youth, a duty imposed on me by the position of Rector. So it is as a teacher that I tell you I am saddened by all the talk about the past, and by the way we ignore and close our eyes to the shameful present of our Spanish America. Have you all asked yourselves what we are doing to be worthy of the glorious inheritance of our fathers? Take the people of Venezuela, trodden under foot by a despot who is stupid and coarse, cruel and dishonest; he owns half the republic and keeps all the patriots in prison or exile. As we can't do anything else against him, take a Venezuelan flag and carry it through the streets, so that it may float freely in Mexico, since it cannot do so in its own country!"

A stupefied silence filled the hall; excited "Vivas!" applause, and shouts burst out; the meeting broke up and as if by electricity the word got around in the schools. In the School of Fine Arts, a young lady belonging to the aristocracy grabbed a Venezuelan flag and rushed into the street, followed by the students. Other schools converged at the University and soon a powerful column had been formed which marched across the city and stopped in front of the newspaper offices, shouting "Down with Juan Vicente!" and "Long live a free Venezuela!"

The reaction came the next morning. All the papers gave prominent space to a summary of the events of the previous evening, but major attention was focused on the note of protest presented by the Minister of Venezuela, and the obsequious, practically servile reply signed by our Minister of Foreign Affairs, one Dr. Hidalgo, disapproving of my speech and giving assurances that it did not have the backing of the government. I sped to the University office, called the stenographer, and dictated my resignation.

The situation became interesting and De la Huerta solved the problem skillfully; he returned my letter of resignation without a reply; I announced that I had withdrawn it, and everything was peaceful. A few weeks later, the Minister of Juan Vicente left Mexico. And what is most important, the government of Venezuela, along with his retirement, decreed the freeing of political prisoners.

We were in a period of genuine revolutionary reconciliation. The conditions under which Obregón had triumphed, supported by the country that wanted to see itself free from the Carranza government, led to harmony. The simple and generous character of the interim President, De la Huerta, had made a fine contribution toward uniting us all in forgetting our differences and working for the good of the country. The general unconditional amnesty granted by De la Huerta had led to the return of a great number of people who had fled abroad.

At the time I am reviewing, *Zapatismo* no longer referred to the blind, unconscious, bloody policy of Eufemio Zapata, nor yet to that of the drunken brother of his, Emiliano, but to a group of men of good will and known capacity within the framework of the intellectual poverty of our political circles—men determined to rescue from the chaos of the barracks the agrarian reform which demands the destruction of the big estates and the creation of small farms, the restitution of the land, the *ejidos,* the Indian received from the Colony, which afterward was usurped by the landholders of the Díaz period.

And so when I was the Rector who already carried some weight throughout the whole country, and they invited me to come to Cuernavaca to visit the State and see for myself the progress they were making in agricultural organization, I naturally had to accept. And one Sunday I went with a couple of friends in an auto, without arms and without bodyguard, trusting in the loyalty of my old adversaries.

I restrained myself from saying what I thought, since by a tacit agreement we were all refraining from mentioning the name of don Emiliano. What was going on at this time was re-affirming the old ideal of the revolution, giving the peasant land and economic help with his sowing, education for his children, freedom to enjoy the results of his labor.

Hardly had the news of the Zapatista celebration been published when the city papers and various writers of the old Díaz gang threw themselves upon me, alleging that I had dishonored the University by associating myself with the glorification of a man like Zapata, who had ordered massacres worthy of Attila, at Tres Marías, a few miles from the city, where children died and good, defenseless women were attacked and violated. The accusation hurt me, precisely because of its apparent justice. With this difference, that I had been against Zapata while he held power. I did not keep quiet; I explained more than once the reasons for my joining in homage to a man who had fought on the opposite side, the purely personal character of my acceptance, and the fact that the purpose had been to wipe out the bitterness of long-past struggles.

However, for months, and over the years from time to time, the calumny that I had associated the University with an act of homage to Zapata has continued to plague me through the mouths of disloyal enemies, whose insistence, after all, pleases me, for it shows that they haven't found any more serious charge to bring against me. And I have never compromised with those who have tried to revive the fame of Zapata.

I have never been fond of billiards, nor of any game which causes us to waste time. The concept of "pastime" is meaningless when life offers us so much of interest; but I have taken a look at everything, and so I do know the green cloth of the billiard halls of our ancient capital.

I recommended to Asúnsolo the group of sculptures which now stands at the top of the façade of the Ministry of Education: a Minerva whose proportions put the engineer on the spot (since he had to strengthen his cement), with Apollo on one side, and Dionysus, on the other, figures that were to be conceived in Nietzschean terms which I afterward adopted in my *Aesthetics: Apollonian and Dionysian Art*. In the center, Minerva, representing ancient wisdom, meant to us the aspiration toward the spiritual, the longing which was later to culminate in Christianity. It is clear that the right and obvious thing to do would have been to put a cross behind and above, but the Jacobins would have torn down the building before it was finished. At the ends or corners of the façade there were to be statues representing Aviation, which were not finished, since the building remained incomplete because of my separation from the job. In the forecourt was to go a monumental staircase, and in the courtyard four statues dedicated to each of the races that have contributed and are to contribute to the formation of the New World: the white, the Indian, the Negro, and the yellow, united in a synthetic ideal which I began to entitle the cosmic race, or the final inclusive race.

Asúnsolo finished the Minerva group and made plaster casts of the colossal statues to represent the races. We exhibited the casts in one corner of the patio so as to study their proportions, and this ruined us. Certain schoolmarms became alarmed about the completely nude forms planned by Asúnsolo and complaints began to reach me: "Was I going to permit this kind of immorality to be flaunted in a building frequented by boys and girls?" I hesitated, postponed my decision, and ordered the plaster casts removed for the time being. Then Nacho Asúnsolo rebuked me, "It can't be true that you will let yourself be pushed around by these old maids; what would be strange about an exhibition of this kind if it were in Europe?" I let him talk, but in the end I expressed my own cause for alarm,

"Look, Nacho, there are going to be four statues, all nude; up to now we have shown only the white man; then will come the Indian and the yellow man; but what are we going to do when the Negro is installed?"

Nacho went away disconsolate, and instead of the statues, the sculptor Mercado made the bas-reliefs which can be seen today, dedicated to the four continents.

To make a simple plan which is coherent and complete, and then carry it out as circumstances permit, and to create the circumstances when they do not appear—such is the secret of a really great piece of work. On the other hand, if you proceed without a master plan, the effort, no matter how sincere and determined, will get lost in details, will be scattered in fragmentation. The work of the Ministry, as I have already pointed out, was to be basically threefold, fivefold for the present. The three essential parts were Schools, Libraries, and Fine Arts. The two auxiliary activities were bringing the Indian into the current of Spanish culture and bringing literacy to the masses. There was still throughout the country a scarcity of books comparable only to the scarcity of schools. In any American town of fifteen thousand inhabitants you will find a Carnegie or Public Library with fifteen or twenty thousand well-chosen volumes. When we began our work there was not a single well-run, modern library in the capital. The National Library, located in a beautiful but quite inappropriate building, had been and still is a storehouse of books rather than a center for public information and reading. They gave me time to build the truly great library that the country needed, but it was necessary to begin by erecting an edifice that would cost several million pesos, the best building in the country, something that would be a rival to the Cathedral or the Palace. Moreover, the Director of the Library was a person incapable of understanding the problem. I asked the president to get rid of him for me, since he was one of his friends, and, as a matter of fact, he did offer him a Legation. The good man, already on in years, replied, "I see you want to do me a favor, Mr. President, but I beg you, don't take me away from where I am. I like this obscure position."

And I had to wait. I was not in any hurry either, to take over that unfit building and to install a good modern library in it. We should build our own buildings. Aside from that, the strength of our National Library lies in its six hundred thousand well-chosen volumes, inherited from convents and colonial collectors. This part of the treasure was safe, for the honesty of the sluggish director was beyond suspicion. But the library is extremely poor in modern books. We needed, then, both a building and books. To get both, we had to awaken the public's interest in reading. Where should you begin if you want to get people to read? Is there a cultured person anywhere in the world who would deny that the starting point for good reading is the classical authors of humanity?

Jokingly I said to Obregón one day, "What this country needs is to sit down and read the *Iliad*. I am going to distribute a hundred thousand Homers in the schools of the nation and in the libraries we are going to set up."

Where was I to get a hundred thousand copies of the *Iliad*, and as many more of the *Odyssey*, and so on, the tons of the hundred best books in existence? To ask the Spanish publishing houses, the only ones that might have met our need, would take time and leave the way open to the people who would make commissions on the transaction and so raise the price considerably. In consequence, the obvious, businesslike, patriotic thing was to utilize the government presses that spend their time producing bulletins that nobody reads, or books for government employees; let them print the classics. President Obregón put them at my disposal.

But the various government printing offices had been brought together by Carranza into a big central one, full of bureaucrats and political hangers-on. The plant itself, expensive and heterogeneous, was deplorable. And it was ridiculous that a Secretariat like that of Education should not have its own press. I took real pleasure in violating another regulation of the Carranza regime, and began to build a printing shop in one of the patios in which the University was then located, in Santa Teresa. At the same time, we imported presses and sewing and binding machinery from the United States. And in a surprise move, the first green cloth copies of Homer, Aeschylus, Euripides, Plato, Dante, Goethe, etc. appeared all over the republic. Not by a long shot did I reach my goal of a hundred classics, but issued barely seventeen, most of them editions of fifty thousand volumes. From the booksellers of Spain I got only a hundred thousand *Quixotes* in a cheap school edition, and twenty thousand dictionaries. Special library buildings were constructed in some cases, and in others old houses were adapted to our use. And every school had at least one room reserved for public library service, for adult and student use by the whole neighborhood.

I could not even start the building of our National Library. The grandiose plan that I had for this work, I give in detail in my book *De Robinson a Odiseo*. But while I was in office I at least succeeded in saving the ground that had been set aside by the foresight of don Justo Sierra, the most illustrious of our predecessors.

I did not take Malhora into account. On the eve of the discord and the circumstances that forced me out, I read the notice in the paper that the government was putting the valuable property up at auction. De la Huerta and Obregón saved the property at my request. Time passed; Calles came in; the people in education changed; but Malhora became more powerful. Finally, he won; a private hotel belonging to him or his associates today usurps the space on which Justo Sierra and I dreamed there would rise Byzantine cupolas in the style of our finest churches to shelter the treasures of the world's printing presses.

And so, O my country, the efforts and dreams of your best sons go down to defeat, crushed by the political system that delivers the power into the hands of imbeciles and evildoers!

Hardly had the discussion of the Ministry of Education begun when an unforeseen peril appeared that filled me with anger. No less than ten deputies demanded an important role in the debate, advancing their own ideas about how the new Secretariat should be organized. One wanted it to concern itself only with rural education; another wanted it to devote its efforts exclusively to the Indians, while others coveted the honor of planning the new organization, creating its departments and sections as they chose. I immediately began to fulminate, attacking the meddlers both in the press and in private. "Those who oppose the new law will not be re-elected," we repeated in the corridors of the Congress. We had to bring pressure to bear on individuals. The best system was to take the deputies to see what we were actually doing. Within the city itself there were plenty of impressive examples.

Men of good will prevailed in the Legislature that approved the Education Law. Among the deputies were many schoolmasters who, out of class loyalty, helped us against the politicians. The proof of the excellent quality of those first congresses under Obregón is the number of deputies it was necessary to kill, kidnap, torture and buy when, later on, the time came for the brutal act of imposing Calles upon the nation. Our work was strengthened by the conviction that you could get somewhere in Congress by means of rational argument and appeals to patriotism.

The activities of the new Secretariat soon became known abroad, the principal magazines of North America noticed them, and there was talk in Washington of the possibility that the United States also might create a Federal Department of Education. It is really hard to understand why there are federal departments of forestry and hunting and fishing, and not one to look after culture.

When Sarmiento carried out his educational work in Argentina, the first thing he did was learn by heart the theories of Horace Mann; then, in case he forgot anything, he transported to Argentina two or three hundred North American school teachers and established them on the Pampa. Later, at the very time that I was working in Mexico, Leguía in Peru contracted for the services of I don't know how many teachers and a supervisor of education from North America. But Mexico's case was not the same. Mexico had a University before Boston, and libraries, museums, newspapers, and a theatre before New York and Philadelphia. In Mexico you have only to scratch the soil to find living roots of the old culture covered over by the barbarity of the government. And in spite of this barbarism, we have never been without well-trained people, professionals who have completed their apprenticeship in Europe. Thus for example, the generation of teachers trained in the Normal Schools of Justo Sierra was notable.

When I was exiled in New York, I learned that a hundred young teachers, supposed to be revolutionaries, had passed through there, sent by the Carranza government to Boston, *on a study trip for one month*. And it was to these same young ladies that they confided the running of the schools, with the excuse that they had been to Boston. They came back full of conceit, and since they knew nothing else, they talked about setting up North American methods, systems which they had not digested, and could not digest because they did not know enough about their own country. They were not expert in the tradition of their fatherland. These folks were distributed in important positions. To strengthen the staff, I brought in teachers of the old regime, preferably talented youngsters that our own work was developing.

I courteously declined an offer to furnish me with hundreds of North American professors, who certainly would have been failures in our country, as they were in Peru. But the selection and purifying of the staff did not turn out to be easy. For several weeks I was exhausted by the insistence of another type of educator whom we shall call for lack of any other name, "the research man." He, too, has spent a short time in the United States. There he devoted himself to what the universities call "research," not in physics or chemistry, but rather in social science and social service. The people connected with this are a dangerous lot who generally have political support. Often they are also minor politicians, but they are capable of conducting intrigues and doing considerable damage.

I told one of them, "Go to the country and do your investigating; take the months you deem necessary to draw up reports and graphs; when you get back, we will have transformed the conditions you are going to study, and we won't read your report, in the first place, because it will already be out of date, and second, because we are too busy doing things to find time to study."

But she did not understand; she came back from her excursion laden with papers and ideas.

"For goodness' sake, don't give me ideas; ideas, I create myself, or I buy them in pamphlets for fifty cents; give me creative activity! Don't tell me what the Indians are like, I know what they're like; they suffer hunger of body and soul; don't tell me what life is like in the poor parts of town; I don't spend my time in the cabinet meetings, I visit the poor; I don't need reports. What the country needs is people who know what must be done and sincerely devote themselves to doing it!"

A commission from a powerful foreign institution offered me free technical advice. I gave them the same answer, "I have technicians, better ones than you could give me, for they are familiar with the environment, they belong to it. If you really want to be helpful, send me a gift of teaching materials; we need globes, compasses, maps, school benches. The teachers, musicians, technicians, and all that makes the heart and soul of teaching we have in abundance and we are not going to change it!"

And, indeed, the staff could not have been better.

There have been honorable and capable men in all periods of our history—even in the darkest crises—but when have they been at the forefront in public life, when has the army allowed them to be the ones to govern?

In a few months I found the salary of Minister sufficient; they paid at the time a hundred pesos a day, plus auto and chauffeur. I did not spend more than fifteen hundred a month, and I began to put aside the rest.

I had determined that I would put only trained people into technical positions. We gave distinguished teachers the principal administrative posts; in lower positions we used professional people with a good reputation in their specialty, rather than those who keep turning up in government and politics because they have failed in the consulting room or the lawyer's office. If we were going to demand quality, we would have to turn a deaf ear to recommendations, even if they were supported by friends or members of the family, and harden ourselves so as not to yield to eyes which plead for a salary, even when they know they cannot give the service that will constitute a fair return.

I began my day at seven in the morning; I breakfasted on fruit and coffee, and by eight I was visiting the works, climbing scaffolds, urging haste, taking notes on what was needed, in order to expedite its delivery. At nine I reached the office, spattered with lime. I had not wanted to adopt the humiliating system of the time clock at the employees entrance, but I adopted another. When I got to my desk, I pushed the bells and called all the Department Chiefs. They came in punctually because they had been chosen from among honorable men and it is inevitable that a boss who does his job forces his subordinates to follow his example.

At noon on days for holding audience the doors were opened for all comers. Sometimes two hundred would come in, most of them asking for something. The use of public audiences is a democratic consolation which permits the public to get in contact with the officeholders, but it is useless, and moreover painful, because of the constant saying "no." The important jobs, even the smaller ones, are not handed out because somebody came to see you; you are a poor functionary if you don't know how to choose for yourself or through your aides. And the ideas the public contributes are of little value for the man who already has a plan.

To newspapermen we gave a bulletin with the news of the most recently completed buildings. Often they would insist upon coming in to talk to me. My relations with the press were at first rather unpleasant.

After the midday meal, which I rarely took at home, I had a siesta for twenty minutes in an armchair in my private office. The girls would come back at four and I would begin dictating. Often, special appointments took one or two hours, but the rest of the afternoon was devoted to conferring with the higher employees of the Ministry and to discussing the work of the various departments. At seven I left and went home. There I had some fruit for supper, played with my children for a while, and then closed the door of my library. Nobody except my little children came in to interrupt me.

My unknown young lady did not come to the public audience; but she turned up in the anteroom one afternoon at the end of work.

Soon she confessed: she had seen me at some public meeting or other; she was charmed by the power of my oratory; she couldn't resist the temptation to call on me. She didn't want a job! This in itself was good reason for relief and for liking her. We went out, got in the car, and I took her to the private room of a restaurant.

She was unmarried, eighteen years old, had fine manners and smelled clean; I soon took her home.

She came back one or two days later, and when I was on the point of proceeding as the case seemed to call for, she looked very much upset and cried, "What are you doing!"

In a flash I guessed; then, I inquired, "Is it the first time?"

And she answered, "Why, what do you take me for?"

And she burst out crying. Immediately the thought went through my mind, "I don't love her enough to take on such a responsibility." I helped her pull herself together, and said goodbye in front of her house. The Ministry that I was creating was my only love.

Instead of the old custom of importing chairs and desks from North American factories, we made it a rule that the Ministry would have to produce in its own shops whatever it needed, even furniture.

In those days I was printing a contraceptive pamphlet, and distributing it exclusively among workers. I did not see any good reason why the lower class should be deprived of information that any lady of the upper class gets from her doctor or her library. And Felipe, with the enthusiasm that was one of his best qualities, asked me to send him thousands of these pamphlets. It was done. A correspondent of one of the metropolitan papers, all of which were secret enemies of everything we were doing, spread the news, distorting it with the assertion that the pamphlet was being distributed among high school pupils. A storm of attacks descended on my head, all of them based on lies, but painful just the same, on account of the nature of the accusation. Felipe did not budge, and went on handing out the pamphlet, still among working women associated with him, including many school teachers. At least this is the explantation he sent me, adding an invitation to come to visit Yucatán.

The schools there were in a state of the most complete abandonment, but like those of the rest of the country, they could count on a first-rate staff, trained in the Normal Schools of the time of Justo Sierra. Indeed, the only group showing any promise was that of the Normal School graduates, tidy, intelligent, patriotic. The warmth with which they welcomed us was moving. In each of the school yards of Mérida there was a celebration with songs, music, and flowery speeches. Our Secretariat was at that time carrying out a distribution of pianos to the schools of the country. The promise of a dozen for Mérida aroused enthusiasm, but actually they needed everything. Some schools had a modest endowment, but most of them were in miserable condition and could not accommodate half the children of school age. In the villages the situation was still worse.

Instead of utilizing it, we expelled our aristocracy, just to grab its heritage, and the result is that the best blood of the country has emigrated to the United States. In that neighboring nation, the Mexican of Spanish origin, more or less fair skinned, is quickly accepted into the ruling class. At the end of two or three generations he has usually remade his lost fortune, but, as is natural, he does not remember the country of his origin.

If they had told me then that all the disorder, all that robbery disguised as social transformation would come to be the rule over the entire country during the period of Calles and afterward, I probably would have resigned from the Ministry at once, and devoted my life to saving my family from poverty, seeing that the country was becoming or already was beyond saving.

But in Yucatán they were beginning to play with the idea of communism, incorrectly understood, and the contagion swept the country. And we have returned to tribal rule in the guise of a doctrinaire political philosophy which those in command do not even understand.

I escaped and went to the Plaza of Campeche; I entered the Cathedral. It was almost deserted, and the great nave dilapidated. At a side altar a few candles were burning and two or three women were praying. The abandonment of the Cathedral was typical of the state of the city, of the state of a race which was losing its God, along with the consciousness of itself and its future. The great emptiness of that forgotten church hurt like a wound; you felt your will becoming enfeebled. I left the church; I passed through the dark and deserted arcades of the customs house, and went on toward the avenue which faces the sea. I was looking for the house where we had last lived as a united family. I passed in front of it, along the sidewalk by the sea. It hadn't changed much. I sat down on a cement bench, worn out by the bustle and sadness of the day. I passed in review the phantoms that were my mother, my father, my siblings. Behind those closed balconies, in the uninhabited rooms, which looked as if no one had occupied them since we left, a great love had sustained us. Where were the dead, father, mother, brother? What were the scattered living brothers and sisters doing? Concha was in Madrid in a convent; Mela in another convent in Tacubaya; the rest obeying their separate destinies. And as for me, I was just passing through; a few hours more, and the sight of that house would be only another memory. And the voice which was trying to bring us together would call in vain: "Time for supper, children! Everybody come to the table!" And then I broke into sobs, irrepressible, deep, tearing sobs, as if once and for all the illusion of a miracle that would reunite us had disappeared. Weeping is the outflow of an infinite and inconsolable sadness; the lament for all that is broken up and disunited for ever. Of what use is infinite love if it does not redeem eternity?

I do not know how long I remained with my head between my hands, once again the big boy, alone and comfortless. The silence of the deserted beach, the unlighted houses, the city in ruins, made me feel like the last dweller on an earth in ruins, who, without understanding it, weeps for the great disaster.

As soon as we returned to Mérida, we organized an excursion to Uxmal and Chichen-Itzá, the region that has the best Maya ruins of the Peninsula. We left our mounts in the village of Uxmal. Then, taking advantage of the last gleams of the setting sun, we climbed a height from which one sees, among the swaying tops of the impenetrable forest, the top of the Castillo, a handsome vestige of Mayan architecture of light colored stone covered with carvings; a quiet tower, lost in the jungle and in the pages of history. A pleasant emotion flowed from mind to heart. What did the legendary Mayans think about as they looked from a distance upon the highest point of their city? The inhabitants of the town that now lies near the ruins do not seem to think of anything important; they care for their bodies, to be sure, taking a bath at dawn in an artesian spring, and another at night before they go to sleep. Men and women go by dressed in white, speaking their dialect mixed with a large number of Spanish words.

Relying on the state of conservation and what the decorations seem to mean, we have invented names for the remains of the biggest buildings: the Temple of the Warriors, the House of the Nuns, etc. The Pelota Court occupies a vast and well-preserved amphitheatre, and so, little by little, as the pickaxe of the archaeologist advances, year after year, new miracles make their appearance; but the whole is uniformly barbarous, cruel, and grotesque. No sense of beauty; the decoration is simple paleography. As they had no reliable alphabet, they used drawing and relief as their language. The decoration is utilitarian, and for that reason induces no aesthetic emotion at all;

only amazement at the sight of the careful calculations and the aberrations of the human mind.

In the dominant structure called the Caracól, we begin to suspect that there may have been thought. We are reminded for a moment of one of those fantasies of Brueghel on the Tower of Babel. The political life which took place on the plain below must have been equally satanic. In any case, the soul of the Mayans felt the need to rise in order to free itself from the confused and brutal earth; they did not know the wheel, they were not masters of the circle, but they understood the spiral sufficiently to construct the stairway which leads to the now broken portion of the tower. It is thought that on top there once existed as astronomical observatory.

In Vera Cruz bad news awaited me: my wife had fallen from a chair while she was hanging a picture. With sadness in my heart I made the return trip from the port to the capital, where I found her with a serious fracture of the hip. She was kept in bed for several months and suffered a great deal because of the stupid way they first set the fracture. Afterward the skill of Dr. Amor at least restored her ability to walk.

Imagine the risk run by a man who has as part of his job the distribution of material treasures in the form of subventions for the development of the dramatic, vocal and other musical arts! Only the passion my own work inspired in me prevented my falling into the habit of handing out gifts with no definite plan in mind; the money was barely sufficient for the development of my own projects. I don't know what preserved me from the temptation of granting personal favors in exchange for "gallant services." Perhaps it was the same sense of honor which forbids taking money for oneself. But I defy my critics to say there is any woman who can boast or be angry with me because of any exchange of favors. Or even any case in which someone collected a salary without doing regular work in an office or school.

However, my reputation for austerity was not enough to guarantee me against certain happenings, like one I shall tell about next, provoked, actually, by an indiscretion on my part.

The sensation of the day was an exuberant dancer, middling as an artist, but physically exciting, warmly sensual, generous with her favors, but expensive. . . . As I was dismissing the clerk so that we could be alone, in spite of being rather confused I noticed a movement on her part which was her undoing. She crossed her legs, fixed her

skirt so that her beautifully turned thighs showed in all their splendor. And a thought passed through my mind like lightning: "She
thinks I'm an idiot, a sexual idiot! . . . but I'm not—at least not
this time!" She explained meanwhile that she had a manager, but
to get started she need a couple of thousand pesos, which you might
say is nothing for a Secretariat that is promoting a renaissance of the
arts. "Art, art!" I thought to myself, "she means pandering!" Out of
the corner of my eye, I could see the magnetic thighs, almost dazzling, warm and promising. I had only to stretch out my hand and the
treaty would have been sealed between us at the cost of the country.
Above the excitement of the flesh, anger won the day. I did not
stretch out my hand; in a movement of self-hatred, I raised both
closed fists above the table and forgetting the crudity of my response,
cried, "We don't care about art here! Two thousand pesos? With
two thousand pesos I can get a hundred school benches, and there are
a million school children who have nothing to sit on! Pardon me, I
can't do it. No, it's impossible!"

And I rose; she got up, too, shamefaced, and left without saying
goodbye.

One sure thing is that at the beginning of the Obregón government, not one of the ministers, and certainly not Obregón himself,
committed any speculation, or devoted himself to his own private affairs.

When I gave up public service I would have time to make money
for my family; for the present, I had to devote every possible minute,
the best of my thinking, to the task the country had set for me. And
the country soon became greater, and embraced the continent.

Both official and private communications and press clippings began
to reach us from all the countries of Spanish speech. Several factors
worked together to make the Secretariat of Education the center of
attention of the Spanish world. In the first place, the Venezuela incident had attracted the attention of the continent. In the second
place, the work of the University Bulletin gave some account of
things we were starting, of our work, and was circulated in all the university and scholarly centers of the world. In the third place, our publication of the classics brought us fame; they circulated everywhere,
sometimes given away, sometimes sold at low prices among Spanish-
speaking people everywhere, filling a need. In the fourth place, there
was the journal, *The Teacher,* distributed in large numbers, with
news of our work and the famous people taking part in it, and a special section devoted to Hispanic affairs. Unlike so many technical

journals, it was without scholarly pretentions, but had the goal of fostering the moral and political rebirth of the Latin world in the face of the powerful nations of the moment. Add to all this the nationalistic character which it imparted to the arts, literature, and education; our intervention in popular dancing to banish exoticism and jazz, replacing them with the Spanish *jota* and folk dances of Mexico, Argentina, Chile, and so on—the whole culminating in public festivals and reinforced by proclamations urging people to have confidence and pride in their traditions, language, and culture—and you will understand why one day a message fell from the sky, in the form of a telegram in which the students of Colombia notified me that in accordance with their custom of designating periodically a "Teacher of Youth," they had fixed upon me for the occasion and begged me to accept the responsibility of being the "Maestro."

To be sure, the honor seemed to me excessive, and moreover, compromising. And I did not reply until I could get the details. Then I saw that I ought not refuse, since the appointment meant an effort to overcome the provincialism of American countries, a generous impulse on the part of Colombian youth to approach Mexico, the old ally of Colombia and a country related by blood, tradition, language, and the vicissitudes of the political life of the century of independence. So I replied with a message which appears in one of my books and which was widely published. In my formal acceptance I avoided the title of Master, for in my judgment, none is Master save our Lord Jesus Christ, and secondly because, even in my modest position of a temporal teacher, this business of acting as Master seemed a confession of growing old. Besides, my willful and arbitrary character was hardly suited to the deliberation and solemnity which we often associate with the status of the master.

In the United States, the independent journals devoted space to the work going on in Mexico and praised it, but soon the bankers began to prick up their ears, as will be seen in the sequel. Frankly, nobody in the North was pleased by the nationalistic and southern rather than the northern-oriented turn which our activities were so conspicuously taking.

In Mexico, the students maintained a reserved attitude. They did not dare to organize strikes against me, to declare themselves my enemies, because they saw me moving among them, laying cornerstones, creating for them gymnasiums, laboratories, and improvements they had never dreamed of. All this commanded their respect, but not their love. And only much later, when I was out of the Ministry and fighting Calles, did the students of Mexico overflow with enthusiasm and become my allies.

The Department for fighting illiteracy, aided by an innumerable body of "honorary teachers," extended its activities throughout the country. Eulalia Guzmán, its enthusiastic and competent director, had created brigades of instructors. It was a patriotic service demanding energy, we told them, and it had to go on as if we were on the eve of war or facing a calamity like the plague. Ignorance is a plague which sickens the soul of the masses. The most patriotic action is to teach people to read, with everyone who knows how teaching those who do not know how. You could see private classes in which the lady of the house brought together her own and the neighbors' servants to teach them how to read. In the public squares, at twilight, we held veritable mass meetings.

The inspiration for teaching the Indians came to us, as was natural, from the Spanish tradition. It was because it had denied and forgotten this tradition that the Republic had accomplished nothing in its century of independent life. The tradition also served to give us support against the system that had been permeating the teachers of Mexico, leading them to imitate the North American approach to the Indian problem. That system is founded on positivistic ethnography, which exaggerates racial differences and makes the savage a creature apart, a kind of link between the monkey and man. Spanish educators from before the time of ethnology, as a result of insight that amounted to genius, and also as a result of experience, had, after a trial, abandoned the system of applying special methods to the Indians in separate schools. In place of segregation they set up a system of integration of the races in school and worship. From this fusion, the homogeneity of our people, the relative harmony of the races, has arisen. Protestantism on the other hand, with its scientific pretensions, both before and after my period of activity, has been setting up special schools for Indians and this can lead only to copying the North American plan, a plan for better division based on color and race. Adopting the North American system is therefore equivalent to undoing the most profound and effective work of the colony, the tight union of Indians and whites. The ethnological thesis which is implicit in the system of educating Indians and whites together is one that I expounded later in my book, *La Raza Cósmica*.

We were aware of the fact that in no case could we do as good a job as the Spanish missionaries, because we lacked an adequate staff. However competent the normal school graduates of modern times may be, each of them has the mountainous weight of a family bearing down upon him; this is the major obstacle to becoming an apostle. The strength of the missionaries lay in the fact that, free of wife, children, and relatives, they formed a spiritual family. And this was a civilizing and redeeming agency. Aside from this, who among the lay missionaries can revive the fervor of the true missionaries who believed they were saving not merely the bodies, but more important, the souls of their students? If the missionary taught the work of field and shop so well, it is precisely because he looked upon all manual labor as secondary in comparison with the primary importance of that spiritual teaching which redeems the conscience.

We began to send out groups of teachers: one for crafts, who would teach tilling the soil and forging iron; another who was an artist and could inculcate a sense of beauty, the only approach that the layman has to the divine; and still another who would arouse people to social action and cooperation in serving the country; and finally, one for reading and arithmetic. And so was born the modern type of missionary, usually a normal school graduate who acted as chief of the team of educators and lived with the Indians, helping them to erect the school with local resources, and teaching the rudiments of pedagogy to young people in each locality, who would then take over the basic education. After this advance agent came the mission with its experts in agriculture, arts, and crafts. A public reader also went about, reading chapters of history and geography in the plaza, reading the newspapers, arranging film showings. With him was usually the musician, whose job it was to awaken local interest in his art, and so on, according to the financial possibilities and the staff we could recruit in each particular case.

Such a crucial task called for talent of the first order. Some of our best poets and young artists served for longer or shorter periods as teachers of this kind. Among the foreigners, as eminent a person as Gabriela Mistral filled this role more than once.

Obregón slipped in as we were leaving: "I invite you to dinner on Wednesday, at home; bring her along," he said, pointing to Fanny.

The dinner took place in the little house that Obregón occupied with his family, below the Castle in Chapultepec. A nice family table, enriched by the kindness and grace of Obregón's wife, pleased us very much. Halfway through, the President announced, "I have been thinking of naming you Special Ambassador to the celebration of the Hundredth Anniversary of Brazil. If you like, you can go on afterward to the inauguration of the new President of Argentina. They want you in the south! And you would not be away from your work for more than three months!"

"The opportunity to visit South America is invaluable!" I said at once.

Fanny was very pro-Chilean, very pro-Brazilian, but did not have quite the same love for the Argentines. In that I differed from her; my enthusiasm for them was one hundred per cent, for Argentina has always been a free country and very Spanish. Although we argued about the merits of the three rival countries, we did not quarrel. Late for the dinner, General Valles arrived just as we were finishing, complaining of his chronic ills—rheumatism, shooting pains, his back. They informed him of my appointment and he seemed pleased about it. I did not suspect it at the time, for I was not thinking about the political future, but he must have been glad to see me away from Mexico. The activities of the Secretariat had been keeping me too close to the workers. On my trip to Orizaba for the opening of the Industrial School, the whole staff of the Orizaba trade unions had given me a banquet. In the working-class centers around Vera Cruz we were developing a workers' school. A working-class mayor of Vera Cruz had given my name to a newly constructed school. And every Sunday morning we filled the theatres of the capital with crowds, largely from the working class, to whom we gave lectures on general culture, concerts, and ballets.

Before leaving, I asked De la Huerta, "Show my executive officer, Peralta, the same confidence you show me; see that he gets exactly the same sums you have been giving me for schools; I don't want to see them paralyzed by my being away."

De la Huerta promised, and he kept his promise. Months later, however, when he returned from his ill-fated trip to New York as Minister of the Treasury, De la Huerta told me, "Now there can't be any increase in expenses in Education, Pepe, because the bankers are opposed to it. One of the most serious objections they made to me was that too much was being spent on education."

I'll have more to say about this later. But the first lightning flashes of the storm that menaced the recently raised tower of the Ministry broke out during my trip to the south. The details of that trip I shall not repeat; I have written them in my book, *La Raza Cósmica*.

My farewell to the city was the magnificent celebration of the inauguration of the Ministry Building. For months we had been occupying the front section, and little by little, as a wing was finished, we would enlarge the offices. The opening ceremony, however, kept being postponed because we disapproved of the custom of having an official cornerstone laying ceremony, after which the building remains in the stage of a project only. We believed in celebrating the laying of the last stone, and that's the way it was. At the summit of the

Secretariat a Minerva was unveiled serenely and beautifully presiding over the front of the building, escorted by Dionysus and Apollo. On the day of the opening, after the concert and speeches, they served a dinner prepared in our industrial schools—a dinner for seven thousand teachers, employees, and workmen.

On the eve of embarking for Rio de Janeiro, Pansi told me that a cast had been made of a replica of the statue of Cuauhtemoc on the Paseo de la Reforma, and that this would be the gift of Mexico to the Centennial of the sister Republic. When one of the delegates of the Socialist Party of Argentina saw the statue and I explained its significance to him, he said, "Listen, I think this is a *gaffe,* for around here nobody knows who that Indian is, and anyway there aren't any Indians in Argentina, and the only ones in Brazil are Negroes; it is a mistake for your government to represent Mexico by a symbol which carries no weight in the rest of America which is Latin."

A little piqued by his observation, I started to prepare a speech which would explain to southerners what Cuauhtemoc meant to us. And I confess that my ideas on the subject were not very clear. I made a speech which had as much success as it did, precisely because in it I presented, I believe, a rather fantastic Cuauhtemoc; one whom I raised to a symbol of our desire for independence, not from Spain, which, after having nurtured us, left us in peace a century ago, but from that Monroeism which is a living and obvious menace. A good proof of the fact that I did not stick to history is that I put into the mouth of Cuauhtemoc those words about not wanting to go to heaven if he would have to be there with Spaniards, words which, if I am not mistaken, are ascribed to some Antillean chieftain. To those who pointed out the irrelevancy, I said, "I am not writing history; my object is to create a myth. My speech held up all right in spite of what I say about Cuauhtemoc and Poinsettism in my book on Mexican history. I point out there the danger of an Indianism which does not build on the work of Spain, and by means of which the Indian now has an Indian country that destroys or abuses the work of Spain. Otherwise, having no worthwhile tradition of his own, the Indian would be left to the mercy of new and strange ideologies which are the forerunners of a new and more dangerous conquest."

A few months after my return, I began to open new school buildings and libraries. I took Obregón in triumph through the poor districts where reading rooms and school lunch rooms, vocational and rural schools were functioning. The city acclaimed us and in the rest of the country the energy of the Secretariat was famous. Invitations to visit recently created Federal schools in the States often took me away from the capital. I only made trips that had for their object the opening of an already constructed school or a completed improvement, never just to make promises nor to find out what was needed. That is the work of Inspectors, not of Ministers. The Minister ought to know.

Still, I went about sadly; I was sad because I could sense the unworthy maneuvering that was going on behind the scenes, and sad because of the contrast between the little that we were doing and all that I had seen in Brazil and Argentina. And I replied to every editorial or news item in which the government was praised because it was spending a lot on education, by issuing a grave warning: "Don't let public opinion be deceived, what we are doing is barely a beginning, not the crowning of the work. Our public education has been neglected for a whole century; it cannot be restored in two or three years. In Argentina, in Brazil, the primary schools, which are better supported than ours, are large, numerous, rich, and happy. In Brazil and Argentina the budget is double or triple what ours is. Mexico, which with its colonial tradition should be at the head of Spanish America, is outstripped. The public must come to our support, not so much because of what we have done, as for the sake of what remains to be done." We did not suspect that not only would it not be done, but what had been accomplished would slowly be nullified when regimes like that of Calles came into power and proved to be accomplices of the old intrigues directed against everything Mexican.

It was the moment when my budget was due to increase, but, nevertheless, I had to allow it to remain the same or to be reduced to a little less, with the certainty that in the following year I would in fact get even less. Obregón was beginning to be worried about obtaining recognition from Washington, and the first thing that was suggested to him was that arrangements be worked out with the bankers who had got hold of the bonds that constituted our foreign debt. In discussions with the Wall Street people, the government pleaded lack of resources to cover the enormous sums, which had been owing under the heading of interest payments since the disorders of the Carranza period, and the bankers took it into their own hands to discuss the official budget and to point out where cuts could be made. They did not have anything to do with the Secretariat of War; the army keeps the country quiet and submissive for them. According to De la Huerta himself, the first thing the Wall Street people called attention to was the amount that was going into schools. Why did a population of mestizos want so many schools? Besides, the Department of Education was functioning without consultants, without the advice of Yankee educational commissions. And worse still, the Lamont people working on refunding the debt did not forgive me for the position I had taken when a certain delegation from New York visited me just before the Council of Ministers meeting, which they supposed would be dealing with the refunding of the debt service. In my best Bowery dialect, I expounded to them what I repeated in public: that the whole foreign debt was a swindle by the International Bank.

In vain did I protest against the trip of De la Huerta to New York. Obregón, having decided to break with his people in order to put a friend of his into the Presidency, had no other recourse than to smile on the bankers in order to obtain immediately the aid which Washington later gave him without reservations and contrary to the real interests of the Mexican nation.

While we in the Ministry all worked with spontaneous discipline and close co-operation, in the University all was disorder. The Preparatory School in particular continued to be a mess. We had not been able to find a good Director for it and the choice did not depend on us. We had put Antonio Caso in the Rectorship, and in general we appointed to university posts people recommended by the Rector. In some cases the results were so notoriously bad that in moments of despair I had thought of making myself Director, and in fact, I went to the Director's office for two hours each morning. By relying on the hard-working students as against the groups of politically-minded ones, I could re-establish discipline in exchange for half a dozen expulsions. But Caso would not hear of it. "What kind of situation would I be in," he said, "if one of my Directors was the Minister, to whom I could not give orders?"

But he did not give orders, and never had, and that was what was wrong. He fulfilled his duties as Rector very decorously, even ceremoniously. There was no one like him for giving an academic discourse, for presiding over a literary meeting; but his administrative capacity was nil and he would not be helped. He was surrounded by little flatterers who aroused his jealousy of me, so that gradually our friendly relations turned sour. In order not to break with him, I had retired from the Directorship of the Preparatory School and by agreement we had named as Director Lombardo Toledano, a favorite of Caso's. Now Caso had a weakness for relatives. He recommended Lombardo because one of his brothers had married one of Lombardo's sisters. Another sister was about to marry Pedro Henríquez Ureña, who also had influence in the Ministry. I thought then that Lombardo's becoming Director might be conciliatory and might bring me together again with my top collaborators, Caso and Henríquez Ureña.

Now my relations with Henríquez Urcña had also become disturbed. At his request I took him along on the diplomatic trip to South America. This trip served him well in building up his relations with the Argentine universities. He had plans as early as this to settle in South America, for the papers in the capital of Mexico basely attacked him; they criticized him for his Dominican nationality, his mulatto physique, his atrabilious, nervous character. But even they could never deny his capacity.

Pedro said to me, "And do you think they publish all that for you because you are a writer? They publish it because you are a Minister. . . . Don't get the idea that you know how to write; your books are very bad. . . . Even this business of the Ministry; don't fool yourself that you're doing it well; you're very arbitrary!"

After these arguments, I received a letter from Pedro asking me to pardon him; he recognized that he was often unjust to me. And on the trip to the South, I took him along to rehabilitate him in public opinion and to frustrate those who were attacking him, and attacking me for protecting a "foreigner."

The first thing Lombardo did was to revive some circulars from the time of my administration as Rector in which I recommended to the students a rapprochement with the workers, a union of students and workers somewhat in the Russian manner. I was the first Mexican imitator of the good aspects of the Soviet regime. But Lombardo did not merely follow the example of his own chief; he claimed to be the initiator of university activity among the workers. And at the Preparatory School they began to form political societies and to make pink speeches.

I rarely went to the main building of the Preparatory School; Orozco gave me black looks every time I turned up to see his frescoes. But I went to the annex nearby every day because they still had not finished the sanitary installations. For the first time in history, we were providing the school with toilets—luxurious ones, American style. I planned to wipe out the barbaric custom of permitting the students to cover the walls with obscene signs or the simple scratchings of badly brought-up boys. I had ordered that anyone who posted a sign or dirtied the walls of the new building would be expelled, and I gave the order to Lombardo, who made no objection. One morning I caught sight of a printed notice stuck on a column. We had a special bulletin board for this kind of thing, but the insolent advertisement was also spread over the walls that had just been prepared for the fresco. I came closer; it was a circular that called the students of a society together for a meeting in the near future. Among the signatures was that of a brother of Lombardo, who was a young student.

I asked no questions, but on returning to the office, I signed an order for a week's suspension of the signers and sent it to Lombardo, of course including as a courtesy a statement to the Rector. At that time the farce of university autonomy did not exist; the Rector was an officer appointed by the Ministry; still you respected due forms. But I was determined to be obeyed.

After two or three days of secret conferences with my political enemies, Lombardo called the students together with an open appeal from the balcony of the Director's corridor and gave them his explanation of the situation. I was suspending three students without a hearing, but since one of them was his brother, he was disqualifying himself from the case and leaving it to the students to decide. There was a lot of shouting, and the tools of the Director—youngsters who enjoyed official stipends paid out by the Ministry, perhaps obtained through Lombardo—worked up groups and proposed a general meeting in the amphitheatre. In the hot session which then took place, two or three professors made furious attacks on me. Among them was Alfonso Caso, whom I liked personally because of his worth and because, since he was a brother of Antonio Caso, I considered him a friend. I don't remember the names of the other two professors, but when I found out what they had done, I fired them for inciting the students. The professors whom I thus disciplined had spoken out at an inappropriate time, and before the united student body, taking open issue with my management.

In the meantime, Lombardo avoided seeing us; he left the capital, making a pretext of going to see his family and what not. But his agents continued to be active. One morning they informed the papers that a big student manifestation against the Minister was under way. The place, the Preparatory School; the hour, eleven. Lombardo, the Director, was still absent.

"They were on the point of lynching you, sir," said the loyal Muñoz.

There were ten or twelve reporters there, and I could just see the headlines in the principal papers: "Vasconcelos nearly lynched by students!" I immediately rejected this version.

"The students are not capable of lynching," I asserted, "this was only a misunderstanding."

But it was useless; the phrase spread everywhere.

Interrupting the interview, I drew up a written statement for the reporters. The school was not being closed; classes would be resumed that very afternoon. The Ministry ordered the dismissal of Director Lombardo and the expulsion of all the students who had headed the revolt.

About two o'clock we went to lunch with a group of friends; afterward I went to Tacubaya to have a good siesta, since the afternoon promised to be stirring. Lombardo's crowd would use their last weapon: a general strike of the student body.

Obregón had already been warned that something disagreeable might happen.

"What we did in the Preparatory School," I had admitted to him several days before, "has not been unsuccessful, and I propose to eliminate the bad elements; but they will accuse me of being arbitrary, they will rouse the mass of students against me."

Obregón's reply was "The only criticism I could make is that you did not do this earlier; do what you think best. Call on the whole garrison if it is needed to keep order.

As long as Obregón was in command, Lombardo was lost. But I was not worried about Lombardo; what worried me was the position in which a statement by all the students attacking my policy would leave me. If the student body really repudiated me, I would resign, not because their agreement forced me to it, but because of my disappointment at not being understood. I did not say this to a soul and wore a stern expression before everyone. Sentimentality is not a good ally in a fight.

The regular work of the day occupied the early hours, and about eleven Antonio Caso arrived. I had him brought into a small private room. My first thought was that he was going to tell me immediately, with all the unction he used on the platform, "Forgive me for recommending and almost forcing a fellow like Lombardo on you." But Caso in private is not the same man he is on the platform. He himself justifies his reserve by saying that one must keep one's distance. He does not omit the solemn formalities even in friendship. Scarcely had he taken his seat in front of the little desk I was occupying, when, without saying a word, he handed me a sheet of paper. I read it; it was his resignation. I handed it back, laughing, and said, "Very well; I understand the annoyance you feel at the behavior of your friends, but what do you have to do with all this? I won't accept your resignation; here it is, I give it back to you, tear it up, or I will."

Caso took the sheet, only to lay it on the table, insisting, "No, Pepe; I have come to resign, and my resignation is irrevocable, unless you do the right thing."

"The right thing? What do you mean?"

"Put my brother back in his classroom; you don't dismiss a professor this way."

The news of Caso's resignation and its acceptance was given at once to the papers.

Caso had managed to keep his self-control, although he had never been servile; only now, with me, had he been intransigeant. No one would ever give him back the official position which I had secured for him.

Still, I had to excuse him, to do something to make him accept a commission of nine hundred pesos, more or less the amount of his salary as Rector, so that he could write his *Aesthetics*. "After all," I thought, "the day I resign there won't be anybody to beg me to accept anything; they may even throw me out of the country again." And then, I know by experience, there won't be anyone who will remember that one can starve.

One or two weeks later, Caso accepted the commission; he went back to teaching his classes, but not before a story had been circulated which was to my discredit: Caso had had to sell his private library in order not to perish of hunger; I had reduced him to this. I was ungrateful to my friends.

In the last year I had had to forego horseback riding because the work of the Secretariat was so demanding. The same with the symphonic concerts which were beginning to be presented in the mornings, with a brillance never before achieved in the city. I took Obregón to one of those concerts; without having the sensitive approach to music that Madero had, he had sufficient appreciation of culture to endure it. What he liked, most, however, were open air festivals. At the moment I liked them too, because they were creative and were the germ out of which many national arts could develop—costume, dance, and song. To bring shows out of doors into the sunlight was one of my concerns.

A talented Catalonian actress passed through the city at that time. Years later she stated to the newspapers that in Mexico she had played out of doors, under the aegis of the government. Although she knew that I was in Spain, she did not invite me to see her; she mentioned the Mexican revolution, which at that period was named Calles. For that matter, all the members of the leftist, Jewish, Yankeephile group were doing the same thing. For example, Valle Inclán, who saw the beginning of our efforts in mural painting, was speaking, and he pled for Spain to imitate Mexico in this respect. He had just left me, and he knew that the Calles government was not interested in murals; I had ordered them painted, but it was not fashionable to mention me. For their part, De los Ríos and García Lorca were doing people's theatre and art missions, and De los Ríos spoke of having seen something of the kind in Mexico, but he too neglected to mention me.

We had given the city a joyful Sunday. It reached the point where certain Catholics began to complain that we were alienating people from the Church with our fiestas. This was not my object. The public had the early morning hours on Sunday for mass. Our fiestas never started before eleven. And it was not our fault that the ancient splendor had departed from the churches; we would have been the first to prefer it to our humble attempts at secular art. The decline of the artistic level, the poor quality of the solemn masses, said with an abundance of priests and acolytes but without adequate choruses and orchestras, was quite obvious. Under the circumstances, it was not we, but boredom which alienated people from the church. As far as the spoken word was concerned, we offered, without meaning to, something more interesting than the Church. Our lectures, in addition to giving cultural information, discussed urgent problems of the day.

I was not a professional socialist but a practical Christian, who was sorry that the Church was not open to the groups who were demanding their rights within an orderly social system. Why wouldn't people be driven away by sermons consisting of nothing but admonitions, accompanied by emphasis on the offering, without a word about the conflicts of the day, the perplexities of the modern soul?

The trouble with Mexico is so deep seated, there is so much to do if we are to get back on the track of simple civilized normality that discouragement seizes you when you start thinking about it. What I was trying to do as an official was to devote every effort to achieving success in this task, but I was resigned in advance to seeing the results disappear as soon as the political wheel turned.

If you do not maintain this high level of culture, you get the result that came about in Mexico: the vogue of folk art initiated by us, as a step toward the creation on a broad scale of a national devotion to art, dropped to the level of commercialized popular art, for lack of constructive efforts and a well-thought-out program. Songs turned out by the hundreds—jazz, blues, tangos, and rumbas from the North

American market! This was a brutalizing art, a syncopated, mechanized vulgarity, a reversion to the bleating of calves, the kind of thing you get in the songs popularized by Hollywood movies. I had recommended popular art as a basis from which to go on to the classics, without crossing the bridge from the mediocre. I forbade jazz and banished it from the schools. But the mestizo population of our land is far from possessing the vigor necessary to create ballet. You must first of all produce joy in the soul, health and vigor in the body.

I have never been very enthusiastic about sports, which I consider palliatives for the absurd life-system created by big business and the deplorable climate of England. The only healthful exercise is work in the country or in the case of women, domestic work. The machines in the shop or at home have produced those skinny or fat but flabby monsters with weak muscles that we modern men have become.

To save ourselves from tuberculosis we have invented those boring games of tennis, baseball, and football.

It was necessary for the government to secularize physical education, the scanty beginnings of which were dominated by the personnel of the Young Men's Christian Association, a Protestant institution (although it claimed to be nonsectarian), and in any case one that represented foreign influence. As I am no friend of prohibitions and persecutions as a means of persuasion, and as I hold that a doctrine and a practice are defeated and replaced by means of better doctrines and practices, before opening my offensive I devoted myself to building better gymnasiums than those of the "Y," and open-air swimming pools that were superior to the dark ones of the North Americans. At the same time we set up a School of Physical Education to train teachers who would replace the athletes schooled in the Protestant institution.

The story I am telling here is at least one of a marvelous awakening which was later plunged into darkness; its labor was abortive. It was all the work of some three years, and the labor of one Minister, not of a President. And the power of a Minister under our Constitution is nil; that is why, in spite of the national attention that our efforts received, on the day after, there was no one to come to their defense, much less to continue them.

According to our plans, every school in the capital was to have a sports field, and we had already opened and completed at least half a dozen. Before our administration there was not a single one. Later, the Ministers, imitating the Hollywood stars, built luxurious swimming pools—but in their own houses—not a single one for the school children.

If I have one regret about my work as Minister, it is having let slip the opportunities the office provides for serving certain friends who need and deserve help. To take money from public funds for private purposes is simple theft and is inexcusable; but to allow a friend to make a commission, to profit from a sale or a business transaction, is that as bad as it seemed to me? Or is it rather that I lacked generosity in individual cases, being so obsessed with saving pennies to make the work of the government more effective? Almost everyone in the government is sometimes deaf and dumb when a friend or relative makes an undercover profit. As I write this little history I find a kind of relaxation from the perplexity which used to torment me when I saw my best friends, forgotten and impoverished, perhaps deeply hurt because I did not let them operate as others did, filling their bellies in anticipation of possible bad times.

No friend ever showed rancor as a result of my cruelty, nor changed his attitude toward me. But I still feel a kind of wound and doubt about whether it is right in situations like ours—situations of chaos and misunderstanding, of general dishonesty—if it is legitimate, I say, to cast off the deserving individual because we are so involved in the illusion that we are working for society!

One of the things I insisted on with the engineers of the Secretariat was that they resume the custom of making the entrances of all the buildings we put up as generously wide as in the old days when we were a country of gentlemen. We did not want schools of the Swiss type, like those that Justo Sierra hastily threw together, nor schools of the Chicago type, like some few that were perpetrated later. In architecture, too, we should find inspiration in our glorious past.

In the Town Hall, a fairly decorous colonial building, the city government gave a reception in the morning, enlivened by the presence of the staffs of all the schools. Recitations of Mexican and Spanish poets, solo and chorus performances, naïve attempts at art which still prove our people's great capacity for culture—such was the entertainment which for an hour or two made us dream of a Mexico reborn, illustrious and powerful. The human material was there, as it is present everywhere; all that has been missing is a little effort on the part of men of good will, a little confidence in one's own worth.

When my little daughter María was about eleven, she broke a leg on the slide at a playground. They telephoned me and I ran to the house, which had already been sold. Apparently she was not suffering, and even her mother was not disturbed. But I felt nauseated and profoundly annoyed with the universe. I am weak in the face of suffering.

Death does not alarm me; pain and sickness horrify me. I do not see the good in suffering that, for instance, Dostoievski does. This part of his philosophy is repugnant to me. Life is the evil, not death. Life seems to me bearable, but only if its soul be noble and its body healthy. The atmosphere of a hospital is hateful to me, and when I see a big room full of people seriously ill, a desire which is part pity and, if you will, part cowardice, rises from the bottom of my heart, and I ask myself, "Why don't they die and get it over with?"

I find no horror in death. I think of it as the moment when the butterfly emerges from the chrysalis. Those who have died and have been saved keep a certain relationship to us, but there is also a gulf between us, like that between ourselves and animals.

The fact is that death seems horrible to us and we can't endure it because of the consequences it immediately has for the body, and because of the pain and sickness which accompany it; but the soul rejoices in it. If we forget the circumstances which surround death, including the services, the lamentations, the whole paraphernalia of funerals, death in itself ought to appear as an instant of sudden transfiguration of the soul.

What I have said gives us the makings of a curious theory of suicides; a theory that it is hardly appropriate to develop in these pages, so I limit myself to pointing it out. Suicide is not wrong because it puts an end to life, which in any case, considered as an end in itself, is a dirty, nauseating business, but because it disturbs, interrupts or frustrates the chance of a natural assumption into the beyond. And the soul sets forth without the full development it should have attained within the body, a kind of eternal foetus. From the point of view of the beyond, suicide is then an abortion.

My confidence in Obregón was based on my personal experience; he had never given me the slightest indication that he was helping Calles achieve his ambitions. Lo, and behold! the politicians were besieging my school teachers on all sides as a major factor in the election, if indeed there was to be any pretense of having elections. It is certain, too, that with the exception of two or three immediate protégés of Calles, not a single one of the country's school teachers was Callista. Nor were the workers.

De la Huerta left the government, still uncertain about his candidacy. I was not a partisan of De la Huerta; it was my opinion that it would amount to re-election to put up a man who had just been provisional president. Besides, I thought it a bad idea for presidents to come from the cabinet. And I was irritated by the indifference of revolutionary public opinion that did not call a formal convention to choose the candidate of the revolutionary party, excluding on principle all of us who were in the Government.

The majority of the army rebelled against the idea of having to be under Calles.

In spite of this, Obregón persisted in his mistake. The blindness of an uncultivated man, his distrust of true loyalty, his ambition for direct rule, led Obregón to the defeat that his protégé Calles, whom he hated, was preparing for him. He liked me and he hated Calles. Because he did not follow his heart, his head deceived him; he destroyed himself and threw his country into an abyss. But it is quite certain that at the time I had no desire to be President. I wanted an honest government which would not devote itself to destroying my educational work. From the hands of such a government I would have asked for a Legation in Spain, in order to study and rest. Perhaps after four years, and from outside the government, I would have acquired the courage to enter politics with ambitions of becoming the chief; for already, from my position in Education, I had pointed out that the solution of the country's problem does not rest in the hands of subordinates, the Ministers, but in the hands of the President, who is the head. If the President is not of the first order, is not the author of the program to be executed, it does not matter in the least whether he be surrounded by illustrious Ministers or not.

One by one, the regional chiefs who did not give their personal adherence to Calles were removed and fell into disgrace. Obregón was maliciously causing events, provoking them, using all his moral and governmental power to set up a successor whom the country repudiated.

De la Huerta began to suffer from all the trouble that falls to the lot of an honest man who, in a despotic environment, dares to defy it. It was characteristic of *Callismo* to accuse innocent persons of precisely those crimes which it shamelessly committed. Every imaginable vilification fell upon De la Huerta.

The resignation of De la Huerta did not drag me down and had no reason to do so. No political obligation bound me to anyone but Obregón.

My hope was to make Mexico City the metropolis of the Latin Continent; an Athens, not because of a ridiculous desire to emulate ancient Athens, but a city renowned for its love of culture, for its liberality and hospitality toward alien talent. We attempted to give each of our South American or Spanish visitors detailed information, and have them travel through the interior. The young and brilliant Brazilian poet, Ronald de Carvalho was in the capital and had given us three lectures on the development of Brazil; I decided to take advantage of my inspection trip to Guadalajara to invite the distinguished visitor to join my official entourage. And I asked the railway people for a car. Usually, I climbed into whatever car they wanted to give me, or took a compartment in an ordinary train; but on this trip, because I was taking a guest, I insisted on their giving me a sleeping car in good condition.

On our eastern coast, in Campeche and Vera Cruz, for instance, we have regions that are thickly Spanish, but the climate has slowly broken down the vigor of the race, and Indian and Negro blood has been mingled with that of Europeans. Puebla is the typical mestizo city; it has a subtle intelligence, but is characterized by weakness and trickery. Oaxaca was a colony of Spaniards gradually absorbed and displaced by the Indians who inhabit the surrounding highlands. Oaxaca was and is not. But Jalisco and the western coast represent a remnant of the Spanish element that has become native. They do not remember their origin, but it comes out spontaneously in songs, in the rhythm of dances, and in the gentleness and kindliness of their manners. And of all this region of forgotten Spanishness, Guadalajara is the Queen.

The city was gay and self-confident. It was amused by its new plaything, the Industrial School for Girls which our department had founded and was maintaining with particular interest. From Guadalajara we got the talent for teaching occupations for women such as cooking, drawing, singing, and dancing, and we took the graduates off to the schools of the capital. From the laboratory of our new Industrial School, the educator would be able to draw tomorrow the seeds of culture that the rest of the country so sorely needed. All social classes met democratically in the buildings of the Industrial School; workers and aristocracy were united by the dream of a Mexico that was beginning to fulfill her long delayed promise.

A group of armed men composed of old enemies of Villa had cut down the ex-guerrilla fighter as he was entering Parral, driving his own car. A shiver went through the whole nation. Not so much because of Villa, as the revelation that we were once more in a regime of assassination after some years of simulating decent government. Everybody understood the reasons for the crime. A rebel movement would not be long in breaking out if the government insisted on imposing Calles as President. And the main barrier to this imposition, that natural leader of an armed protest, could not be anyone but Villa, the fighter who had withdrawn but was not tamed. The death of Villa, unreservedly applauded by the Callistas, was proof enough for everyone that the government was determined to impose its will upon the people, and would mercilessly crush opposition.

Toward the end, my relations with Pancho Villa had been cordial. I never saw him again because he never came to the capital; however, he would send me telegrams asking for school materials for the children of the hacienda the government had given him when he surrendered. People recommended by the general always found a friendly welcome in my offices. The warrior's messages ended with an "affectionately yours" that was sincere. The betrayal that cost him his life affected me like a disloyalty.

Through a leak from some reporters, it was learned that ten days before the assassination of Villa, a group of fourteen uniformed men had rented the house from which the attack was made. When it was over, the fourteen soldiers mounted their horses and rode off without anyone bothering them.

North American lawyers, when they are not top rank, write a lot and get all tangled up in "Whereases" and "Whereins," and finally say in many pages what a good Latin lawyer expresses with exactitude in half a dozen clauses. However, when the Yankee lawyer is shrewd, this very confusion of style serves to disconcert and confuse his adversary. In contracts that are difficult to interpret, it is the cleverer who has the advantage; and when the interpretation is even slightly doubtful, it is the stronger who dictates the interpretation that favors him. So it is that the advantage in a tangled document was all in favor of the United States.

De la Huerta knew the treaties. De la Huerta hesitated. And although he did not then denounce them, and I do not remember his ever doing so, it is clear that he refrained from approving them.

The Yankee oil companies, which never act without instructions from Washington, granted Obregón's government an advance of ten million on future taxes. His desire to crush the rebels, therefore, won out in Obregón's mind over his earlier policy of independence from Washington.

The first blow was stopping payment of the item meant for the journal *El Maestro*, which had been carrying the fame of a cultivated Mexico to all civilized lands. We distributed seventy-five thousand copies. And although the journal never achieved a high philosophical or literary quality, and its purpose was not to discover new talents, it did perform a real service in spreading basic culture and sending Mexican propaganda abroad.

The fame of our capital was for the first time attracting artists from the south of the continent. Among them was a famous actress whom we shall call Luciana; she packed the theatres and aroused the interest of the whole city. Luciana's secret was her diction; nobody recited the way she did. In my youth I had heard on occasion the famous golden voice of the French actress, Sarah Bernhardt; although she was world-famous, she had seemed to me inferior to the Italian actresses who came to Mexico City. Now for the first time we were hearing in Spanish declamation that was worthy of our literature. Listening to her I became convinced of her merit; then harsh criticism put me on my guard against the danger that is so common in Ibero-America, that of praising artists as geniuses and then seeing them cut down to ridiculous size in Europe. I realized that we had made no mistake in the capital of Mexico when I learned a year or two later that in Madrid Luciana had put a celebrated poet, thought to be the prototype of the most exquisite purity of taste, into a state of absolute delirium.

During a visit that Obregón made to the capital, I took him to hear Luciana. He thanked me for keeping the capital amused with affairs that cost the government nothing. That was the way it ought to be!

Disgusted with myself, I decided to draw up a telegram in which to present my resignation to Obregón. I signed it on the twenty-eighth of January, 1924. I told him that I could not loyally serve in a situation which ran counter to my most deep-rooted convictions, and that I remained at his orders as a private citizen and friend.

There was nothing else to do. Only a nation-wide movement which would sweep away factions and change the hearts of the citizens could offer any hope. "In the meantime," I said, "everything has been dead for some time, ever since Obregón decided to throw his support to Calles, for the civilizing efforts of a Department cannot be reconciled with the plan of handing over the presidency to a savage. It would have been good if we could have raised the level of the country by means of education."

Two or three days went by and what Gastellum had foreseen happened: Obregón sent a request that I withdraw my resignation, promising on his word of honor to punish the assassins of Field Jurado, who he said were known to him. And he really did know them. With Obregón's promise to see justice done, honor was saved, even if it should take some time to carry out the promise. As soon as the rebellion was over and the Government on its feet again, there would be time to get around to demanding the punishment of the assassins; for the present, I could not refuse to trust for a while a man who had trusted me and had permitted me to carry out the work of my Ministry. So I called in the press and told them, "I have just withdrawn my resignation because I have confidence in Obregón. He will see justice done in the matter of Field Jurado as soon as the revolt is over. Poor Field Jurado!"

In general, the country was not sorry about the defeat of De la Huerta. Obregón himself, horror-struck by the actions of Prieto Laurens, told me at one of our last staff meetings, "You see now, De la Huerta is to blame for all that. If he had not taken it into his head to attack me; if he had had the strength to hold back his partisans, we would not be where we are now, in a situation in which there is no stopping what is about to happen."

He was referring to the Presidency of Calles, which was his own work and which he regretted. And it was to destroy him.

The city and the country lacked a stadium. I began as I did in other cases, by first getting hold of available free land. There was an old abandoned Pantheon. Because of our aversion to tombs and the low price of land in the district, an immense plot had escaped the covetousness of those who were exploiting national property. But where would I find the money for building? I detest those iron buildings, in the style of American skyscrapers, that will have to be demolished in fifty years. I admire peoples who build for eternity whether with stone, like the Romans, with brick, like the Babylonians, or with simple, massive, and durable adobe like the Incas of Peru. But the strength to support stands for sixty thousand people can come only from concrete, which is frightfully expensive. Still, I insisted on the concrete even if it should mean not finishing the construction. We signed a contract for about four hundred thousand pesos, without knowing how we were going to pay it. The structure would be wonderful; in any case, it was indispensable for a city like ours; it would be enough if they gave me fifty thousand pesos from time to time as an extra addition to the budget.

We had lots of discussion then, and since, about the shape and size of the stadium. I refused to make it a mere race track. What I cared about above all was having an open-air theatre in which to give ballets and gymnastic events, and to present the choruses of different schools. Therefore, we made studies of the right proportions from the acoustical point of view, not just from the point of view of the rules of different sports. I preferred to have an open space in which the human voice would not be lost, rather than a bigger space in which amplifiers would be needed. For that matter, amplification was just beginning at that time.

My desire to leave the government somewhat advanced the date of the opening.

A huge crowd of more than sixty thousand applauded the beginning of the games. A parade of male and female athletes, young and supple, performed exercises to music. Then a chorus of twelve thousand children sang. A group of a thousand couples in national costume danced a *járabe*. Other groups did Spanish dances, for the only types permitted were Spanish and Mexican. No useless music, no performance that did not develop from the daily activities of our schools. The Department of Physical Culture proved what Mexican athletes could do without any guidance from foreigners.

We had maintained cordial relations with the Universities of North America, especially with the University of Texas. A Rector of that university had been our guest, and in connection with his visit we worked out an exchange of scholarships. Four or six young Mexicans went to Austin with stipends from the Secretariat. Professor Handman of Texas, an eminent sociologist and distinguished writer, had made two trips to Mexico and had become interested in the educational work which he saw progressing there. Professor Hackett, an expert in the history of our country, taught that subject at Austin, and had visited us several times. So there was nothing strange about the fact that this year the University in our former province decided to confer on me the highly honorable task of speaking at commencement, a task that in Yankee universities is given to prominent educators, thinkers, and teachers, from outside the host institution. The invitation pleased Obregón and he put his private railway car at my disposal for the journey.

That June, 1924, the University of Texas was not yet the splendid institution that is today admired by Texans and foreigners alike, but the eminent men who started it on the road to greatness were already there. Professor Ellis took us driving through the city, took us back to his house, and told us his plans, and we caught some of his creative enthusiasm. Our old friends, Handman and Hackett, gave us dinners. The official reception was simple, but the warmth and friendliness of our welcome left a pleasant memory. Even at that time I could brag about certain things in which we had the better of Texas: for example, the stadium, for Texas was not yet building one. Since then Austin has grown and become one of the great institutions of the world. Its library today is a model of sumptuousness and efficiency.

One of our companions on this trip was Haya de la Torre; disgusted with the savagery that was suddenly developing in Mexico, he left for London, with a grant from the Yankee Methodists. We said our farewells in Austin. When I reached the capital, I found a letter from him in which he thanked me very nicely for the pleasure he had had in Mexico, and said in most moving words, "I have seen how you suffer in the new offices of that Ministry which you built and which is now besieged by all the avenging furies of barbarism." At that time Haya was sincere. Before his trip to Russia, which poisoned his mind, Haya was a noble lad. The Marxist doctrine which is without honor, loyalty, and honesty, on the ground that these are bourgeois virtues, never absorbed Haya totally. Later I called him to task for his silence with respect to the Mexico of Calles, and even more for his second trip to Mexico, when he took a salary from the Callista university. Apart from this, I have nothing against Haya, and if I have any regret it is that I was not able to help him as one should help a political refugee, providing him with sufficient resources to get around and keep up the fight. Much as I have been attacked by the people who vented their rage on me for "paying foreigners to flatter me," it is certain that I gave our foreign guests only very minor positions in which they legitimately earned a living. Haya never got more than ten pesos a day and always worked for them.

I called on Obregón before leaving for Oaxaca. I found him reserved but still cordial.

"Who knows, Counselor, what disappointments local politics will present you with! You know it is always easy to fall a victim to lower and irresponsible authorities. The central government cannot always provide the necessary guarantees."

"No, General; in my case there is no difficulty, for I can count on the whole State; I don't really have a rival. The candidate they want to put up against me there will withdraw because he is a trustworthy man whom I know and who seems to esteem me. In any case, if I win, you can be sure, in your retirement, that you have a personal friend in Oaxaca, one who will never change."

"I do not doubt it, Counselor. And, by the way, you are probably not too flush with funds; if you like, we could give you something for campaign expenses; this has been done in many cases."

It was indeed all too well known that governors had been made this way in recent months, without consulting local opinion and with plentiful funds from the National Treasury.

"In my case, General," I replied, "it will not be necessary to spend much money; before accepting the candidacy I made the stipulation that I would not bring money, because I don't have any, and also because I believe this is what unpopular candidates do; I don't have to win popularity; I have it already; but I have just one favor I should like to ask of you. You know I have devoted myself for four years to my official work, neglecting my private interests entirely. I have about twenty or thirty thousand pesos that I have saved up, but I am going to have considerable personal expense. I want to ask what any employee has the right to request of an enterprise in which he has worked. I want you to give an order that they pay me two months' salary, or say six thousand pesos."

"Of course, it is the least we can do; but it is a mere nothing, and besides, as you say, it is a right; you may count on it."

He behaved so meanly afterward that he did not even keep the promise to send me this salary payment, and I did not keep after him about it; I never collected the money.

In every town of Oaxaca, Vasconcelos committees sprang up spontaneously; it was two or three months before the election. There was really not a chance that another candidate would come out ahead. With the object of firming up this situation, I tried to win the newspapers over to my side. At the moment nothing was easier. Since I had just left the Ministry of Education, everybody knew the importance of what I had done there, and no one hesitated to give me the title of outstanding educator and leader of our national intellectual life.

We were entering upon a democratic struggle, we bore no ill will toward anyone. The State, at a time of political crisis, was calling upon one of her most illustrious sons.

Democracy was a reality on our Mexican soil!

We failed to take Obregón into account. His will moved in secret. And Governor Ibarra was his tool.

Each one of those who helped me, the élite of Oaxaca at the time, fell into the shade, into oblivion and impotence, with the exception of those who became traitors.

My rival, who had been completely apathetic, began to go about the city and to speak in private. He never made a speech to the people, but to his friends he made a remark that was enough to defeat me:

"The Counselor is too big a candidate for Oaxaca; the Counselor drinks champagne; I drink mexcal; I ought to be Governor."

Really, the poor fellow did nothing, did not have to do anything. The incumbent Governor, whose protégé he was, and the Commanding Officer, did everything.

I returned to Oaxaca to watch helplessly the trickery, violence, and cynicism. The government did not even bother to hold elections; boxes were missing, ballots were missing, votes were missing, for voters were threatened and frightened. Even so, with the few who turned out, there would have been enough votes to assure us a legitimate victory. But they never complete the count under regimes of barefaced force; the official party carts off the voting urns and never even bothers to open them.

As usual, a few days after our defeat, the same papers which had encouraged me and had proved the unlawfulness of the defeat, instead of insisting on reprimanding those who had gone against the public will, opened a campaign to declare that I had done wrong in launching my candidacy; that I didn't know what the real situation of our politics was, etc.

One day in Oaxaca, while I was looking at the old houses with their noble coats of arms and the patios with their beautiful stone arcades, I noticed how small the white population was, and how many Indians from the surrounding highlands were invading the streets, wrapped in their blankets, silent and impassive. And I understood the whole tragic process of the history of Mexico; it lies in this displacement, in the exhaustion of the conquering and civilizing Spanish blood. In the time of Juárez and the reform movement, Oaxaca contained a nucleus of Mexican-born people of Spanish blood that could not have been better. This group fought for the improvement of the country and the defeat of Santa Anna, fought against the Empire, and later spread throughout the Republic, taking all kinds of managerial positions. The city was drained of its white citizens and the houses that remained deserted were slowly taken over by Indians. The unifying bonds, the educational work necessary if the racial change was not to be a landslide were lacking. The racial mixture, which is indispensable and can be our salvation, has not had time to bear fruit. And the result is that, with the departure of the old families, Oaxaca has turned into a manor house in ruins.

Obregón himself, doubtless feeling that he had committed an injustice toward me, sought an opportunity for a rapprochement. Dr. Gastellum invited me to dinner; Jaime Torres Bodet was there.

After dinner the Doctor said, "We are about to get some new autos in the Secretariat; I have instructions from General Obregón to tell you to come around and see them and pick out one which he would like to give you."

"And on what constitutional power does the President base his right to hand out automobiles?" I replied.

I had some consolation; to the extent that doors were closed to me in Mexico on account of the terrorism of Calles, the best groups of South America began to show me the same interest and consideration they had once shown me as Minister. It is clear that this deference resulted from my Hispanic-American work, as for instance, in the publication of the classics. This had had widespread consequences. In any case, the gesture of opening the doors that the sister republics made was both noble and gratifying to one who had been called by Gabriela Mistral the "sweetheart of Latin America." Mud slingers have spread the rumor that I spent money on publicity for myself in the South. They can never prove I spent a cent on publicity, either in the South or the North. The best propaganda is accomplishments, and this is what the sterile and impotent cannot understand. Our work had been known for its creativity and optimism. In the emptiness of the continent it shone like a solitary star. No other official up to that time had done anything like it to develop the spiritual solidarity of the continent. Neither Rodó nor Manuel Ugarte had a chance to put into operation the things they so excellently preached; I had had the good fortune to be able to accomplish a part of what so many had dreamed. This explains why it was later so easy for me to move about the continent, earning my living, which in itself is a triumph for an exile. And all this has nothing to do with the legend that I had filled the posts in Education with foreigners. More foreigners came to the University later to give lectures than in my time. This was not because the University became more liberal, but because Institutes were founded, supported by the Spanish colony, following a movement which came from Argentina. What I spent on foreigners was limited to the three or four persons I have already mentioned, who earned the extremely modest salaries I have revealed: Haya de la Torre, ten pesos or five dollars per day, Gabriela Mistral, twenty-five pesos. As I understand the facts, the Secretariat spent more on bringing Haya back again, although they dropped him when it became obvious that they could not make use of him against me.

In those hard months of the beginning of 1925, I made preparations for a journey to Spain.

I had no relations with the Spanish Embassy, for my *Revista* had attacked Primo de Rivera and his coup d'état. But good friends in the Spanish colony of Mexico City undertook to do groundwork and encouraged me to make the trip.

I could omit from my story certain episodes which might wound the feelings of circumspect people, but he who writes, not for a given audience, but in order to contemplate his own life from a critical point of view which will orient him for the future, must recall circumstances that seem trivial to others, but that left indelible traces on him, or constituted valuable experience. Traversing the hell of the flesh is a part of the soul's history that arouses more guilt feelings, but also more interest than all the ups and downs of politics.

I do not belong to a markedly sexual type, nor have I devoted my life to seeking adventures with women. With my unglamorous appearance, my shy temperament, my moral character, I could not be taken for even a caricature of Don Juan. From an early age, my intellectual ambition, my dream of creating great works of the mind, has made me saving of my strength, incapable of devoting myself for long periods to sexual excess—excess which has always impressed me as leaving the brain empty, the soul crippled. Between following up an adventure and writing a page that seems beautiful to me, I have always chosen the latter. My own egotism, moreover, keeps me away from erotic involvements. My real vocation is very far from the love relation between the sexes. I have always believed in the love of the absolute. Even if the expression may seem pedantic, anyone will understand what I mean if he suffers from the same illness. And in practice, eroticism and mysticism are opposites and enemies, although in the last analysis they are connected, like water from springs originating at the same subterranean level. And every time I have fallen into the trap of amorous obsession, including matrimony, a voice from deep within me has accused me of betraying my calling, which from the cradle has been that of a hermit.

For that matter, the man who today is called an intellectual is a kind of anchorite, who in order to be effective has to subdue the body and give himself entirely to the abnormality and torment, sometimes so glorious, of mental activity and creation through thought. Our whole organism, insofar as it is animal, is made for digestion and sleeping; the efforts which the soul imposes on it become notoriously painful in the case of a man working with his conscience. If to this biological condition you add the upbringing of early years, severely religious, forbidding even the tasting of sweets in Lent, leaving us with a deep-rooted conviction that all sensual pleasure is sinful, you will understand the disturbance that all voluptuous delight arouses in my nature. And this is just what happens in the consciences of all Christians.

From this drama comes all that is best in our civilization, a striving in the direction of the heroic goal of contradicting and conquering nature so that the spirit may come to its full flower.

The scandalous sin seems to me rather the invention of the priesthood than a dictate of the Gospel, and, in any case, it is the worst offense that one can commit against the rigorous, cruel code of all kinds of Pharisees. The feminine temperament, for its part, demands exclusive devotion to love; fame and mental activity seem to it secondary matters, and women give themselves wholly only to a man who has in advance consented to sacrifice himself as their victim. From Dionysus to Don Juan the law of the true lover has been to let himself be devoured by women.

The distinguished liberal and fine gentleman Don Eduardo Santos was one of the first newspaper owners to invite me to write regularly for his publications. Quickly I became the most widely read of all Mexicans. Nevertheless, the thing I most wanted to do was not newspaper articles; my true calling was the book.

My poverty has not been a vocation, but a punishment, an accident imposed by circumstances. The natural thing in my profession, for a man with my capacity to work hard, is that I should have become rich. But already a fortune-teller reading my palm had told me, "Rich you will never be. When you have money you will have to spend it, and you won't always have it."

The moral obligation to continue the fight against *Callismo* forced me to earn a living by my pen. Otherwise, I would have been a writer of philosophical books, and also an active businessman.

When Lanz Duret, editor and owner of *El Universal*, came back from a trip to Europe, he kindly confirmed the arrangement that I could travel, sending my articles from wherever I happened to be.

Only very seldom did I go to the theatre. I have never had the time nor the inclination to do so regularly. The commercialized theatre of our days only rarely presents a drama of O'Neill, a comedy of Lope de Vega. Night after night the leisure classes who are in easy circumstances waste their time on shows that are essentially pornographic. This may perhaps be a way of avoiding worse perversions— this looking from a distance at pretty women, more or less undressed, but the habit of doing so must lead to an exacerbated and superficial, abnormal state of sensuality, since it is not nature's way to pass one's time in excitation which does not lead to satisfaction, as if you looked at fruits or turkeys without eating them.

Mexico had decidedly become uninhabitable. Everywhere the appearance of the new functionaries, copied from the mask of their chief, was one of sullen arrogance.

A month or so later I embarked for Europe, thinking that that second farewell would be the last.

We had left the house in Tacubaya because my family was to follow me after a few months, as soon as I had finished the tour I was planning to Asia Minor and Greece, perhaps even to India. I put in my pockets three or four thousand pesos in gold and letters of credit for an equal amount.

The papers scarcely mentioned my journey, if I had been carrying a diplomatic passport, traveling at peace with my Government, there would have been lots of notices and pictures. I didn't miss them. When we disembarked at Havana, friends and newspapermen were on the dock, gathered there to lionize me. The next day the leading Havana papers gave the place of honor to my statements and my picture, and in a less important corner of the paper noted that the same ship had brought the commission sent by Calles, headed by a Señor Aaron Sáenz, to take part in the inauguration of Machado. Cuba was entering a period of ferocious dictatorship and did not know it. In the press, the arrival of an intellectual was still more important than that of so many diplomatic and political missions. People did not seem to pay much attention to Machado, although that seemed suspicious to me, and I pointed out to my friends in the minority party that in the official proceedings the delegations of the bloody dictatorships of America, those of Vicente Gómez of Venezuela and Calles of Mexico, had the choice places.

"I pity you," I told them, "if Machado starts imitating Calles. Cuba, which has been happy since it gained independence, will know for the first time the agony of despotism."

What they told me about educational work on the island depressed me. Much as we in Mexico boasted of a budget that was high for us, it was miserable compared to Cuba's. Advancing the attack against *Callismo*, I gave the papers my point of view on the educational activities of the new government, "In my time the appropriation was only fifty million pesos. Now, after six months of the Calles regime, it has been reduced to twenty-five."

I was leaving Mexico as a protest against militarism. And in Spain, the King, in alliance with the military, had just destroyed the Constitution. How could I accept official attentions from such a government? With a bit of prudence on my part, I could doubtless have spent three or four royal months on that delicious peninsula, surrounded by the kindest and most cordial hospitality. Honors of this kind are usually showered on an ex-functionary. But wasn't my place among the defeated, the oppressed? I had no personal contract with the Republicans, but my duty lay with them.

What I would do was to enter the country like any ordinary traveler, visit the sights and the museums. More than anything else, I wanted to look at the architecture. Feeling our way, we had done a great deal of building in Mexico. Even if I never again had a chance to direct a building operation, the immediate contemplation of the churches and palaces would serve me well in providing material for the book on *Aesthetics* which would be the culmination of my intellectual life. My own reading on the subject, largely interrupted during my work in the Ministry, went no further than Ruskin and Taine and the classical Italians like Vasari.

My friend Fontoura, the Brazilian Ambassador, had recommended that I should on no account miss Coimbra and Lisbon, so neglected by the Hispanic-American traveler. Gratefully, I followed his advice. Limiting yourself to Paris is all very well for those in search of vulgar pleasures or those who have some well-defined object of study. The true traveler chooses the routes that legend and art have consecrated, that have superstructures of the spirit. The peculiar "feel" of peoples is not to be found in their cosmopolitan capitals, but in the poetry of the villages, in the miracles of the cathedrals and convents. The traveler finds true treasure in the squares of famous cities, in the towers that have stood watch for generations, in the places where men have suffered, and enjoyed, and thought.

Portugal—a great little nation—the nation of the most glorious empire of all times; its character, proud in action, but affable and tender in daily living. It had such lofty ambitions that it finally lost everything. And we were charmed by the deep humor of Eça de Queiroz, like untarnished, old gold. Portugal lacks a literature worthy of its epic history, but that is because its lyrical vein was spent in action; its history is its poetry, and its complicated, elegant art, parallel to the plateresque, moves us with the feeling that we are related to it.

Who knows if the Latin awakening which today throbs in history, may not restore Portugal's energy? If our America has a future, it lies with him, the Portuguese, our ally and our brother, as he was in the days of splendor when the Pope divided the world into two parts, Spain's and Portugal's.

In the castle of Cintra, my delirious vision of the future grew calmer, and I surrendered to the delight of the gardens. I envied the spacious, vaulted bedrooms. Grace which once was power, such seems to me to be the definition of the charm of Portugal.

What is left to us is the good wine that helps us remember, helps to make less horrible the present that is before our eyes. Great cities that have become proletarianized, or worse, depraved, oppressed, miserable and ugly: ugly cities that once upon a time were princesses of India and mistresses of the Iberian plain.

In Europe the tourist contemplates the work of centuries; the apse of the cathedral of Avila has walls from the eleventh century, and the portal is from the fourteenth; the principal palaces are of the seventeenth century and the hotels of twentieth-century style. The mania to build by demolishing the old is, I suppose, of North American origin, and its cause is obvious: building is so badly done in that country, in such a temporary manner, that the short duration of each building is taken for granted. And in the United States they do not have those walls made for eternity which are so much work for us to demolish, when we wish to replace them with mean buildings.

The café, in the fashion of Portugal, Spain, and France, was a new institution for me. It existed in Mexico before the process of Americanization upset all our habits. It belongs to a civilized phase of sociability. In the United States the rich man has his club for talking to his friends; the men of the middle and lower class live in brutalizing isolation. They hurry home from work and when they get there they sit alone on the steps of the front porch in summer, or beside the stove in winter. There are millions of human beings who never talk to their fellows. People huddle together on street corners and in squares that more or less take the place of the café. But, really, even we have not found a substitute. Friends in the same business or profession go to the café to exchange views for an hour or two a day with the excuse of having a cup of coffee or a glass of wine. In Spain and Portugal they abuse the leisure of the cafés, which morning and afternoon are full of customers who talk, talk, talk.

For myself, I consider the function of the café as that of a club in which you converse, but I do not understand the Spanish and Portuguese love of coffee, that blackish, depraved drink, worse than all the drugs in the pharmacopoeia, for it robs us of sleep, instead of bringing it. The man who does not sleep well is a sick man or a candidate for the madhouse. Wine is sacred because it brings sleep.

If they are devoted to coffee in Spain and Portugal today, it is because each country in its way is decadent and lazy. Both have lost the taste for fruitful work, and the man who loves his work tries to sleep so that he may be wide awake for it. He who has nothing to do doesn't care whether he sleeps or not. And moreover, since the Iberian cities have become so noisy—with the population squeezed into shells that were built for carts and wagons, not for the automobile— every night becomes an inferno of noise and rumbling which makes us jump out of our beds. The poor victims of decadence have not been able to build themselves quiet homes in the suburbs in North American fashion; nor can they make up their minds to pass strict laws against noise. When dawn comes they have not slept a wink, their eyelids are swollen, their brains dull, and in coffee they find the hashish which keeps them awake and prevents their nodding in full daylight. In France it is different; there people in cafés take wine and sleep soundly in their cities, which are crowded, too, but have effective ordinances against noise.

I understand very little about color. I can see well enough, but line and shade are lost on me, both in painting and in music. The magic of rhythm is everything to me, but I miss the fine gradation of tones, which is a matter of harmony. There must be harmonic temperaments and melodic temperaments. It is worthwhile meditating on this classification; for the moment, I assert that even for a man who is blind to color tonality, two painters that Madrid quite rightly adopted are the greatest of the city: Velásquez and Goya.

The left-wing paper, *El Sol*, was my best ally, and would have kept on being so, if I had not quarreled with all leftism when it visibly took the side of Calles. I met casually, on a Madrid roof garden, Pérez de Ayala, whose novels I don't like; but his newspaper articles are good, always full of original, well-informed thinking. Pío Baroja was introduced to me one night. We called on Ortega y Gasset at the editorial offices of the *Revista de Occidente*. He was surrounded by young disciples. He did not make a very good impression on me, nor I on him. This was exceptional in the general atmosphere of cordiality and easy access which all the other important people of Spain had extended to me.

You soon feel at home in Madrid, recognized on the streets and in the cafés, praised by the papers, smiled at by friends.

A committee was formed to arrange an *homenaje* and some recep-

tions for me. People of various political parties were on it. The first
event was a tea, by invitation, at the Ritz. The leftist element was
predominant among those attending, but we all had a surprise. At
the head table, the presiding officer was General Magaz, a Minister of Primo de Rivera. The service began very correctly, with that
excellent Madrid chocolate. General Magaz, rather old and a bit stout,
very good-humored and polite, begged my pardon for not eating, because, he confessed quite frankly, "I don't want to spoil my dinner,
but we are all very happy to have you with us!"

And we conversed amicably about superficial matters until the time
came for the toasts. When the General rose to offer one, don Ramón
del Valle-Inclán, who was at one of the little tables at the rear, got up
angrily, "I protest," he cried, "in the name . . ."

And his explanations were lost in the tumult. He was objecting to
the presence of Magaz, and accompanied by opposing murmurs of
approval and disapproval, don Ramón left the hall, followed, I think,
by Américo Castro.

The papers asked me for interviews, which I invariably gave, talking about the military regime under which we suffered in Mexico,
and other things which fitted the Spanish situation, too. "The day
that these Hispanic peoples spend more on teachers and less on
soldiers, we shall begin to rise from our decadence. I am depressed by
the history of Spain, both on the Peninsula and in the New World. I
have just seen a plaque which commemorates the place in which
Cervantes was imprisoned; this is the rhythm of our history: 'Into
the prison with genius! Put the imbeciles into positions of power!'
England, on the contrary, gives power to genius."

And the students got excited. They sent me friendly messages
and I replied with a fiery manifesto in which I made an appointment
with them for an exchange of embraces on the day of victory. While
public meetings and university demonstrations were being organized
in Madrid, a commission of the friends of Unamuno invited me to
visit Salamanca. The illustrious old man had just been exiled by the
Dictatorship. And by military decree a substitute Rector had been appointed.

In Avila correspondence from Mexico reached me; my family was
enthusiastic about the coming voyage which would reunite us in
France at the year's end. The papers were attacking me. My mistakes
grew; my extravagance reached the proportions of a legend which
served to cover up the thievery of my successors.

When I returned to Madrid the students had already had a run in
with the police. The great public meeting they had planned for my
return was forbidden. Still, in spite of everything, they wanted to
have a celebration in some indoor place, but I opposed this. I also had
to refuse a great popular luncheon for which more than a thousand
people had already signed up. I decided to leave Spain, but by way
of the South, so as to catch at least a glimpse of Sevilla. But before
that I stopped incognito in Córdoba.

The temptation which had come to me in Avila, really to give up
for good and enter a monastery, to pray, making up for the years in
which I had not prayed, returned in intense and urgent form. But I
reflected, "The Gospel says 'Thou shalt leave thy father and thy
mother and thy wife . . . ,' especially thy wife. But it does not say
'Thou shalt leave thy children.' "

Chacón y Calvo, my learned companion, wanted in passing to visit
Moguer, the native territory of Juan Ramón Jiménez; he wanted to
absorb the atmosphere for an essay he was writing about the poet. I
once dared to argue with him about his favorite and he almost broke
off our friendship.

"I don't like algebra in poetry," I told him. And he replied with a
whole lecture delivered in a tone of condescending pity for my lack of
understanding.

"But the truth is," I added, giving up the struggle as far as poetry
was concerned, and jumping to the prose of Juan Ramón, "I would
rather swallow a millstone than admit that this *Platero y Yo* is a
classic. If it is, it's only because it's so boring. It is true that the oratorical style, which is held in abomination these days, and to which I
have a certain inclination, is often vain, pompous, and tiresome, but it
is also certain that nowadays people fall into another defect which is
perhaps worse, namely, style for the sake of style. The reader has to
suffer because of the efforts of the literary virtuoso. No masterpiece
has ever been written this way. I abominate 'style.' Stylists make us
sweat and don't even leave us a memory of what we have read. A
good style is identical with the action of thinking."

León Sánchez, the bookseller, had given me a letter to one of the
architects in charge of the Alhambra. The architect enlightened me
with all his wisdom. I spent two or three days looking and coming
back to look again. I don't claim to deny the celebrated charm of

one of the most beautiful sites in the world. Nevertheless, it is not one of the things that thrill me. A hidden aversion remains, and is aggravated when they tell us that in the bathing pool they gouged out the eyes of the musicians so that their curiosity would not interfere with the sporting of the Sultan with his concubines. There is nothing more anti-Christian than that palace, since it is typically Muslim. It is dead, with that death from which there is no rebirth. It does not deserve to come to life. The soul of the building is ephemeral, like the stately vice which it sheltered. Bad foundations and a lot of plaster, its decoration of foliage, its atmosphere of repose, give that ruin the splendor of decay. Its glory, which lacked a spiritual aspect, is withered. The civilization that erected it left us nothing. Some translations, perhaps, translations of Aristotle and science that the Arabs had imported, but had not created themselves, and had then passed on to Europe, which at that time was still uncivilized; but in any case these were to reach Europe later, in purer form, from Byzantium.

Ninety per cent of the charm of the Alhambra is literature. Even in that area, the officials in charge of public buildings who encourage North American tourism do what they can to sell us an Alhambra translated into English. The best inn there is not the Mesón of Boabdil, but the Washington Irving Hotel. I never had the patience to read his mediocre reports on the Alhambra. In the field of Arabian love stories and legends, would it not be better for the tourist to acquire the *Romancero*, in either a cheap or de luxe edition, and at least have it in addition to Washington Irving's book? In those days, the educated men of Spain, at the same time that they were working for the Republic, were making the mistake of worshipping everything foreign, that is Saxon, and for that reason they were soon to destroy the Republic.

In Valencia they display a statue of the Virgin covered with very rich jewels. I was quite won over by the idea of setting the most costly precious stones in the Sacred Image, and dressing her in the finest brocades. Some of this can be seen in India, and it is a permanent trait of Oriental culture to clothe the most important idol with the garments and treasures of greatest value. The most beautiful things to look at—diamonds, rubies, rich embroidery—are taken away from the area of private greed and put on public exhibition, not in museum showcases, which are the tombs of art, but on the body of the idol, which is a symbol of the highest concept of the culture. I cannot conceive of any better use of jewels, and if I were a magician and dictator of an empire, I would requisition the pearl necklaces and the diadems to put them on the head and mantle of the images of the Virgin.

A traveler can remain for years in Europe and never stop enjoying surprises, discovering wonders. In the United States, on the other hand, anyone who knows one town, knows the way of life of a hundred and thirty million inhabitants; everything there is washed, but with a soap that leaves everything tasteless, if not indeed contaminated by the aseptic odor, which does not prevent there being more sick people and more hospitals in the United States than in Europe. One might say that the evil of external uniformity ends by sickening their bodies as well as their souls.

In general, the lot of the average man in Europe is better than that of the average man in America. Money buys more in Europe; the general welfare is greater and the enjoyments there are incomparably more elevated. We in America live in a narrower, more restricted environment, on a soil infertile for things of the spirit.

To read up on Mallorca I had hastily gone through Azorín's book. A quatrain of Rubén Darío that Azorín used as an epigraph says more than his whole book. I don't remember it, but it leaves an impression of a place where the elements make music. Even better than Azorín's book, the one by that female devil, Georges Sand, helps us understand the characteristics and habits of the people of Mallorca. Chopin, in his turn, gave us in his *Préludes* the deepest feeling for that scene. His *Préludes* are strange, terrible creations, the wonder of the ages. Her ability to guess that she was in the presence of a creative genius of the first order says more for the talent of Georges Sand than all her literary work.

This is what the world wants; that he who protests do it without making a scandal; that he who does not rob allow himself to be robbed; that he who does not kill keep quiet and get along peaceably with the killers. This sort of discretion wins all the top prizes in the contemporary world. But to be at peace the soul requires that we establish equilibrium with the eternal values, not with the conventions and the circumstances of the hour. Success attained at the cost of a decorous silence and tolerance of evil, is, in the language of truth, Pharisaism. Good food sickens the Pharisee and luxury gives him leprosy. On the other hand, the bread I bought with my well-earned pennies was clean and tasty, and I brought a cleansed soul with me to enter the treasury of the most beautiful landscapes and the best art in the world. Free from obligations and, if you will, discredited as a man of the world, I visited the museums and thrilled at the country-side and knelt to pray in the churches. A sinner, to be sure, but no whited sepulchre!

It would never have occurred to me to stop in Marseilles at all if it had not been for a chance meeting with César Arroyo.

After an apéritif of Amer Picon, the speciality of Marseilles, he took me to the restaurants of the port. The way you can eat there makes up for the fact that you cannot get any sleep in the city. We were trying a marvelous bouillabaisse when Manuel Ugarte arrived. César was making an effort to arrange a reconciliation between us. As soon as we saw each other, we exchanged a warm embrace. I know few men so good, so likable, and so intelligent and well edu-cated. It was years later that I discovered that after talking to me, Ugarte had written to one of his friends, "Here is another man driven out of America because he wanted to do something good for it." This was the case with Ugarte. He lived from his writing after having spent his personal fortune in a quixotic journey to work for the Hispanic-American cause. No one had supported him, because among us, those who have money are in cahoots with Monroeism or else they are little men, incapable of promoting a noble cause. Numerous pa-pers in America refused Ugarte's writings because his signature was not acceptable to the powerful advertisers, the publicity trusts, and the Wall Street bankers.

"Can you imagine," Ugarte said, "the place where I found the most liberal reception for my preaching? It was at Columbia University in New York."

"And your book, *El Porvenir de un Continente!* [*The Future of a Continent*]," I added in confirmation, "is to be found in all the libraries of the United States. In the nations where Spanish is spoken, on the other hand, you have to search for it in the second-hand book-stores. And the intellectuals of note in Hispanic America may not know your books, but they all listen attentively to the preaching of Roosevelt, Wilson, and Brisbane."

In those days an Indian rebellion had broken out in Bolivia. The Bolivian consul in Italy had promised Ugarte that if the rebellion triumphed, and it began acquiring a continental and communistic character, a Pan-American government would be set up in Bolivia, in the very center of the Continent, and Ugarte would be Minister of Foreign Relations.

"And think," added Ugarte, "who would make a better Minister of Education for the whole Continent than you?"

In the air of Florence there is a kind of electricity of the spirit that sets you on fire, and sharpens your thinking. You are more awake there than anywhere else. It is a kind of intelligence that is very different from that effort à la Paul Valéry (the Frenchman), an effort to be intelligent which leads to the suspicion that one is not very sure of his own intelligence. Generally this refers to purely logical and reflective activity, the analytical activity of the mind. In Florence intelligence is different. In Florentine thinking, synthesis dominates analysis.

In the spiritual realm, Florence is more than Athens, for it unites humanistic culture with religion and the demand for the impossible. The transcendental feeling that Athens did not attain is attained by Florence in the highest degree.

One quickly comes to love Florence as a spiritual home, just as so many assure us they love Paris as a second home, the home of liberty.

Four or six hours of reading at night, added to the effort of looking at canvases in galleries and at murals, images, and statues in churches, had tired my eyes so that I could no longer follow the melody of the lines of all that precise drawing which is the Tuscan scene faithfully reproduced in the work of Tuscan artists. The mind also experiences a kind of saturation. After several days of deep emotion, of complicated reflection, we felt exhausted.

I had returned to look at the famous *David* after hearing unbounded praise of Michelangelo's imagination, and once more it had given me an impression of size without majesty. And the tomb of Lorenzo the Magnificent, summing up the pageantry of the Medicis, is excessive for what they were, petty princelings of a province which never reached nationhood, much less empire.

The machinery our souls have to work with is fragile. Two weeks of constant attention to the things of the spirit had left me weak and exhausted. The work of the mind is contrary to our physiological organization; our body, like that of animals, is made to move about in search of nourishment and then to rest and sleep.

I broke the sublime spell and left Florence. Walking would restore my lost strength. To rest the mind there is at times nothing better than giving the muscles more work to do.

My inamorata and I had planned to spend the last night in Florence together. She came on time to our appointment, but only in order to excuse herself; she could not make up her mind to get home late and to have to invent explanations; it was better to say goodbye right there. The shops were still open and I wanted to buy her a present; she refused and asked only for a package of Turkish cigarettes. We went into a tobacco shop; I insisted on making her take one of the finest and most expensive brands in the shop. And we went out again. In the shadows, she held out her hands and offered me her forehead for the farewell kiss. Although she had given me her address and we had promised to look each other up in Paris, something told me that we would never see each other again, and that soon even her name would be erased from my memory. But sometimes feelings last longer than names. I do not even remember her face, and still the grateful memory of a pure sympathy is as alive as ever; it was that rare thing, the meeting of two souls that touched, that gave each other whatever they had, then separated never to meet again.

I hate like a kind of spiritual filthiness the Anglo-Saxon love for dogs and cats that occupy space in the home and daily take the time and attention of their master and mistress and demand work on the part of the servants. All this represents spiritual poverty, and is as bad as the fleas and bedbugs that spring from economic poverty.

Thousands of tourists of all races, of all languages, pass through Assisi every year, and all are left with a kind of purification of the conscience. There they take a silent vow to try to be good, long-suffering, simple, and if necessary, heroic, with that true heroism which means not caring about one's own troubles and trying to alleviate the suffering of others. Resignation with no lessening of effort. Patience without indifference. And infinite love, without any concern as to whether it is returned.

It has been said that in Rome history dominates us. But history is hateful. History is a summary of current events which are therefore unimportant for humanity. Only a man without spiritual inventiveness, a mere logic-chopper like Hegel, would conceive the idea that history was not the instrument of destiny, but its realization. But being faithful to their history, most nations fail to go beyond mediocrity. And it is not strange that Marxist economic materialism, a doctrine of man's vulgar destiny, has been based on history. Everything valuable in culture, on the other hand, is based on creative processes, on invention, on revelation and miracle, which contradict history, repudiate it or do not take it into account. Without history and with contempt for history, the Hindus created their mental and artistic world, the best thing humanity accomplished before Greece and Christ. And Christ had no need of history.

History gives us the social process of crowds and nations headed by chiefs who are worth no more than the herds they represent. The destiny of nations is, thus, usually nothing more than a confused quantitative addition without differentiating and redeeming qualities. On the other hand, spiritual events, the appearance of great moral quality, are exceptions in history. History is, then, a catalog of the drowsy mediocrity of the earth, unaware of the true values of life. For the historian great moral qualities are exceptions to custom, violations of ordinary behavior. History, in a word, is blind and deaf to the things of the spirit, and is only a piling up of unimportant events. For that reason mythology, poetry, fables, art, and literature are so far superior to history.

For getting acquainted with an age I know no better history book than its best novel. We all know more about France through Balzac than through Thiers or Guizot. And even the romantic and attractive Michelet really tells us less than Chateaubriand. The fact of the matter is that the material of history is mediocre.

Judea wrote almost no history. Greece begins, creates history, but however interesting and well-written the work of Thucydides, it never achieves the profound meaning of myth. The best history leaves us with an impression of something past and dead. Mythology strikes us at every moment as living teachings and the explanation of perennial reality.

I undertook the trip to Greece, not as a devotee of Athenian culture, but as one who takes a logical step on his journey through Byzantine Art. I was not even prepared by any recent reading to absorb impressions of the classical world. I was prepared to believe that the highest model of architecture is not the Parthenon but rather Hagia Sofia, the Parthenon of Christianity.

In spite of the lure of ancient Greece, I could not rid myself of the presence and the conversations of the race which today inhabits the country. Among the people on the boat there were some coming from North America, the well-known "Greeks" who have filled the whole northern country with bad restaurants. Some were coming back to

take a vacation in their home country and others had retired from
the business to settle there after working hard in the "New World."
They form a hybrid race made up of native and Turkish elements—
one of the most complicated races of Europe. They speak all languages without knowing any one well, they simulate all temperaments; they have come to be the symbol of the outcast, the urban
nomad devoted to small business, money changing, interpreting.
Those who were coming from the United States treated me cordially
as more or less a compatriot; there were some who had been to the
Mexican border and they were eager to have travelers take a serious
interest in modern Greece, not merely in the country of the archaeologists. It is quite certain that the population in general is ugly, like that
of our cities, noisy and poor, real rubbish of the Turkish conquest
which has destroyed its victims and is creating nothing in their
place.

The main buildings of the era of recent independence are classic in
style, for example, the excellent National Museum; the library, a
beautiful structure; the handsome white marble stadium. A Greek
who became a millionaire in the United States gave the stadium.
In all the reconstruction that was going on throughout the country it
was easy to see the influence of North American energy; construction
that was rapid, modern, sanitary, within the framework of respect and
love for the old. The great number of Greeks repatriated after a long
stay in North America, and the cultural interest of France and England, where Greek classicism is practically a part of their own history,
doubtless contribute to the notable progress which the country has
made since the last Turk left fuming, after the Treaty of Versailles.

The Archaeological Museum is glorious! In general I have always had a horror of archaeology, perhaps because in Mexico we
associate it with the grotesque figures and broken pots of Indian Art.
In Greece, archaeology means the classicism which is the foundation
of our thinking, as the heirs of occidental culture. All that is, therefore, much more our own than the most authentic Aztec or Toltec
antiquity. For that matter, even upon an Asian, a Japanese, or a
Polynesian, Greek statuary of the different periods must produce an
effect which cannot be compared with that of any other art. The most
beautiful colored Chinese sculpture, the best Buddhas of India, all the
higher art of the world owes to classical Greece the traits that lend it
nobility.

I looked at the Parthenon over and over again—from below, from in the front, from behind—and I always reached the same conclusion; instead of praying on the Acropolis as Renan did, I would save my prayer for Hagia Sofia, the greatest church of Christianity.

It is a disgrace to the whole of Western civilization that its greatest artistic monument should be in the hands of a people who have profaned it. I am no partisan of the Orthodox Church, the origin of which is an ugly schism in which all the right was on Rome's side. Giving the Emperor the power to lay down articles of faith—identifying material power with spiritual power—has brought upon the Orthodox Church all the calamities of politics and the consequent subdivision into Patriarchates. Nevertheless, it is obvious that for historic, geographic, and artistic reasons, Greece ought to have become the mistress of Constantinople.

VIENNA   In the Rathaus, Iso was quite at home. A magnificent Gothic palace meant for the municipal government. The most astonishing thing about it was its interior planning. One luxurious hall after another; a first-class public restaurant, lecture halls.

Along the Ring, you go down to the Gothic Cathedral of St. Stephen. This church has handsome architecture and is the center of a great musical tradition. Mozart was often there. During my visit, every week a famous organist, playing Bach and then improvising, would fill the church. Iso was not religious but he did love music. On Sundays he hunted for a church in which we could find a mass with orchestral accompaniment and there we would take our places in the midst of a crowd of the faithful and curious. In Vienna if you see a crowd fighting for a place, you know there is a good concert.

At night after dinner Iso was an habitué of a famous café. Eminent people came to it, like Adler, the psychologist, who asked me for information about life in the United States because he was getting ready for his first visit to the Yankee universities; know-it-all women, homely and pretty; writers and artists. I hated not knowing German; sometimes, to please me, they would speak French or English.

In Germany they study a lot of Latin; they do the same in France and the United States. Only among us in Mexico, because, according to the men of the Reform Movement, we lead the world, does no one now study Latin, with the result that professional graduates of our schools arrive at the Sorbonne and can't take the anatomy or sociology courses because at every step they run into Latin quotations which the professor sticks into his lecture, supposing that he is talking to an educated audience.

I read my lecture in English without too much trouble or glory; the interesting part was the discussion afterward during a university dinner. Iso translated for me the speeches that were made in German. They were talking about population. A specialist in economics who spoke only French gave me very interesting information about the weak foundation of North America's economy, predicting almost exactly the depression which came four years later in 1929. I have a very pleasant memory of that night at the University, but I also made up my mind not to go out socially when I visited other European capitals. It is not like me to go around as a semi-official visitor. I don't like to represent anything. My idea in traveling is to be alone and do your own sightseeing, as I had in Italy and Turkey.

VENICE   There were still bathers at the Lido, and in spite of the lateness of the season, there were still vestiges of a superb season as far as women were concerned. Desire to be young, handsome, and rich becomes very intense on the immense, smooth, comfortable beach. Some wonderfully fine women—and in lounging pajamas, which made them more charming—were lying about in chairs under the awnings. There is not that gross exhibition of toasted, sunburnt, sometimes scratched flesh, not the abuse of sun bathing and that certain primitiveness without modesty which have made the North American bathing beaches so coarse. One sees Italian women as if they had a halo of poetry. And they reconcile us with feminine beauty. They make us forget all that vulgar pornographic propaganda of the Hollywood movies, with their low-class girls who have gotten rich and have no other charm than a complexion coarsened by the abuse of make-up. But those women at the Lido!

PARIS   Two friends had come to the station in Paris to meet me, Chacón y Calvo, my companion on the trip to Andalusia, who had just been transferred to the Cuban Legation in France, and Alfonso Reyes, my old friend from the Atheneum, who was still Mexican Minister in Paris, but who had been converted into a devoted follower of Calles.

Alfonso Reyes maintained the Mexican Legation with less luxury than Zaldumbide did the Ecuadorean one, but with equal intellectual brilliance. Famous writers of France, young and old, flocked to the modest house of the Minister-Poet, one of the few Mexicans who has succeeded in interesting French criticism both in his own work and in his studies of Góngora and Mallarmé. His wife, Manuela, helped him to make the atmosphere of the Legation delightful. She was a wonderful woman, very understanding, very intelligent, instinctively skillful and affable in disposition, which is the best way of being polite, without coldness or excessive formality.

There was a close friendship between Alfonso Reyes and Zaldumbide, so that it was natural that the Ecuadorean Legation be chosen for the first public reading of Alfonso's tragedy *Ifigenia*. It was an extraordinarily brilliant reception.

About that time Blasco Ibáñez arrived in Paris, and at once we made an appointment to meet. They had told me he was anxious to talk to me, and although I had some prejudice against him, I decided to speak to him, including in the conversation his book on Mexico— an unfair book because it presents Carranza as a statesman; a great book because of the accuracy with which, after only two weeks' stay in Mexico, he guessed the true character of the military. In Mexico they gave us a Blasco wrapped in calumny. He was supposed to have written his book because Carranza had not been willing to pay him twenty-five thousand pesos for a eulogistic book, a stupid version of the affair, since Carranza paid more to at least half a dozen mediocre authors who published books in his defense.

"It disgusts me," I said to the secretary who brought us together, "that he published his book on Mexico in the *New York Times*, the organ of North American infiltration."

All my objections, as I learned later, were passed on to the great man, who answered them one at a time in our first and only, very pleasant, very long interview. It took place in the Hotel Lutétia. Blasco was in his shirt sleeves, as his enemies portray him, but not excessively rude; he was simply free and easy. And he talked like a genius. Blasco never sold his convictions; when he could, he saw to it that they were well paid for, but this never made him pull his punches.

They kept on paying a good price for my articles. I had just made a bargain with a New York agent to place them in various periodicals of Hispanic America. I had in mind to isolate myself and go into seclusion, since I wanted to write something other than dull, mercenary, weekly articles. The publication of *La Raza Cósmica* had brought me a certain fame in Madrid; I received flattering reviews, but that, too, was not my object. What filled my thoughts and pursued me through the concerts of classical music and the cafés and boulevards was the writing of my *Metaphysics*. My ambition was to shut myself up to write it. Alfonso's family and mine frequently had Sunday dinner at the Mexican Embassy. Alfonso used to reproach me for a certain stinginess, for example in not treating myself to a centrally located apartment. I replied, "I have enough to live on comfortably for two years, but the fight in Mexico is going to be long; I shall not go back to Mexico except as an enemy of the government, and when I am able to cause some damage to that infamous set-up! For that I must economize and plan ahead."

The Secretariat of Education at this time was spending on pamphlets and propaganda books for the Calles regime all that I had not been able to spend on schools. The staff of the missionary-teachers was cut and the whole appropriation was meager, whereas thousands and millions were spent on paying for articles and books telling the story of the educational projects of the government. In my time, the only propaganda had been that which resulted from action itself—from the work accomplished; now, with the work suppressed and distorted, a good part of the appropriation was devoted to paying propaganda writers to such an extent that the press of the country accepted the official version that I had wasted the country's money to pay for propaganda abroad. That version is still current, but no one has ever been able to produce the slightest proof of it.

As the decision of the government to discredit me became ever more obvious, the Mexican newspapers, one by one, began to give space for all the hidden spite, rancor, and envy which they had not dared show months before, when my accomplishments were indisputable and admired. Now they refreshed the public's memory, and proclaimed that I had been a spender, that I had created jobs. On the other hand, there was not a word attacking those who were now getting rich at the expense of the educational system. Still less would anyone admit frankly the cause of my having left the country. There was an effort to seek childish motives for my annoyance, since no one dared to admit that I had withdrawn from the prevailing situation for deeply patriotic reasons.

The Spanish system of maintaining a censor on each paper was preferable to ours, because it was more open and avoided the hypocrisy which did not countenance bringing suit against newspapermen, but held them in the grip of fear of trouble, murder of their personnel, and underhanded economic attacks that ruined papers that did not submit. The atmosphere of lies in which Mexico has lived since that time has no other cause. The public gets used to seeing the thief proclaimed an honest man, and ends by believing that it is normal and

irremediable for officials to steal. Each week the official bulletin re-
peats the story of ten or twenty people brought to justice, after a
"summary" trial, and one comes to accept the idea that the army's job
is to kill citizens in carrying out orders from the President. The soldier,
with complete lack of conscience, states, when a new administration
slightly lifts the veil that covers the crimes of the preceding administration and names come to light, "I killed him because they ordered
me to, and I am a soldier."

And no one asks, "Where does the statute say that one ought to
obey one's superior, and act outside the law, when he orders a crime?"

I was invited to give a short course at the University of Puerto
Rico, a course on something connected with education in Mexico.
The pay was fine. I crossed the ocean in boredom. On the way I put
the last touches on the lectures which, after I had given them, I pub-
lished in the volume called *Indología*. The details of my trip to
Puerto Rico are in that book.

In Puerto Rico I received an invitation to take part in an Institute
devoted to Mexico at the University of Chicago the following month.
The Chicago lectures, which paid well, are to be found in the volume published by the University under the title, *Aspects of Mexican
Civilization*.

In spite of the pro-Calles conspiracy, the spirit of free discussion,
the novelty of my attacks, or something or other, attracted considerable attention. The vigorous, enlightened people who dominate the
Yankee universities were not grudging in their praise. Three or four
professors of social sciences were my friends and there was a sort of
counter-conspiracy to get me a class the following year. It had never
occurred to me to be a professor, least of all in a foreign country.

One of my repeated visits was to the Hull House of Jane Addams.
Jane Addams was still at the height of her powers, and she talked to
me for a long time, with her quiet manner and keen intelligence. She
scolded me for the violence of my attacks on the Mexican government.

"Are they not doing something good?"

"I don't know," I replied, "if a fake and a criminal can do good;
there in the place of honor you have a portrait of Tolstoy . . ."

"Yes, he was a guest in this house, as you are now."

"Well, since you are a pacifist and a friend of Tolstoy, doesn't the
chorus of praise for a murderer like Calles arouse you?"

Jane Addams, a fine woman, still could not throw off her Protestant
background which made her indifferent to the persecution of Cath-

olics. Besides, her state of mind seemed to me to be one of total ir-religiosity; perhaps she had had faith and then lost it, and this was the explanation of the coldness of Hull House, a center of theories about charity, rather than of charitable activity.

No one would have imagined that free, glorious Santo Domingo, so rich in culture and schools, would, within a few years, fall into the ignominy of the Trujillo government.

On the contrary, it seemed then that Santo Domingo might again be what it was in colonial days, a center for the diffusion of culture, a refuge for the persecuted.

I intended to publish *Indología* at my own expense, but finally I gave it up because I could not take the time to distribute the book for sale. It ended up in the hands of my same publishers because I was in a hurry to get out of the whole business. The idea that time was pass-ing without my being able to get started on my *Metaphysics*, which was only the forerunner of my *Aesthetics*, was torture to me. Deep down, I felt that the main task of my life was the writing of those three books: "*Metaphysics, Ethics, and Aesthetics.* Naïvely, I thought I had the elements of a new system of the universe, and still more naïvely I imagined that this business of formulating a system was im-portant. I had not reached the period at which one forgets one's own theories and system. But if we did not suffer from these delusions of grandeur, who would accomplish anything in this world?

Chicago had asked me if I preferred to have my course begin at once, in January, or in the quarter beginning in April. I chose April, so as to have three months more for explorations and study in Europe. And as I have always thought it is wrong to stay for an indefinite time in Paris, when there are so many other valuable and extraordinary things to see, I decided to rush off to Egypt, with a side trip to the Holy Land. I persuaded Pellicer to go along. I went ahead a few days earlier to call on Romain Rolland in Switzerland. We had cor-responded a good deal, and this visit was practically promised. In gen-eral, I have not been concerned with getting acquainted with per-sonages of the intellectual world, for I know how useless it is to talk for a few minutes with busy, sought-after people. I should have liked to greet Bergson, but what could he have told me that was not in his *Evolution Créatrice*? Besides, I think he was not seeing anyone be-cause he had just had the first attack of his paralysis or was working on a book. Rolland, on the other hand, follows the practice of per-sonally getting in touch with people in all parts of the planet, and I owed to him innumerable kindnesses. So I was very happy to present myself at his villa in Vaud, in the Swiss Alps, on the shore of Lake Leman. He was tall, pale, white, lean, with a broad forehead, dreamy eyes, and a bright smile. The sister who lived with him was slender, tall, dry, very intelligent, affable, and polyglot. We talked of many things; he showed me his garden, displayed his father, a little old man, whom they were preserving under glass, as people say, and he invited me to have tea with jam and pastry. I posed to him the problem of progress: "Is there such a thing as social progress, as we are influenced by liberalism to believe, or is history nothing but a series of examples of growth and degeneration, a little as Spengler would have us believe, or as religion teaches us, for example in the Book of Revelation?" He believed in the necessity of producing aristocracies and selected types to be the salt of the earth. In those days we got along famously because he still had a critical attitude toward the Soviets, who idolized him. Afterward, his unlimited support of Soviet doctrine drove me completely away from him—that, and his irreligious point of view.

Thanks to the insistence of Carlitos, we did not miss Taormina. It is a city built on terraces that climb up the hillside facing the sea. The ruined Greek amphitheatre is deserving of attention more for the view than for its construction. From it, one's sight is refreshed by one of the most beautiful scenes on earth. Etna, cloud-covered, snow-capped, turns its back to us; below, the mass of houses, and before us, the sea, over which on clear days, you can even see the tip of Italy. The fields covered with olive trees and vineyards remind us of the agricultural basis of Latin and also of Greek civilization, and the way they depended on these two selected crops. Wine and oil have been taken by religion itself as the symbol of its highest sacraments. Perhaps there cannot be a really superior type of life except where the land lends itself to these two products.

I entered the grotto of the Holy Sepulchre.

"Lord," I said, "I am here because I was able to get together the money for the journey, but others who have not been able to come are doubtless closer to Thee, for they have sought Thee by the road of goodness and sacrifice. I am going again into the world, Lord, to sin, for this is the law of my flesh, but also to fight a little for truth and justice. In this fight, I promise Thee loyalty at all costs. And may the struggle avail me in the hour of judgment. I know that in the final judgment Thy mercy weighs more than Thy justice; and so I shall live without fear. I surrender to Thy light, as the butterflies of my country's jungles do to the morning breeze. This is not because I fail to recognize my responsibility, but because I use it to love Thee, Thou who art the personification of good, above all the abstractions of the Stoics, the good made man, the Lord Jesus Christ, whom we love as a person and worship as God. This is the highest concept of all the philosophies, and a reality more living than the whole life of the cosmos."

Such was my prayer, but other and very diverse were my doubts.

The narrow alleys which we could see from our windows, with their rubble and their poor dwellings, completed the familiar impression made by a city of stone. But the buildings of Jerusalem are more robust and beautiful than ours. The patina of time is not the thin layer that four centuries of Hispanic culture have left in America, but a deep covering created by millennia. One might say that just as the Holy Land has, in the realm of ideas, set the standard of morality and religion, so also in architecture its massive walls, tiny, mysterious windows, sober exteriors and charming interiors, the very clothes of the families, are so many paradigms of the civilization to which we European Americans belong. You feel at home everywhere in the Mediterranean, as if in the house of ancestors who were much more illustrious, more powerful and wiser than we.

Culture degenerates with transplanting; this sociological truth strikes you as you travel through the lands from which our culture is derived. Thence comes the effort I was making to work for Americanism, not in the sense of a regression to the primitive, which would be stultifying, suicidal, but with the aim of creating a new race and a new culture, on the solid basis of our Spanish tradition, which was itself a magnificent synthesis of the most fertile antiquity.

In Jerusalem the ruins and the walls recall the birth of our faith, which is still the only hope of the world. More even than in Rome, the feeling of eternity revives in Jerusalem. This same eternity takes on life in the magnificent stones which seem such a contrast to the type of dead eternity represented by the Egyptian pyramids, an eternity without a soul, the mere lasting of inanimate things, tumuli of a people that longed only to rule the world.

Jerusalem stands for that true eternity which is of the spirit, while Egypt with its mummies and pyramids, older than present-day Jerusalem, merely expresses a vain effort to immortalize that which perishes, as all that takes form in material things must do. Thus, the modest church of the Holy Sepulchre possesses a more fertile beauty, a more lively artistic reality than Memphis or Karnak, and a more human feeling, a more divine breath, than the Parthenon, which is a temple erected to celebrate one idea, not the totality of man's fate.

As soon as we entered the Holy Land, I took as my bedside book and tourist guide the text of the Gospel, in an excellent French edition which I bought there. I read it in fragments, according to the place we were visiting, but in prolonged periods of meditation I became increasingly disturbed, as if my conscience were troubling me. I reviewed my love life and I felt free from sentimental ties; with all erotic passion gone, it was a happy state to feel one's soul free from bonds, and wholly devoted to thought. Nevertheless, one serious cause for worry remained. I might not feel any sentimental bond of a sensual sort, but an oath had bound me to Adriana, a contract uniting us for eternity, and I was trying to break this bond without going back on my pledged word.

I had cherished a feeling of deep rancor against Adriana for many years and had refused her offers of peace, but now the rancor was gone and I decided to seek her with the olive branch in my hand to ask for mutual pardon, without resuming our old relationship, and only to purge my conscience. In that instant all became clear, I felt released from Adriana in the very depth of my feelings, and the old temptation was converted into a desire for her welfare, which henceforth would keep us separated, but not enemies, nor yet friends; we would be only destinies that recognize their mistake and separate, wishing each other well.

BAALBEK   Great literature, great philosophy, great art, are Greek or Hebrew; the Roman, standing on the shoulders of those two cultures, is a vulgarizer who often deforms his inheritance. This is the message of Baalbek with its huge columns that have neither the strength of the Egyptian ones nor the grace of the Hellenic. A great palace surrounded by galleries that are too high, and very narrow for their height; decoration which aspires to imitate that of the Greeks but is no more than mediocre; the obsession with the colossal that ruins civilizations which have achieved only power—like the Egyptian, like the Roman, like that of the modern United States.

MARSEILLES   In Marseilles César Arroyo had prepared a great bouillabaisse for us, but we had to skip it because I was in a hurry to take the Paris express. The 1926 Anti-Imperialist Congress was being held in Brussels, and I did not want to miss it. The Nationalist Party of Puerto Rico had appointed me their delegate, along with César

Falcón, a Peruvian who had begged off, and I did not want to leave my good friends in the martyred island without any representation.

Accompanied by my son Pepe and the young Uruguayan writer Deambrosis, I presented myself at the Congress on the very opening day. Some distrustful persons imagined that I would find an excuse for not taking part, seeing that I had well paid relations with the Yankee universities. In due time I lost those connections, but only after I had acted on my convictions, without a thought for the consequences. I left the Congress before it was over. I did not attend the party that the Chinese gave; they were the largest and richest delegation but I did not take to them, because of their Soviet tendencies.

The majority of the delegations from China, Egypt, and Syria were mere flocks of sheep belonging to Moscow. We of South America were on record for our independence. The general impression left by the Congress was one of discouragement. Without wishing to, we could not help thinking of the sad fate of the colonial nations when they are handed over to their own devices. Brutal leadership, discord, and hate seem to be the sequels to the independence of peoples who do not have the cultivation that deserves freedom.

CHICAGO I settled in a hotel for professors, close to the University. My class in Hispanic-American Sociology started with a good number of students. Purposely I avoided any obligation to deal with history, for that subject has never been to my liking, and at any rate, sociology lends itself better to ramblings which end up in the study of ideas and theories; facts do not interest me. The class, for which I was very well paid, took an hour a day in the morning. In addition, I was supposed to spend an hour at the disposition of my students who wanted to consult me in my office. Add an hour or so devoted to preparing for my class and I still had many good hours free every day, and in addition a completely free weekend from noon on Friday until early on Tuesday. As I had no social obligations and did not mean to create any, and on coming home did not find the pleasant distraction of my children, I began to do what I had so often desired, live the life of a hermit in the heart of a city. After the siesta I read for a few hours; then I took a turn in the park, went to some restaurant at dusk, and again had the whole evening free. What better opportunity to begin my oft-postponed *Metaphysics*? To put myself in the right mood, I read again Bergson's *Les Données Immédiates de la Conscience* and *The Critique of Pure Reason*. I brought myself up to date in biology and psychology. I reviewed the latest pragmatists and Russell, who claims to be clear and gets lost in higher mathematics. I got acquainted with Whitehead, reread Aristotle's *Metaphysics* and the summary of medieval philosophy by Gilson. Soon it developed that my reading was serving only as an excuse and a stimulus. My hand raced over the pages, covering them with writing in pencil, which at night I copied on the machine. But the best ideas came to me, as if falling from heaven, when I walked at twilight along solitary paths in the park beside the University. Happy in my solitude, I heard a divine voice dictating to me; I caught a phrase and repeated it, fearing that I might forget it. I shaped whole paragraphs and then ran to my bedroom to write them down on paper before they should be lost forever.

I stayed in New York a week after finishing my course at Chicago and before taking the ship for Europe. At Chicago they had given me a formal contract for six months the following year (1928) and I expected to rest for several months in Europe and then return with my family to settle definitely in the city beside the Lake. But a great disaster overwhelmed me: I had just suffered a grave financial loss; all the savings which made up my reserves had gone up in smoke in unsuccessful business enterprises which my own brother embarked on without authorization. Six thousand dollars was gone forever! And this forced me to give up Europe, to shut myself up in Chicago as soon as my contract began, in order to draw my salary as a professor.

Adriana was still in New York, temporarily separated from her foreign husband. In the beginning, a whirlwind of passion had brought us together, causing us to imagine that the fire might be re-kindled. It did not last long, like the fire in coals that have been covered with ashes and is momentarily brought to life by the bellows, only to burn out and be extinguished for good. What do disloyalties of the flesh matter if the soul remains faithful?

There were many charms in the European trip made possible by the thousand pesos friends found for me, but not least memorable were the concerts. However, the concerts of modern music in the Salle Gavea were reduced to something laughable: selections by that hopeless family, from Debussy to Ravel. The latter has freed himself; at heart a Basque, he could not go on in deliquescence, and Spain and Africa have contributed elements which saved his work.

MANHATTAN   The Associated Press had announced my arrival and a reporter of that celebrated agency asked me while I was still on shipboard, "What do you think of the re-election of Obregón?"

"You don't think about this, you spit on it," I replied.

Only one newspaper picked up the phrase, but that was enough to spread it.

A gentleman invited me to speak at International House in New York. This Institution was then run by an admirable couple, husband and wife were both Protestants, of pure Yankee strain, very liberal, very kindly.

"We cannot pay our speakers," they warned me, "but on the other hand we will give you a chance to speak to a select and numerous audience, and the freedom to say what you wish."

The House would pay only my travel expenses from Chicago. I presented myself in New York, under the necessity of leaving that same night for Chicago so as to be on time for my next class.

The affair began with a long and excellent banquet. A few chairs away was Inman, who still pretended to be my friend, although he was entirely in the service of Calles. Inman was also on the program, but only among those who were to say a few words. When the dinner was over, he approached to ask me: Would I tell him? Did I intend to attack the government?

"Just what I came for," I replied.

Inman spoke before me, and I could see that he was nervous; he beat around the bush, telling things about South America which we had heard from his lips ten years earlier. Without being a university man, he had managed to gain access to Columbia as a professor, thanks, undoubtedly, to the great weight of the Protestant influence in Hispanic-American matters. Diplomatically, he cut it short and yielded to me.

When I rose, to my great surprise, the hall broke into an uproar, there was wild applause, and many stood up. The spontaneous reaction of the audience proved the latent horror of the Calles government which never appeared in the press; in me they were applauding the brave man who threw mud in the face of the criminals.

I spoke with passion for twenty or thirty minutes. The audience, a little astonished, hung on my words, and at the end there was repeated, prolonged applause.

One of those North Americans who had wandered around the Hispanic continent and had no happy memories of his wanderings got up. Suddenly he shouted, "Do you think it is very decent of you to abuse the hospitality of the United States by throwing blame on the conduct of our statesmen?"

The blow was hard and I felt it. I kept quiet for a moment until the hall had recovered from its surprise and the silence was complete. Relishing in advance the blow I was going to deliver, I put my hands in my coat pockets, and replied with another question, "And which is worse, sir, to come here unarmed to condemn injustice, or to go down there with squadrons to commit outrages and to shoot patriots, as you did, for example, in Nicaragua?"

There followed weeks of hard work. In addition to my class, I was responsible for directing a seminar which met for two hours twice a week. We studied the agrarian legislation of Mexico from colonial times to the present. My background in law school came in very handy. Among my disciples in the seminar were persons as distinguished as Eyler Simpson, the author of learned books on Mexico. The career Simpson was undertaking opened my eyes, and at the same time filled me with admiration. Supported by a generous fellowship, Simpson had already devoted two or three years to the study of Mexican questions and was getting ready to spend three years in our country. As Simpson himself explained to me, this very intelligent youth was going to devote his life to being an expert on Mexican matters. I thought to myself, here is a man who in the course of years will know more about Mexico than any Mexican; among us there is no one to provide the financial backing for a life devoted exclusively to study.

My rank as professor gave me the right to work in the stacks of the library, to take books as I liked and to work on them at a private desk. There I brought together the materials necessary to finish my *Metaphysics*. The work advanced as rapidly as was possible in view of the constant interruptions. Often, on weekends, I left Chicago to give a paid lecture in one of the different nearby universities. In this way I was in Madison, in Iowa, in Indiana, in Cleveland. Everywhere I found a lively interest in my subject. The most pleasant part of these occasions was the private conversation after the formal lecture, usually over a good dinner. The guests were professors and writers, people of exquisite sensitivity, intelligent and tolerant. The United States possesses a real aristocracy in the personnel of its institutions of higher learning, well-informed men and women devoted to study. They are paid so well that each of them makes regular trips to different parts of the world.

As vacation was approaching, a good friend got me an invitation to give a summer school course at Stanford. They welcomed me there with open arms, but before leaving Chicago, I received another invitation, this one for the fall. I was to take part, with a good honorarium, in an International Conference of Educators, which was to meet in Seattle. When the invitation came to Chicago, my Dean supported me as the educator who ought to represent Mexico.

All things considered, my activity in Chicago could be summarized as a worthwhile experience. My *Metaphysics* was finished and ready for printing. For my regular class I had been getting five hundred dollars a month, and each lecture on the road on weekends had brought me a hundred dollars, sometimes a hundred and fifty, after subtracting the cost of railway fare.

I packed my clothes and books in trunks which the express company took care of, and by handing out a check for a little more than a thousand dollars, I had at my door an automobile from the factory in Detroit. My children's vacations were beginning and while I was fulfilling a preliminary engagement in California, I gave them two weeks to practice their driving. I came back as agreed, and loading the car with the hand luggage, we made the auto our home on the long trip from Chicago to Los Angeles, going by way of Texas. For several weeks we lived in this mobile house, stopping to sleep and eat wherever we liked the scenery, and heading south.

The man-made scenery is monotonous in the United States. All the cities, cut according to the pattern of New York, have their Broadway, with bright signs announcing the same plays, films, and merchandise. In addition to Broadway, there is always the commercial street, the Main Street made famous by Sinclair Lewis in his novel. And it has been repeated to the point of satiety that customs, foods, ideas, are also all the same, cut according to pattern. However, one must add that a trip through the United States is made agreeable by the uniform courtesy of the people. It is a courtesy that is not formal like the European variety, but spontaneous, as if from the heart. Standardization, warm-heartedness—such is the story of my drive through Illinois, Kansas, Missouri, Texas, and New Mexico.

A friend had told me a lot about the circle of Mabel Dodge to which he had belonged before going to Mexico with Lawrence. The case of Mabel Dodge never interested me; she is not the first, nor the last white woman to marry an Indian, and her role in the novels of Lawrence, whether as inspiration or as torture, seems to me completely vulgar and secondary. And the fantastic idea of Lawrence, who wants us to accept her as Queen of the Aztec people, restored by an Irish Quetzalcoatl, or what you will, and substituted for the Virgin Mary in the prayers of the multitude, is simply grotesque and in the worst possible taste, in spite of what the snobs of Buenos Aires and the ambiguous international clique that delights in the pornography of

Lawrence may say. He was nothing but a sexually inadequate man devoted to sublimating the potency that he did not have, and making a divinity out of it.

I talked to many influential professors about the situation in Mexico, explaining the harm that is done us by North American policy, which has always given its support to uneducated governments incapable of doing anything for the good of the country.

"As a destructive policy it is admirable," I told them very frankly. "As a sincere policy, it is detestable and in the long run ruinous because sooner or later our ills will infect the United States, as always happens with colony and mother country."

Everywhere I found understanding and sympathy, except when it was a question of religious matters. If Calles had not set about to destroy Mexican Catholicism, he would certainly never have won the strong support he had in the United States. Without admitting it, all the Protestant elements—and the Anglo-Saxons are at heart Protestants—are grateful to Calles for his attack on the Catholic religion, which in their country is growing and is feared. What they would not have dared to do in their own country, they enjoyed observing in ours.

I taught altogether twenty hours at Stanford, rather poorly paid, for the University is not as rich as the University of Chicago. As I entered the room for my last lecture, at three in the afternoon, a student handed me a newspaper extra which carried the news of the assassination of Obregón in the capital of Mexico. Trying to forget the important news, I brought my course to its close. That same night I was due to leave for Berkeley. At the University of California I gave only three lectures, summing up the doctrine I had developed more fully elsewhere: the problem of Hispanic America from the economic, racial, and political points of view. The University of California is an ensemble of beautiful buildings situated on one of the most magnificent sites in the country. The houses around are luxurious and modern to a surprising extent. On the third day, the newspapermen accosted me: What did I think of the death of Obregón?

"A tyrant fell," I said, "but, unfortunately another is still alive, and he will be more baneful, now that he is free and is rid of his chief."

"How is that?"

"He has gotten rid of an obstacle; the death of Obregón was foreseen. And the man most guilty of it will preside at the funeral."

My allusion to Calles was clear and, as I learned, the university authorities did not like it, since all of them were under the thumb of the intensive Methodist propaganda.

The Seattle seminar was attended by eminent men from different parts of the United States, residents of neighboring colleges, and writers. And it was a series of brilliant discussions, lectures, and evening affairs. I got my best lesson in oratory in those days by listening to Yankee orators, who are not orators, but instead are specialists, learned men, newspapermen or teachers, who, as a result of knowing their subject so well, become models of oratory. In general, the North American's way of speaking is admirable. Without emphasis or rhetoric, with a simplicity which is captivating and a vigor and exactness which are convincing, each one expounded his subject. Their sentences contained few adjectives and were full of meat, their gestures were natural, and an inoffensive humor was always ready.

An unknown fan thought it was a good idea to arrange an interview for me with a famous California Senator. I spoke frankly about the handing over of the country to the bankers of Mr. Morrow, of the limping enforcement of the oil laws, and above all, of agrarian reform and the way foreigners were gaining title to the most valuable farm lands of the country. I added my disapproval of brutal assassinations; I reminded him of the educational disaster that overtook Mexico because of the incompetence of my successors and because money was spent on the Army, which kept the government in power by force and left no resources for education. I thought I had convinced the Senator, when in reply to my explanations he observed, "Nevertheless, there is one advantage in the present situation which you cannot deny, and that is that Calles, with his anti-religious laws, has got rid of the Catholic schools. How much we would give in the United States to be able to close our parochial schools!"

I did not reply; there was no use; my interlocutor had hit the nail on the head; he had shown up himself and the dominant majority of his country. It was a religious war that was being fought. The North American ruling class wanted to see Catholicism disappear from Mexico, for it represented Latinity, the type of civilization which makes us what we are, and which stands in the way of their moral conquest, a conquest which would consolidate their interference in the fields of economics and politics. Everything could be forgiven Calles, because he served them as an arm with which to strike at the Church.

What was the duty of the Mexican, of the patriot? To rally to the defense of his Church, of his tradition, of the very soul of his race! Let them regulate, if they would, the relations of Church and State, but in accordance with our doctrine, in a maneuver suited to our circumstances, and not under the influence of another's policy. More decidedly than ever, I began to declare that I would fight to free the Mexican Church from persecution and to see it established in our country with guarantees like those it enjoys in liberal countries like France and the United States.

The die was cast; my campaign would be an effort to bring Mexico back to her own identity; for that purpose I would have to take a radical stand against all the enemies together: Wall Street, which supported Calles and Morrow; the American government, which supported Wall Street and carried out its old plans; Yankee liberal opinion, inclined to Protestantism; our political thieves who plundered Mexico as if she were wartime booty; the murderous assassins who terrorized the country—the whole flock of disloyal enemies of a fatherland that was strangled, oppressed, and suffering.

PART FOUR

THE PROCONSULATE

THE PROCONSULATE

We repudiate the pretensions of the Mandarins, the presumption of the intellectual who believes himself above common people. Cleverness in expression is not the distinguishing mark of the elect, but only a mere chance, a technical advantage; the authentic élite are those who are good and noble in character. I claim no special privileges, boast of no special gifts, beyond my experience and my motives.

To me, as to Job, life has given the experience of knowing infinite happiness and exhausting pain. In the rhythm of my tragic story complaint and rejoicing alternate.

Whatever may be the motives of the professional writer, I have the special duty of proclaiming certain facts with respect to the public life of my country. In an anxious moment of its history, it was my role to arouse hopes where only crimes had been encouraged. And since the criminals are still victorious, my shouts are the only homage that I can render to the victims of a defeated cause—defeated, but not forever, for evil knows no permanent victories. My testimony will recall heroism; my gratitude seeks to please my friends; my condemnation pursues the traitors; my intransigeance continues in the face of the enemies who proved disloyal.

The book that follows may appear pitiless toward evildoers; on the other hand, it is full of pity toward those who suffered for the common good. It is natural that at times the reader will be caught up in the feeling of dizziness which swept over us, the passion which exalted us; but let us drop our self-criticism, since tranquility for even simple criticism is lacking when one is urged on by the greatness of his destiny, the fascination of his story, and moreover, stands perplexed before the impenetrable mystery which surrounds the goings and comings, the blunders and the achievements of human life.

General Ruelas, another distinguished refugee, had taken me away from Stanford to San Francisco, to initiate me into the Society of Old Devils in California. This was a kind of free fraternity, made up of the best elements of the Hispanic-American colony of the port city. The periodic ritual was a fraternal dinner, with wine picked up at a bargain, outwitting the prohibition laws which weighed so heavily upon the country.

I spent two or three days in San Francisco, always accompanied by the good Doctor Urrea. We hardly left the Mexican quarter, a poor district and what was worse, not even independent, but politically under the thumb of the Italians, who treat it as their province. Everywhere our people are at the bottom of the ladder. Many times I have said, "If we cannot give ourselves civil liberties and education in our own country, how can we hope that in other lands they will treat us as civilized human beings?"

Could we be on the eve of a renascence? From one end of the United States to another, from Chicago to Texas, from Texas to California, the wind of hope was blowing and demands for redemption were increasing. Clubs sprang up spontaneously to encourage the civic struggle which would culminate in my candidacy for the Presidency. It was believed among the expatriated that the time had come for my return to Mexico, not to submit to those who had slain our brothers and had harassed and persecuted us, but to impose an order within which culture and liberty could flourish. And I advised them, "Write to your relatives and friends who live in Mexico, and tell them to keep working for justice until you come back." And they did. And the national clamor reached such a point that if they had not crushed it with army bullets perhaps there would have been no Mexican colonies left in the United States; our country would have been regenerated.

In Los Angeles—"the city with the largest Mexican population after Mexico City," as they called it in those days, thanks to its two hundred thousand of my compatriots, swept aside into a huge, miserable area—clubs blossomed with the aim of pushing my candidacy. There were Sundays when I had to attend one meeting in the afternoon and another at night, all full of pretty girls, confetti, music, shouting, and speech-making. Political refugees of all colorations offered their disinterested help in an enterprise which promised to unite Mexicans under the flag of work and culture.

On the general situation at the time, I quote part of the writing of the great woman to whom this volume is dedicated, and who in the course of our story will be known only by her familiar literary name of Valeria.

In Los Angeles, where José Vasconcelos was at this time, he accepted an invitation to take part in the next electoral campaign. He would accept the candidacy which different groups were offering him if, after taking the pulse of public opinion, he was convinced that the public demanded it. With no money to spend liberally among the voters who were for hire, without secret influence in North America, without the support of high-ranking officers in the garrisons, who was going to take him seriously? To enter the political battle under such conditions you had to be "that crazy Vasconcelos."

It is essential not to forget that the real enemy of democracy in Mexico, whom this strong man must face, is not his apparent rival, Pascual Ortiz Rubio, the rubber doll inflated by the political boss, Plutarco Elías Calles; it is not even Calles himself, but the representative of capitalism interfering in local matters: the American Ambassador Dwight W. Morrow.

In taking on such a formidable adversary, the future candidate could rely only on his unshakeable faith in the Mexican people and in the imperative destiny that called him. He knew that in the last analysis the independence of his country was at stake, and that only an aroused public opinion would prevent the success of a carefully prepared attack that would take advantage of every one of our mistakes, an attack that seemed certain of success. This hidden enemy lent all his power to break the will of the people and to gag the press of two continents.

The goal which guided the steps of that man, short of stature, broad of shoulder, lofty of forehead, who faced the unequal contest, was to awaken and maintain the tension of the conscience of our race, which is so often slothful and forgetful of its past greatness. His aim was to keep the purpose before them and to turn it into an active campaign, without allowing tears to cloud his vision.

We must also add to the economic program of land redistribution and to the claims of labor, the freedom to obtain the punishment of evil officials and to unmask false revolutionaries. Suffrage must be effective, for no one can replace the judgment of the people when it is a question of electing the right men; to assure an effective vote the people must recover from their apathy and express their will.

What distinguishes charlatanism from reform is that the former has nothing but words, while the latter reinforces every word with standards which ennoble the words and put them into action. There is no patriotism without hard work, no liberty without responsibility, and, finally, civilized life is impossible where usurpation and outrages remain unpunished.

I crossed the border with a capital of some forty dollars.

And so our political campaign in Sonora began as a democratic honeymoon. We did not attack Calles in person, since in his official statements he had promised to retire from politics and to respect the result of the election, whatever it might be.

By often using my handkerchief to wipe away excessive libations, and at other times swallowing the alcohol so as not to seem a poor sport, I succeeded in enduring the interminable orgy of drinking. The extraordinary physique of these people and their rural life preserve them from perishing from their continual drinking of brandy, which they ingenuously call wine. For myself, I summoned all my courage, and acting like a Roman when in Rome, I almost came to like it, but in bed at night my throat burned.

In Hermosillo we added to our party three young men who had spent a long time learning the secrets of Hollywood. They accepted the idea of scraping together their own resources; we gave them credentials as organizers and they were very useful. Méndez Rivas, who liked military expressions, labeled them the "Flying Squadron." They invaded small towns or went ahead to the cities, organized public meetings, and created independent clubs pledged to my candidacy. They were warned and charged to pass the word that we made no bargains, except conditional ones, with any of the existing parties. We were going to change everything and bury the past. My idea was to lead to a kind of national plebiscite which for an opposition party is the only clean way of coming into power.

We would have to repeat the feat of Madero's time, when the whole people rose against the army. Now the army men were worse, and were better prepared, had fewer scruples, and could count on the strong support of the foreigner.

My plebiscite made progress. In various speeches I pointed out frankly that I sought the direct support of the voters, so as to remain free from all kinds of commitments to parties that were not true parties. It was a question of sweeping away corruption; nothing in our muddy political past deserved to be kept alive. As for my programs, they knew them already; my platform and my promise were exemplified in the work I had carried out when I was in public office. If members of my audience found any constructive work that was superior to mine, let them hasten to withdraw their support from me, and give it to whoever was the better man. Above all, what was needed was to elect to the government, the best, not the worst, as we had been doing, illustrious men, not boors.

Estimating resources: When in Mazatlán we counted up the forces on which we could rely, it looked as though they were all those in the place. There was no enemy facing us, and, in fact, everybody in the middle and working classes, and a few among the well-to-do were bound to us, formally affiliated with our organizations. If propagandists of other candidates came later, they would find the terrain completely occupied. Our secret enemy was the army. Officers and leaders were going about, very polite but tight-lipped.

TEPIC The capital of Nayarit is a colonial city, small, but very pretty, inhabited by a large nucleus of Creoles. They are not a genuine aristocracy, but a second-rate bourgeoisie, a collection of Yankee-lovers and Yankee-influenced people, who accept from the United States the optimistic preaching of the Rotarians, but do not have the American energy that accomplishes things. Their ideal is to see their sons educated abroad so that they can become lackeys of imperialism. They derive whatever advantages they can from all governments, and have on their lips the preaching of the hour, now democratic, now socialistic, now Bolshevik, but always militaristic, and following the slogan of the Masonic lodge or the foreign Bourse. None of them, of course, came near us on our tour. My attacks on the Yankee Ambassador and all that Rotarianism, which is nothing but disgraceful colonialism, sounded to them like blasphemy.

GUADALAJARA In front, the enemy continued to harass us, and from those who filled the street behind us, we began to hear hostile yells. Half a block farther on, those whom we were pushing along as we advanced turned to deliver an attack which decimated our advance guard.

At that moment Nacho, who was ahead, came to me and said, "The men in front have been reinforced; and we are cut off in the rear. Take refuge in the first open entryway; we will put up a resistance until you are safe!" And he advanced once more. We admired his courage and presence of mind. Really, going on would have been suicidal, but this business of ducking into an entry was ridiculous. Then, at the end of the little park, I saw a sign "Hotel," undoubtedly a good hotel, patronized by foreigners. Slowly we made for it, followed at twenty meters by the attackers. I was the first to reach the desk of the hotel; I asked for a room. The clerk did not realize who we were and asked as usual, "With bath or without?" "With," I replied calmly, took my key, and went up to the fourth floor, followed by the little group. Meanwhile, the tumult downstairs slackened. The iron gate served as a barrior. . . . The government party, in their version of the affair, tried to pass us off as the aggressors, but they were not successful

in persuading public opinion, largely because this time they did not
have the cooperation of the press.

All in all, the day turned out well. The scandal of the attack, was,
except for the pain of our wounds, as someone put it, worth a million
pesos in publicity. So we slept soundly in a clean bedroom on the
fourth floor of a decent hotel, in incomparable Guadalajara.

Our situation was really as good as possible. This was proved by
the very attack we had been subjected to the night before. Anyway,
the blow had failed, since all the papers, without exception, condemned this outrage in violent terms, and the Central Government
hastened to make excuses and to promise punishment of those responsible. Sáenz, the official candidate, backed by the North Americans,
could count only on a party that was morally objectionable, seeing that
it was supported openly by Ambassador Morrow. The Obregón
group talked of launching the candidacy of Valenzuela, but it was
actually getting ready for a military coup that had little chance of
success, since no one now wanted to hear any more about Obregón,
much less his gang. So the enemy was divided and uncertain while
we were making real progress in winning over the minds of the
public.

The rebellion was now to become nationwide. It appeared that the
only thinking man among my enemies, the one who was astutely
directing everything, Ambassador Morrow, saw this himself. Now we
could make speeches, good or bad, and in due time weapons would
speak out, as the only way to bring down a tyranny that had its roots
in force and usurpation. A number of middle-class ladies called on us
or sent us friendly messages and began to organize clubs. Guadalajara was full of Vasconcelos centers.

It was part of the Ambassador's tactics to let the opposition talk,
to let it shout—anything but pick up rifles, as you will see.

Zuno, the former governor, still had some money, and he told me,
"They are taking out Sáenz; he didn't catch on, he is a follower of
Obregón. And just imagine, they are putting Ortiz Rubio in his
place!"

We both laughed at this strange choice. The story was going the
rounds that when they recalled Ortiz from Brazil, where he had been
shipped soon after the death of Obregón, he thought he was being
fired. Arriving in New York, he was told, "Prepare yourself; you are
going to occupy an important post." And he asked, incredulously,
"Minister?" "No, President!" He couldn't get over it. Nor for the
moment, could we.

MORELIA   Hypocritical atmosphere. Half guarantees. Honeyed
words of tolerance and, underneath, implacable pressure to control
voting by terror. It was hard to find anyone to take permanent
charge of the Club. In confidence, Salvador Azuela told us, "Terror
rules here, the same as everywhere. General Cárdenas, a taciturn
man, worships Calles like a god. He believes him to be a statesman,
and owes him for paternal favors. And in silence, he exercises
absolute power." The reception had been scantily attended, but even
so, the strong arms of my staff had had to threaten some bravos with
their fists when the latter wanted to interrupt the speakers; these
fellows were official people in disguise.

Valenzuela had made family affairs an excuse for taking a trip to
Sonora; he had left the capital, almost in flight, by way of Chihuahua.
In Chihuahua, under the protection of the military who were on his
side, he had made terrible statements against Calles. He asserted that
he had proofs that Calles was the assassin of Obregón. I don't know
whether he published any such proofs, but it is certain that he gave up
his candidacy to follow the military leaders of the Obregón group.

Villarreal, too, perhaps tipped off as I was, had marched north, but
in the posture of a Presidential candidate. The group that favored
him hesitated, waiting to see what he would do in the North. And
soon it came out that Villarreal, forgetting that he was supposed to
be a candidate, had attached himself to Escobar, took orders from him,
and received a command at his hands. The field, then, was clear. Of
the four candidates who began the race, three were out of the fight.
Sáenz had been eliminated by his own people. The rebellious outbreak began just when an official convention was being held in
Querétaro; at this meeting Calles unceremoniously set Sáenz aside
and Ortiz Rubio was named the government candidate. In Querétaro
the hundred or two hundred deputies and politicians who named
Ortiz Rubio vandalized the bars of the old city; their vulgar orgies
were a public scandal, and when they departed in triumph they took
along the sheets of the hostelries that they had occupied, and unable
to cart off the mattresses, too, they ripped them to pieces to avenge
themselves on the "reactionary" population.

I did not take seriously the idea of repudiating the rebels, although
this benefited the Calles party; but when I discussed the matter later
with friends and enemies the reasons for not having done so seemed
obvious and incontrovertible. We had nothing to do with the Obregonists, the re-election party, the true creators of the existing tyranny.
If they triumphed, there would be no elections. Calles, for his part,

had performed the service of eliminating Obregón, who was really dangerous and would have perpetuated himself in power. His lieutenants, on the other hand, would get nowhere. And as was to be expected, I did not have to do anything to warn the partisans of the different regions of the country that they ought to be neutral and wait for the election; the government itself took care of spreading my point of view, and did it even through the movies, at home and abroad. The Callistas were to emerge from the fight powerful, but only in a military sense; they won with the moral and material aid of Washington. Public opinion continued to oppose them.

I must admit that during the whole campaign I had what is called "a good press." Some papers gave us support out of commercial interest, which comes from following the current and giving the public what it asks for, others gave support out of patriotism and friendship. I mention with gratitude only those who remained faithful and were infuriated by injustice, not those who, on the day after the election, when the real struggle should have begun, condemned my incitements to rebellion, declared themselves pacifists, and later entered the service of the regime they had pretended to be fighting. The big press, generally speaking, adopted this last tactic, in many cases going as far as gratuitous servility, which was unnecessary and was not even gratefully received by those whom they flattered.

TOLUCA   Of that glorious day in Toluca, I will let Valeria herself speak, for no one can achieve better than she the bare style that reaches the heart of the most complicated situations, and at the same time, amazes with its novel turns of phrase, with the exactness and clarity of its imagery.

One of the youngsters has jumped up on the platform. "We have come, comrades, because it is indispensable that every man should now realize what is his obligation, his responsibility! The country is in danger. The moment is solemn; in the coming elections Mexico's future is at stake, and her independence!" And the men in blue overalls, with thick woolen sweaters, who a moment before seemed tired and hesitant, are now bound together by the mysterious rhythm of unknown words opening up new perspectives: "fatherland," "destiny," "independence." The very language, aside from its substance, is moving, arresting. The orator communicates his conviction; its novelty and enthusiasm are contagious.

Vasconcelos is defending the honor of Mexico. To be against him is to betray our own destiny; only those who have sold out would do this. Vasconcelos is the true revolution, which transforms life by changing our values, putting conscience in the place of appetite, responsibility in place of deceit. The masters of power are going too far, they threaten us with death because we want an honest government, but even our death will be a victory, for the innocent blood they shed will stain their hands indelibly!

In the afternoon, in my lodgings at the Hotel Princess, which was to be my home in the capital for several months, calls never stopped. I was in bed at ten o'clock when a correspondent of Central American origin arrived; he was one of those I had most favored in my days in the Ministry. He wanted to send telegrams to the papers of South America. Didn't I think that the figure for the number of people who turned out, a figure already sent abroad by Associated Press, was correct—fifteen thousand? "Oh," I replied, "so that is the figure that Morrow has authorized?" "You know that correspondents write up their dispatches in the Embassy!" "Do as you like, I don't care about the opinion of the press agencies. What I care about is what the city saw and what is preserved in photos and film."

The movie houses could not avoid showing the film in which our procession appeared, filling Madero Avenue, spilling over into the Plaza Principal. These visual records are there to be seen by whoever wants to challenge or confirm what I say. This fellow never came back to see me. Now he is an authority on Mexican affairs for the whole Ibero-American press, or what the Protestants call "Indo-American." This business of Indo-Americanism is a trick of the Smithsonian and its division of anthropology, bent on wiping out every trace of Spain, even from their ethnic classifications. By labeling us Indo-Americans, instead of Ibero-Americans or Latin Americans, they reduce us to a subcaste, quite aside from falling into a pleonasm, since what is Indian is already American.

The candidates Valenzuela and Villarreal became exiles. The official candidate, Ortiz Rubio, stayed at home while the decisive encounters were taking place in the North. He did not even put in an appearance in a small square, because a couple of shouts would have put him to flight. And the gunmen, who later inspired him with courage by killing opposition men in his presence, were busy in the North, gathering booty and killing the scattered followers of Escobar.

Once more, the United States had saved the government. In those days, in fine public meetings that we succeeded in holding in Xochimilco and Texcoco, among pure-blooded Indians and people of old

European stock, I renewed at a higher pitch my denunciation of the Yankee Ambassador for shamelessly intervening in our political life. Rumors began to circulate to the effect that the Ambassador wanted to have a talk with me.

In my speech on March 31, 1929, I said, "While others get support for their candidacy in obscure and cowardly alliances with the representatives of our enemy, the North American Capital, we get ours in humble towns; we seek the support of the real people, scorning Mr. Morrow, that Ambassador of the United States, who has his background and predecessor in Poinsett, the foreign Minister who came to divide the Mexican people—scorning Morrow, to whom I have sent word that other candidates will seek his aid, but that I ask him for nothing, and that after the Mexican people have triumphed, I will give him twenty-four hours to pack his suitcases."

VERA CRUZ   The region of Vera Cruz was propitious. There I could count on friends from the time when I was Minister.

I have never honored with public debate adversaries who have no sense of honor. I write what I believe to be true, because I wish to, and without making a major effort to find out everything that happened. My only regret, at times, is my lamentable forgetfulness of the names of certain persons who helped me so loyally. If there are any such, I, pleading a frailty of human nature, beg them to accept my apologies. It is well known that forgetting names is one of the first signs that age is beginning to overtake us, at least mentally.

We were satisfied with our tour of the State and crowned it by an incursion into Córdoba, with its neighboring ranches and villages. Spanish blood is predominant in all that region. And it is curious that when the returns were in, the regions of the country in which voting was highest, so overwhelmingly in my favor that the government people could not deny it, were the regions of Vera Cruz, the north of Nuevo León and Sonora, Sinaloa and Coahuila, which are also, according to statistics, the districts with the lowest percentage of illiterates. Not that the illiterates voted for the government, but it is easier to attribute opinions to them, to cheat them of their wishes, than it is in the case of the literate.

The main problem connected with the Convention we were planning was how to get a locale big enough to hold all the delegates, who, we knew, would number not fewer than two or three thousand.

Every provincial organization had been informed months before that it would have to pay the expenses of its delegation. Rich clubs, like the one in Mazatlán, would have paid the whole cost of the meeting, if necessary. We already had word of numerous delegations coming from the United States with their expenses paid by humble Mexican workers in exile, keen and patriotic in spite of their modest circumstances. The Mexican colony in Chicago, which then included more than thirty thousand workers, awaited our word to send off a dozen representatives. And this was the case everywhere, with the sole exception of regions completely controlled by the savage regime: Yucatán, still under military control, and Tabasco, Chiapas, Oaxaca.

A new party would emerge from the Convention; this was the great desire of the best among the younger generation.

The general situation of the country in those days was described by Valeria:

In 1929, Mexico had a single enemy: the Yankee. The Catholic Church, independent of the State for more than half a century, did not constitute any real political danger. Nevertheless, the bosses who have never hesitated to violate the liberal principles of the Constitution, under the pretext of making it respected, started and kept up religious persecution, the inhumanity of which foreigners refused to see, disguised as it was by the supposedly advanced opinions of its instigators.

We must keep telling ourselves that the fight is to the death and that we must utilize all the vigorous reserves of our civilization if we wish to survive under the pressure of this gigantic embolus. For this reason, Vasconcelos, who is not a practicing Catholic, understood that it is better for Mexico to return to a purified Catholicism, a thoroughly Spanish tradition, than to go on being diluted by an American type of Protestantism, and that the fight had to be to the death, along all fronts, and including everybody; he understood that in order to be saved, we must once more bathe our origins in that fountain of youth, impregnating ourselves with that culture which a reckless independence tried vainly to deny. In a word, we must combat our anemia with the only tonic capable of nourishing us: Spain.

Among us it is rare to find a person who has followed the trial of the Spanish classics. We are in a decisive period of major reforms, and of them all, the most essential is a renewed appreciation of Spain and of the Church in their civilizing work in the New World.

As for the spiritual role of the Church, it is decisive even in the lives of those who have split off from it; it molds their souls and immunizes the spirit against the pox of Protestantism, since the latter—once its historic role as the champion of free will was finished—out of a spirit of exaggerated individualism, engendered the contemporary capitalistic system. So every son of Spain can be Catholic or atheist, but not Protestant.

This was when Vasconcelos began to pronounce that phrase that he repeated until he was made a prisoner: "I summon you to the seventeenth of November! Let the people, in a great plebiscite, declare its will, and then back it up!" His counsel of civil disobedience became clearer: we were not to co-operate with the shameless faction, we were to stop upholding the apparent normality of a condition which was so abject that it embittered life itself."

The situation of the Church, with its bishops exiled and its churches closed, was the fundamental reason for the Catholic uprising.

Morrow imperturbably continued to promise that there would be tolerance in the enforcement of religious laws and at the same time handed the Church over to its enemies.

The news of the forced surrender of the *cristeros* sent shivers down my spine. I saw in this the hand of Morrow, who thus took away all basis for the rebellion which should logically have followed our not knowing the results of the voting.

There had been an earlier contact which left the situation clearly defined. In 1928 at Chicago, I had had Professor Eyler Simpson as an auditor in my seminar on Mexican legislation. Still young, Mr. Simpson had for years been studying Mexico. At that time, he had planned to live in Mexico for three consecutive years in order to continue his studies *in situ*. The Foundation paid two more students to specialize in Mexico and had a dozen scattered around South America. The aim of the Foundation is to create an expert personnel at the university level, for the service of the Department of State in its relations with our various Hispanic nationalities. In addition to being hard-working and conscientious, Mr. Simpson is good-looking and well-mannered, intelligent if not brilliant, disciplined and precise in his thinking—the ideal type of expert or specialist. In Mexico, Simpson was an attaché at the Embassy, perhaps not maintained by it, but certainly in close contact, a fact he did not conceal from me. Mr. Simpson called on me two or three times, renewing a friendship which in Chicago days had been built up during dinners and walks together, enlivened by the company of Mrs. Simpson, a lovely lady and an artist. Valeria, who was dazzling in everything and spoke English and French as if her own language, aided me in entertaining Mrs. Simpson. And one day, while Simpson and I were looking, from the balcony of the Vasconcelos committee office, at the graceful Mexican architecture of the National Theatre, he said, throwing aside all reserve, "You think you are going to win; you have public opinion on your side, but something very important is missing at present—the good will of the American Embassy." "Why doesn't the Embassy like me?" I asked with a frankness equal to his.

Then with the exactness of his thinking as a technician, my old pupil said, "The United States is par excellence an industrial country that needs markets; the natural market of the United States is Latin America. Good continental collaboration presupposes that the United States will produce manufactured articles, and the countries of the South, raw materials and also tropical products which do not grow or grow poorly in the United States. Any government that guarantees the United States a policy of rational economic cooperation, as I have explained it, which promises, moreover, to respect the recently signed treaties, will be an acceptable government. And I doubt that you with your ambitions to build an independent Mexico, can count on the sympathy of the Embassy."

Was that a warning? Was it a simple friendly confession, and no more? In any case it seemed to me useless and untimely to enter upon a discussion and I limited myself to replying, "Yes, I doubt it, too." And we changed the subject.

It was through the painter Adolfo Best that the interview with the Americans was finally arranged. Best had a protectress who admired his work, a very fine North American lady, who if I am not mistaken was the wife of Mr. Rublee, the legal counselor of the Embassy. As Best told me, "You will see how sweet this Mr. Rublee is." I confirmed this sweetness when I met him. "Tears come to his eyes when he talks about Mexico," Best had told me; and very soon, seeing him thus moved, I thought how pained he must be by what Morrow and his country were doing to us. The fact is that I lunched at the house of Mr. Rublee (every time I spell his name differently, and it doesn't make any difference).

The Ambassador turned up. Puny in appearance, shorter than I, almost "undersized," short-sighted and bow-legged. In vain I searched his face for the flame of intelligence which was supposed to characterize him. With simple politeness, Mrs. Rublee indicated to each of us his place at the table; my chair was beside hers. Mrs. Morrow was not bad looking for her age, a little thin, but her austere and dis-

tant manner did not lead to an immediate liking. They offered cocktails and I hastened to take mine, as a due protest against the prohibition law. Mr. Morrow and Mrs. Rublee drank theirs with me. Mrs.
Morrow abstained. In due time, I put down plenty of red wine. Morrow mixed water with his, and Mrs. Morrow drank straight water.

The lunch hour passed in small talk, and afterward they left the
Ambassador and me alone. We discussed only general subjects and
another appointment was agreed upon, for lunch at the Embassy.
During the meal, Mrs. Morrow had not been able to hide her cool-
ness, I would almost say her dislike of me.

The Embassy occupies a whole block. The Americans owe to their
English blood a certain imperial heritage which, added to their own
recently acquired power, permits them to recognize and occupy without any loss of reputation the old mansions that the Spaniards of the
glorious epoch built themselves in Mexico City, the second capital of
their empire.

The meal, scanty in spite of the fact that it was midday, was
served in His Excellency's private office on a small portable table. The
books on his desk did nothing to suggest a refined taste, but were
works of colleagues in law or banking, in the commercial jargon of
capitalism, without that pretense of a love for art and literature which
characterized bankers like Morrow's patron, Mr. Morgan. You could
see that the *nouveau riche* Morrow had not reached the category of
collector of *objets d'art*.

"It is going to be hard for you to collect many votes," Morrow said
at the end of our interview, "because, although I don't deny your
popularity, you know the power of the machine. At the last minute
the adding machines may have lots of surprises. You are doing something important; you are educating the people in democracy; you will
teach them to vote, and although you will lose this election—since
the government is very strong—in the next one, four years from now,
your triumph is sure unless you make the mistake of stirring up a
rebellion."

When Morrow said this, I learned who had given the official party
its hypocritical thesis that they did not look askance at us, that we
would not win, but that we were educating the people. There was
no doubt. A country governed by wicked men of little ability had to
take from the Proconsul not only its national program but even the
arguments that were thought valid against the opposition.

I did not think of the luncheon with Morrow again, but a week
later, also through Mrs. Rublee, I received a present from the Ambas-

sador: a book with an introduction by him. He had not signed it and said nothing about his relations with me, but the introduction contained the thesis he had talked about: that opposition parties were the safety valve that prevented revolutions, that salvation lay in organizing the opposition. The Morrow thesis spread more widely than you would believe. Many friends of mine, timid souls or complacent types, advised the same thing, that I should let myself be defeated, that I should hasten to admit defeat and make peace with the victor.

My advantage was that I had made a living from the movement and had been able to save the money from my articles for almost a year. At the end of the campaign I deposited this money in New York. When I was in Aguascalientes on tour of the North, *El Universal* permitted itself to remark on its relations with me which obliged me to send in my resignation. I refused to try to collect the honorarium for the last article that was published under the title, "Vasconcelos' Last Article." The most hateful thing about it was that the paper continued to call itself independent. I understood that they were laying siege to me by hunger. My enemies knew and I knew that after my unmasking of the influence of Yankee policy in Mexico, I could never again earn a peso in the United States, where formerly the universities had been a refuge for me.

On the occasion of one of my returns to the capital, or because of the publication of my *Metaphysics*, I don't remember exactly which, a group of intellectuals got the idea of offering me a banquet. The political campaign that was going on divided the country into two irreconcilable cliques: that of the coterie obedient to Morrow, supported by most of the army, and the mass of honest and patriotic people. It did not make sense to pay homage to the intellectual with mental reservations about the man of politics. Besides, this business of "homage" and the rhetoric of banquets has always disgusted me.

I received an invitation to dine at the British Embassy. The Ambassador, a refined and prudent man, spoke only of general matters, but his military attaché, a rustic, talkative young man, chattered too much. He had been on the recent campaign in the North with General Calles. There would be no chance to make another revolt because the people were tired and disillusioned with the failure of the military aspect of the opposition movement. Now the government could count on a strong and united army. Besides, with the decided and vigorous support, not only of the United States, but also of England. . . . Altogether, I was given notice that I had against me the only powers that dominate Mexico, the foreign powers: England, which gave us our independence, and the United States, which has made good use of that independence.

Good friends had managed to keep my name in the columns of the best magazines, always taking advantage of the wide circulation that the Associated Press and United Press gave to their information, distorted as it was. And now these agencies were enemies; each of their correspondents submitted his notes to the censorship of the Yankee Embassy. Without doubt, what disturbed certain media of Yankee Pan-Americanism was the clear idea they had of the great Hispanic movement my election would lead to all over the Continent. That was why the North American press was so cold.

Fresnillo, a rich, independent mining town, gave us a great reception. But one thing disgusted and disappointed me there, and unfortunately that place was only a miniature of the feeling of the whole nation in this time of its decadence. Big signs covered the walls announcing a bullfight the next day. The expert, a Mexican torero, with a reputation for bravery, merited unpopularity to the point of lynching, for on two occasions, catching the bug of butchery, which was common among the government people, he had killed chauffeurs, just for kicks. After a week in jail and a lot of newspaper scandal and assertions that justice would be merciless, the torero, a protégé of the government, came out on bail and the trial was forgotten. And what is worse, the bull-fighting public, which is almost everybody in Mexico, applauded him like the devil. It was also well known that the official party used him as a propagandist. The very same people who had taken the trouble to walk a mile to welcome us at the entrance to the town, next day would fill the bull ring to give an ovation to the torero and to the propaganda worker for my opponents.

COAHUILA On the terrace, the welcoming body had taken its stand and made speeches. I thanked them as well as I could, for what happens is that whatever little oratorical capacity one has evaporates in the face of success. It seems useless to add words when everybody acquiesces and feels the same way. Words, the tools of persuasion, seem unnecessary in the face of a spasm of collective agreement. My friends were right when they used to say, "Make him mad so he'll speak well!"

As we were coming back, on the way to the hotel and still in a close column, a group of neighbors barred our way and a pretty girl handed me a bouquet of flowers in the name of Coahuila, and it was not until dark that we were able to use the rooms in the hotel, and to find a bathroom, which under the circumstances was more necessary than food and drink.

SALTILLO I remember that General Dávila said to me, "I suppose you must have some support in the United States, after living there so long."

"I haven't any," I replied frankly. "On the contrary, the United States is solidly behind their Ambassador Morrow, and you already know what Morrow thinks."

"Then it's too bad," he added, "because in that case we are lost!"

We were lost because the people no longer believed in themselves.

When we have behaved badly in carrying out a task which affects a common cause, it is easier to find flaws in the man who acts as leader than to confess our own faults. Every one of those who deserted the movement of 1929 added his grain to the false legend that because of my character I managed to make enemies out of many friends, and that I defeated myself. But I ask, "Who is there who does not see himself deserted, calumniated, and rejected in defeat, even if he possesses the patience of a saint?" Moreover, the responsible person in an enterprise of high moment is forced to demand of others the same strict discipline he imposes on himself, which means at the very least operating in good faith and with the maximum expenditure of one's personal capacity.

Valeria declared that she had decided to settle in New York, to do propaganda work in intellectual circles. The world must be told what was going on in Mexico; this was a vital matter not only for Mexico, but for all of Spanish America. If the United States went along with the band of assassins who shared among themselves our Presidency, our Ministries, the top posts in the army, at least let no one plead ignorance. There was, of course, no one as good as Valeria for a task of this kind. I did not want to see her uprooted from Mexico and publicly compromised. Her financial situation, once so splendid, was beginning to be difficult. How was she to get along if she were condemned to a long period of expatriation?

But who can convince a woman who has already made up her

mind? Valeria left, alleging, and quite rightly, that in Mexico a woman could not count on a secure future if she decided, as she herself had done, to unmask the enemy and not to yield.

I secured a new and very valuable proponent in Juárez, in the person of an engineer, Paredes, who, sacrificing his time and money, agreed to represent me officially in Washington in order to build up a favorable opinion toward us when the revolution should break out following the elections.

Poor country! I learned that Mr. Rublee had said in those days, his sight clouded by those tears of his which feigned tenderness, "On one side, Ortiz Rubio surrounded by assassins, on the other, Vasconcelos, surrounded by boys!" But they were not boys who all over the country had sworn to give me their vote and then to make it respected.

The students, delighted by their new toys of a university in which examinations had been suppressed and where the students appointed their professors and removed them at their discretion, deserted activities in connection with the election, and morally speaking, the university immediately suffered the shame of having a Rector appointed by President Portes.

November was beginning, and already our defeat was taken for granted abroad. Letters from Valeria communicated to me the reaction of the pseudo-leftist intellectual rabble that congregated in New York at Columbia and other institutions, supported by well-paid courses in Spanish. Attentive to the weathervane of success, they had at first flocked around Valeria, had pretended to give her their adherence; then, when the assassinations began to raise doubts, when they saw that only an armed effort on the part of the whole country could save us and that that effort was forbidden by the bankers of Wall Street, the radicals deserted her. Among them there must have been some who would later figure to advantage in the Spanish fellow-travelers' tragedy, although for the moment I did not suspect it. At the time they were all very respectful of the barometer of Wall Street with Mr. Morrow as the Proconsul, the Prophet. The greatest possible honor for them was to dine in the house of Mr. Lamont, Morgan's partner. The Protestants and Jews of Columbia University, in the service of Calles and aware of what was going on in Mexico, in many cases turned against Valeria who received only criticism from me for mixing with that kind of people, whose friendship is useless during the struggle and costly in triumph.

Valeria spent her great talent in a vain effort to remove the racial prejudices of those men sold out to pretorianism and Monroeism. But she did not want to go back to Mexico. She would return, she wrote, only if all that was changed. Otherwise, she preferred ruin and poverty to living in the humiliation of putting up with the faces of assassins grown proud under Yankee protection.

In a way I was a plague carrier, or at least an embarrassment, even for my friends.

Places in which to hide out were plentiful in the country or city, but from the beginning I had stood out against that procedure, which reduces the chief of a movement to impotence, aside from the fact that, by depriving him of the means of communication, it takes away whatever strength he derives from the spoken word. We could not lose contact with public opinion. And it was preferable to escape to a foreign country from which one could speak out, rather than spend months in the tomblike silence of a zealously guarded hiding place. But before doing what Madero had to do, what any chief has to do who does not want to deliver himself impotent into the hands of his enemies, to do what saves his person—but compromises his cause—I tried to find a place where I could be protected by my armed partisans. At the most, we could assemble five hundred poorly equipped men, not enough to resist an attack by the whole army; it was better to split them up into guerrilla bands; I ought, then, to find a safe place for myself, at least to get away from the place where the rebellion was going to start. In our hotel, calls never stopped. At the hotel doors, a couple of constables searched people's pockets and disarmed everybody who was not angry enough to resist. I begged the chief of police, who called every morning pretending to be attentive, to remove these characters. They were there on purpose to be a nuisance and to frighten visitors.

The last night, on the eve of the elections, groups of gunmen in trucks drove up and down under our balconies shouting insolent remarks, firing into the air, and crying "Vivas" to Ortiz Rubio and Calles.

The idea that the vote involves the obligation of sustaining it against force and fraud, an idea that we had so strongly defended, had not carried conviction.

"What do the Americans think? Are you counting on support from the United States?" were the questions put to me by two or three colonels who had secretly communicated with me via common friends. My reply to everybody was "The United States will be against anybody they cannot manipulate; I tell you in advance that we can hope for nothing good from the North; but this is the reason why you should support me, not why you should abandon me." Insensible to this language of honor, which is final in other armed forces, our men preferred to attach themselves to the side that Mr. Morrow sponsored. From that time on, I saw in our forces something like the Philippine constabulary, a constabulary subjected to the suave but efficient proconsul, Mr. Morrow.

On the day of the elections, we left early from Mazatlán by the train for the North, to await the uprisings in Guaymas.

In Empalme half a dozen houses belonging to railway employees were at our disposal. "If you want to hide," said Corrales, "they won't be able to take you away from here; here you are among your own men." "That isn't the question. We intend to go on to Guaymas." It was better to maintain communication with the rest of the country as long as we could. We only accepted their invitation to lunch. After lunch, we took the road, by truck, to Guaymas, which was not far away. A few minutes later, an auto full of military men of high rank came to meet us. A Colonel got out, whose name I forget, and whom I shall merely call the Colonel. At noon, I ordered an apéritif for the military men, and they accepted. When we sat down to lunch, I invited the Colonel to eat with us. After dinner, I retired for a half hour's siesta. During the afternoon, the number of visitors grew to such an extent that the vestibule was full and there was even a crowd of people in the street. Somebody brought some musical instruments. Among the callers and curiosity-seekers there were many women, most of them good-looking girls, although of the lower classes, and it occurred to me to say, in the center of the spacious drawing room, "Why don't we dance?" and we had an improvised party that lasted for several hours.

The military took turns, but did not leave us. A new group of officers continued to sit in a corner of the vestibule.

What displeased us most when we got the papers from Mexico City, was to see beside my declaration that I had won the election and considered myself President Elect, a statement of lawyer Calixto Maldonado, who said, "Democracy has been killed, there was no election; the assaults prevented it." More satisfactory was the fact that they also printed the loyal statements of Góngora, the President of the Party, expressing the fitting and truthful point of view: "In spite of the outrages committed, the people turned out to vote. We won by an absolute majority and from now on, for me, Vasconcelos is President-Elect."

In Mexico City, the government published the count of the election on the afternoon of the very day of the election; but in New York, the papers gave it out at eleven o'clock on election day, as transmitted from Mexico by the official party. The announcement was so much too early that, when it was confirmed hours later by the Mexican press, it was quite clear that the figures had been made up the night before the election, or earlier. The Yankee press, eager to offer one more proof of the lazy character of the "greaser," accepted the official version that we lost because the government people took possession of the ballot-boxes very early and we were late in arriving.

Nobody called attention to the unprecedented shamelessness of accepting as correct a count which was published in New York at eleven, that is to say hours before the legal closing of the polls (taking into account the difference in time between Mexico and New York). Besides, the vast area of our country and the poor quality of communication means that a fair calculation, if it is to be exact, requires several days. This did not prevent the Morgan partner, Lamont, from publishing jubilant statements and a message in which he congratulated Ortiz Rubio on his victory.

In the computation that I mentioned, Ortiz Rubio was awarded two million votes; to the communist candidate, my friend Triana, who had not bestirred himself, they gave forty thousand, and to me twelve thousand. There was not a single paper, of course, either in Mexico or abroad, that commented on the figures, analyzed them, discussed them.

I informed the Colonel, who presented himself every morning, that I had decided to go abroad. And, in the joking tone we sometimes used in talking to each other, while I was finishing dressing to go out, I said, "Don't you see that here by being in your power, I am in the way of my friends who might want to start an armed uprising?"

"No, Counselor. You know we are simply an honor guard, and you are not a prisoner. But I will pass on your decision to the Regional Chief."

The next day he told me I could count on an escort to take me to the frontier. The government circulated the news that I was giving up the struggle and leaving for the United States. What else could they say?

The night before my leaving to go into exile, a mysterious personage came to Guaymas, and set the imagination of the simple townspeople all astir. He got out of a plane, which was rare in those days, began asking for my address, and sent to ask for a chance to see me before eight in the morning. I was leaving for the beach, and I told him I would see him briefly in the hotel on the waterfront. It was Lloyd, the Associated Press correspondent, who said to me in English, "I must talk to you for two or three hours on behalf of Mr. Morrow; it is something very urgent!"

I went to bathe. The curiosity of the officers who accompanied us seemed to be aroused. Word had gotten around that the gringo was a special agent of the Proconsul.

So, then, the Proconsul was concerned about me, when the President and Generals appeared to pay no attention to me! "Why are you keeping him waiting?" grumbled Pedrero, consumed with curiosity. "Leave the bathing for some other time; you've had your dip."

"I'm keeping him waiting," I said, "just for that very reason, because he comes from the Proconsul!"

I listened to Morrow's envoy for more than an hour. His attitude was friendly, extremely so. Morrow recognized the great democratic effort that had been made. At the same time, the power of the government was invincible, but I knew that he had some influence with the victors. What would I think if they gave me the Rectorship of the Autonomous University, so that from there I could continue my work of educating the new generation? And for my friends and supporters and those to whom I had made campaign promises, one or two posts in the cabinet of Ortiz Rubio?

"And what do I have to do to get all that?"

"It's very simple, just sit down and sign, without leaving your desk, a telegram you will give me to send out; a telegram in which you state that there was pressure in the election, that it was not clean, but that in spite of that, out of patriotism and to avoid greater ills, you concede the triumph of your rival and congratulate him, and recommend that your people do the same."

"Tell Morrow I am not his kind."

I was not going to betray my cause in exchange for a public office. I understood Morrow's point of view: he had done what he wished with the country and its men. For him, I represented a minor obstacle, a small stumbling block; but if I yielded and sent that telegram, then the Ambassador could boast of having no enemy, of having manipulated the country as he wished and to the general satisfaction.

"No, Lloyd," I replied. "Thanks for the trouble you have taken to come so far to see me, and thank the Ambassador for his interest, but we have opposing points of view that are irreconcilable. The only policy that I preach now and will continue to preach, is armed rebellion. And the expulsion of Mr. Morrow from the country as soon as we win!"

Later, alone in my room, I reflected repeatedly on the situation. I would not accept any kind of cooperation with the winners of that fraudulent contest.

"Forego the Rectorship," Lloyd had said, "don't accept anything for yourself, but don't stand in the way of your party's gaining an important position in the new government. Withdraw, if it seems best to you, but withdraw peacefully, settle in the United States. Mr. Morrow will be your friend, will open many doors to you, if you just give me this telegram of congratulations to your rival."

To owe your daily bread to Mr. Morrow, after what he was doing to the Mexicans!

I decided to make the trip to the border the next day. The train left Guaymas in the afternoon. Many people came to see me off. A great many women were crying. "There goes the hope of a free Mexico," some were saying; but what distressed me was that no one said, "Soon we will have to bring it about by force!"

In the hotel on the American side, newspapermen accosted me, and I began to dictate, "They did not defeat me; they cheated me." I added, "It is now up to the Mexican people to secure justice. I shall return to the country as soon as there is a party of a hundred armed men who will make me respected as President-Elect."

The immigration authorities behaved in an extremely courteous, even cordial fashion. "What do you propose to do in the United States?" was one of the routine questions. "Wait until people with arms call me back to throw out the usurpers."

The chief of immigration said, "I don't blame you. I can understand how you feel. God bless you!"

I was given the following summary of a private interview with the American President: That consular reports to the United States recognized that my election was a fact; that in every district not only had my majority been overwhelming, but that such outrages had been committed as would invalidate my rival's position; that the American government was tired of Calles, not because he had failed to keep his bargain with them, but because his party had exhausted the Mexican people, and it was therefore time for a change, always within the framework of the same policy of subordination to the treaties and understandings that Mr. Morrow had achieved. For the same reason, the protection of the government in Washington, extended to the people in power in Mexico, was neither unconditional nor eternal: that if I was able to bring about a rebellion before Ortiz Rubio carried out his announced trip to Washington, the American government would remain neutral and would put off its recognition of the government's presidential candidate. But that if the rebellion I was preaching did not occur before the indicated date, "then" (Hoover had said) "if the Mexican people don't cry out against the government's having violated and made a farce of its vote, I am not going to be the one to do so. If by the date of the visit of Ortiz Rubio to Washington, there is no rebellion, Ortiz Rubio will have the support of the American government, and we will not tolerate disturbances nor even propaganda against his government along our border."

Strictly speaking, the North American procedure was correct.

From Washington, Engineer Paredes, whom I can never sufficiently repay for his sacrifice in representing me there at his own expense, also advised me to accept defeat and peace. Days passed, and Mexico, still immobile, resembled from a distance one of those Aztec idols, empty forms of coarse granite, which never housed a soul.

In the general breakdown, Valeria stood up magnificently. She would not hear of making any deal. We ought not to return to Mexico if the people did not insist, with arms, upon justice being done.

Together we traveled as far as San Antonio; there she left me to go on to Los Angeles, while I stopped over for a few days to talk to some people.

The day came which the *Times* correspondent called "the saddest day of his life, when they set up his friends in a row to be shot." We learned the fact in a Tucson café, from the afternoon papers. On the front page, in big letters, they published the news that General Bouquet had just been executed in Nogales, in the State of Sonora. A few days after the murder of Bouquet, the whole press published the decree that President Portes Gil had issued against me. All customs offices, all military commands were informed that I was forbidden to return to the country. Completely frustrated, I had to recognize that I was a rebel. It was what I needed for my peace of mind: the recognition that I had not accepted my unfair defeat lying down. The tragedy of Bouquet brought me to the conviction that for a long time it would not be possible to set in motion that terrorized mass which constituted my country. And much as I blamed Morrow and the intervention of the United States in supporting the evil that had happened, in the last analysis I had to admit that our own responsibility was greater than that of the foreigner. For no one can impose himself on a virile and conscientious country, especially if he acts only by means of the kind of influence the United States had been using in recent decades; it is well known that they did not have recourse to a crushing use of force. They simply took advantage of our corruption and channeled it in a way that was harmful to us.

Quietly and with all the pomp of a nabob, Ortiz Rubio went to Washington to hear what I knew they would tell him—that it was he and not Calles whom they recognized as President, and that he could count on their support to make himself respected. The poor devil could hardly believe his ears. Moreover, they advised him to come to some kind of terms with the opposition; consequently, he made declarations that would open the door to us. Doubtless he was already contemplating what he would propose to me later on: an alliance to rid himself of Calles, who had taken him from nowhere and made him President. But aside from the fact that I scorned making a deal with him, I cared nothing about pushing Calles aside; my goal was to throw out of the government all that military influence that had been debasing our people. In Chicago, the Mexican colony —most of them my followers—gave Ortiz Rubio such a rebuff at the station that he dared not go on to Los Angeles. In that city, our compatriots held firm and kept filling the halls when Vasconcelos meetings were held. It was quite obvious that wherever Mexicans acted without the pressure of an army upon them, they snubbed Ortiz Rubio in the most decided fashion.

The idea of a long exile in the United States held no charm for me. I decided to spend those years among Latin people, in the southern part of the hemisphere or in Europe. But I was short of funds, and moreover it was not a good idea at the time to be too far from the border. Something might come of the attempt on the life of Ortiz Rubio. I decided to wait.

Meanwhile, aid came unexpectedly from a source which it is more logical to call Providence than blind chance. From Paris, my literary agent Deambrosis sent me a cable saying that Eduardo Santos, the owner of El Tiempo of Bogotá, a paper that for some years had published my contributions, had invited me to visit Colombia, either to deliver paid lectures, or simply as his guest. The road to the South opened up before me just when the one to the North was closing, and as Santos had distinguished himself by his part in Hispanic-American affairs, I felt a genuine return for my efforts. What Mexico could not give me—a fitting place of refuge—Colombia offered. Quickly I began to make plans. For personal expenses and those of my family, I had barely three thousand dollars, enough for one year.

Far from considering the kind of return to Mexico that would be easy for any of us if we would issue a submissive statement (for the United States wanted no exiles in their midst, and demanded from Mexico a forgiving attitude toward the submissive ones), Valeria definitely decided on exile. But it was not possible for her to carry out this plan at once; her finances were in a bad state. Whether it was unsuccessful business deals she had gone into with stupid or dishonest associates, ruinous borrowings she had made to get her hands on ready cash, or whatever, the fact is that she was in a bad fix, at times distressingly so, in spite of the fortune she had inherited two or three years before.

When we drew up our balance sheet in Los Angeles, the result was that I resolved to leave at once for South America. The journey would carry my message to the only quarter that remained open to me, and beside that, it offered me an opportunity for earning some money quickly. Accustomed to coping with the difficulties of exile and of struggle against implacable enemies, I have never felt satisfied if I did not have in front of me a year of living that I could count on with some assurance. In line with this customary attitude, scarcely had the two or three weeks passed—necessary to see whether the business of an attack on Ortiz Rubio would lead to the outbreak of rebellion or only to the consolidation of the government's terrorism— when I decided to leave by sea for Panama and Colombia. For her part, Valeria agreed that it was essential for her to go back to Mexico to straighten out her affairs, in view of the long absence she was looking forward to. Besides, she planned to pick up her son.

I consulted all the principal leaders of the movement of which I was the chief, asking their opinion about my leaving the United States, although really I was under no obligation to do so. In the future, I would have to devote myself to denouncing the tactics of Monroeism and Poinsettism, not only in Mexico, but all over America. My enemies had increased and my offensive would henceforth not be limited to Mexican politicians.

I decided to move my family to Los Angeles while I wandered about. My sons were in the university. My daughter, busy with her studies, was still so young that it had not occurred to me that she might become engaged, and I was toying with the idea of taking her with me on my tour of the Southern countries. But one day Herminio put in my hands a little book of Chinese proverbs and pointed out one which said something like: "Have a care whom your son marries, weigh the advantages and disadvantages of every party; but your daughter, marry her while you can." I did not understand. Neither did I pay much attention to the warnings and worries that her mother expressed about the engagement of our daughter. "Was it serious?" she asked. Finally, Herminio had to fall back upon the formal procedure of asking for her hand. Rather surprised, I said to him after a little reflection, "What's the hurry? Wait one or two years, until this situation clears up!" They paid no attention to me, and in the face of the inevitable, I stated firmly, "I have no desire to lose a valued friendship as well as a daughter. I consent, but on one condition: once you are married, if you don't get along and repent of the marriage, don't let your lives be embittered by it. Give her back to me, and I will never get tired of her."

"The only reason I don't get angry is because it's you," replied Herminio, offended. I cancelled my daughter's passage. Unfortunately, my trip could not be put off, and the wedding was set for two months later, in spite of my not being there.

The attitude of North American diplomacy in Mexico did not turn me against Yankees as persons. A great many North Americans showed sincere sympathy for our lost cause. Every time I had anything to do with public officials, as for example when I asked for a permit to leave the country, the most perfect courtesy was the rule, and frequently our conversation was cordial.

In the Norwegian or Danish ship (I always confuse those Scandinavian countries) that took me to Barranquilla I was the only passenger; I sat at the Captain's table and the cooking was wonderful, unequaled in delicacy and abundance.

But the accursed elbow of the sea formed by the snake of the Isthmus, and the empty hold of the vessel, led to a terrible attack of seasickness, such as I had not had for a long time. The result was that I landed at Barranquilla more dead than alive.

COLOMBIA The marvel of the railway trip is an extremely long tunnel, illuminated at intervals, ventilated, almost beautiful, a masterpiece of Colombian engineering, carried out with Belgian cooperation. What a relief to be in a country where not everything is of North American workmanship! We reached Medellín by night.

At my second lecture the audience was smaller than at the first and some newspapers began to exhibit little affection for me. Intrigue was beginning: a wave of feeling like that in Cartagena made them cancel dinners and affairs that had previously been planned.

Discouraged and angry, I was thundering before my students, inveighing against those who sell their souls to foreign influence, when one of the boys asked, "Write all this that you are telling us, draw up a manifesto or proclamation or speech that will help orient the younger generation; we will circulate it all over the country."

"Sit down, sit down there," I replied, "I am going to dictate it."

I gave them the text of the short speech that circulated widely and that Waldo Frank reproduces in his book on Latin America. In it, I recommend to the contemporary generation that they renounce their fathers and grandfathers and all their cowardly forebears from the days of Independence on down, and reconstruct all their values on the basis of Hispanic nationalism. My brave young friends faithfully spread this doctrine.

Why should I not give two or three lectures in Bogotá on educational subjects which would interest everyone? I would get honor out of it and money, too, and then, just before I leave I could give one or two militantly political lectures, without having to worry about the economic consequences. This is what we arranged. In the morning, while I was waiting for the time to leave, the boys brought around Sanín Cano, who was spending some days of relaxation in the hotel. I liked this sixty-odd-year-old character, tall, white-haired, heavily built, with something English about him suggested by his pleasant manners and the fine humor of his conversation.

In some year previous to my own nomination, the students had honored Sanín Cano with the title of Teacher of Colombian Youth, a thing which he, like myself, took partly as a joke. We talked alone for a couple of hours and with the greatest cordiality; he went with us to the station, and, as the train was leaving and he stayed behind, the students asked me: "What did you think of Sanín Cano?" "He is a great man!" I declared. Two or three weeks later some one told me that his reply to the similar question, "How did you like Vasconcelos?," had been, "He is another coward like me."

On the platform as I got off the train, Eduardo Santos opened his arms to me. He was a dark-skinned type, intelligent, very polite and sincerely affable. He had me get into an open car, and slowly, in order not to tire those who were going on foot, we made a triumphal entry into the ancient and cultivated city, the pride of the Continent.

Years before, the boys had chosen as their Master one who was a Minister; he now came to them defeated and persecuted. Suddenly, this aroused their enthusiasm, although perverse spirits would not be long in insinuating doubt and distrust. They shouted "Viva Unamuno!" and then "Viva Vasconcelos!" At the time Unamuno was a refugee in Paris and at odds with his king. This joining of our names pleased me, for it revealed a certain racial consciousness; transcending the situation in their own country, this youthful group rose to the global level and shared the struggles and problems of their race, in Spain as well as in Mexico. And that was precisely my message.

Santos reached his peroration, and his flattering, eloquent presentation obliged me to make one correction. He hoped that I would enjoy my stay in Bogotá because it had fallen to my lot to be the loser, and I was doubtless exhausted, and it was the moment for friends to come forward and prove that they were true friends. I thanked Santos for his invitation, the students for their loyalty and the whole people for their cordial welcome; but I added, "I am not a defeated man. Morally defeated, defeated before justice and history, are the wretches who, in collusion with foreign interests, are gaining public power, whether by force or by deceit. I am a man of victory, not defeat!" I shouted. "Defeat hides its shame, conceals the facts, is silent about its pain; I come denouncing as traitors men who are just that, not merely to my country, but to a whole continent."

My message of spiritual nationalism—not merely economic independence—the need of preserving the cultural heritage of Spain, the peril of penetration by the North, all this awakened interest in many segments of the population. Soon I found myself surrounded by artists and nationalistic enthusiasts. And they showed me all that is typical of the country, which is certainly not much.

The last day came. A final tea party in the fashionable café turned out to be rather melancholy. *El Tiempo* asked me for some farewell lines; I wrote them hastily and in banal, sentimental words, incapable of expressing the strange emotion one has on leaving forever a world which has entwined one's heart.

As I traversed the Colombian countryside on the estate of the Valderramas and others, I noticed that the majority of the landowners were called "Doctor"—at least as high a proportion as the Generals who are chief landholders among us. This demonstrates the differing origins of land tenure in Colombia and in our country; in Colombia it is legal and normal, among us spurious, violent, revolutionary or pseudo-revolutionary.

In the country there were ceibos, palm trees, subtropical underbrush, all of which appear in the pages of Jorge Isaacs' *María*. Of Jewish origin, but converted, and with deep family roots in the region, Jorge Isaacs, along with one or two living poets, is still the interpreter of the Cauca, and its pride. The only historic mansion of the district is the one in which the romantic author lived and which his heirs have now transformed into a museum. I visited it; I am not sure whether it was in Palmira. I could not help but reflect that it was a Jew by race, and an Irishman by origin—I don't remember for sure —who was the first to give expression to the Creole sensitivity of our race. To be sure, overwhelmed as we have been by the task of developing a savage land, we have not achieved lasting works in the field of thought, works which can extend beyond the boundaries of our own tongue. Where are the figures we could put beside a Whitman, a Poe, an Emerson, a William James? Nevertheless, we do have our favorite spiritual leaders, and José Enrique Rodó, who was a provincial writer with rhetorical talent, showed us Ariel struggling with Caliban. Where is the great literature which justifies the heritage of Ariel?

In the desert of our mental life, we must feel gratitude when, from the sidewalk under the shade trees, they point out, at the end of a path, among well-cared-for vegetation, the house once occupied by the heroine of our youth, María; thanks to Jorge Isaacs, she became the incarnation of our blood, and appears as such among so many personages of foreign literatures.

ECUADOR   The formality to which South Americans are so addicted is rather funny; instead of taking a taxi for the minute required to cross the border, I had to wait for a Commission to escort me from the hotel to the sentry-box which faces the Ecuadorean border station. In the latter, another reception committee, composed of the mayor, the military commandant, two assistants, and ten or twelve private citizens, was waiting for me. From the customs house we went on to the City Hall. A hall with a lecture platform at one end, rows of seats, old portraits on the walls: the Mayor seats me at his right; the secretary reads the decree which states that I am a guest of honor of Tulcán. I made a brief speech of thanks; I inscribed a "thought" in the golden book, and although it was eleven o'clock in the morning, they served champagne.

The most memorable thing about that night was the supper they served us in the local Casino, a meal that far surpassed what one might have expected from the small population. The cook was French, they told us, and there was a really excellent soup, and meat pie, vegetables and dessert, with imported champagne. Real champagne is a common enough refinement in small cities of South America. There a trip to Europe is considered a part of one's education and a social duty. There is hardly anyone, let alone the important personages, who cannot talk with easy familiarity about Parisian restaurants and excursions in the Old World. From the United States, however, they import only tractors and agricultural machinery.

As the drunken dancers pass in their slow monotonous rhythm, you recognize in the masks, in the colors and cut of the clothes, a community of style which the Spaniard imparted to the various tribes of Mexico, Ecuador, and doubtless to countries farther south. The dances of Ecuador are replicas of our regional, so-called indigenous dances, as are those of New Mexico; one is tempted to say that they are an invention, not of the Indian but of the Conquistador, who spread the same music, the same taste, the same culture, from California to the Pampas.

The same stamp of Spain is preserved in Ecuador in the dwellings of the population and in the gentlemanly manners of the people. The agents of imperialistic penetration can do nothing to counteract this tradition. We talked about this as we came back over hill and dale from our horseback ride. On a hillside they pointed out the abandoned house of a Protestant pastor, who tried vainly to proselytize the most ignorant Indians. What he lacked was the artistic trappings that the Spaniards brought with them, and the superiority of a culture capable of embracing and transforming all aspects of life, not merely its techniques.

I recalled that once, speaking of a political change in Ecuador, I had asked César Arroyo in Marseilles, "And how will Zaldumbide make out? Won't they remove him from Paris?" "Oh, no," declared Cesarito. "Nobody dares touch Zaldumbide; anyone who did would be discredited; he is the top writer of the country; who could take his place in France?" This was really the case, and it is wonderful when you find a people able to give this kind of appreciation to its men of letters, its eminent citizens. As to the great dead of the country, this admiration and respect of the Ecuadoreans reaches the point of veneration. Above them all stands Montalvo, whose ten or twelve books are the treasure that the country offers the visitor. They gave me this present in Ambato—this collection of Montalviana, which most clearly expresses and sums up the best in the national spirit.

In Zaldumbide's house, after an intimate supper, it was decided that under the auspices of the Rector, who was with us, I would give a lecture in the main theatre, on an educational subject. After this lecture I would be free to give, independently and at my own risk, a popular talk on Mexican politics. Zaldumbide, by bringing pressure to bear on friends and Legations, managed to fill the hall for the first affair, which was by invitation. The first families of the capital were present in the boxes, and there were lots of newspaper men, writers, professors, and students.

There was a tense feeling in the hall, the kind of feeling that arises when something rather special has been announced and expectations are high among the audience, just as they are at the first appearance of a famous matador. I was so keenly aware of my insignificance in comparison with their exaggerated expectations, that I almost panicked. If I had followed my first impulse, I would have run out of the theatre, back to my hotel, and to the frontier. I was prevented from deserting in that way by my belief that I had a message that was useful to an audience that formed part of my own menaced race. So I began by enumerating the ways in which we could fulfill the obligation of unity which our common past imposes upon us; I insisted on the urgent need to preserve our differences, surrounded as we are by manifestations of the universal culture. In the name of this mission, we ought to combat the influences which tend to make us pariahs in body and soul.

The Argentine Ambassador, the excellent Barilari, whom I had met years before in Buenos Aires, advised me, "Keep on going south and stay in Argentina; the Government of Irogoyen is the only one in all America at the moment which can support your propaganda." I was attracted by the idea of a series of lectures in Argentina, and if I did not decide on it, it was because that part of the world seems so remote. And another thing, I wanted to move closer to Mexico for family reasons. My daughter had been married and was happy, but my son and my wife were in Los Angeles and I needed to go and fetch them. Besides, I wanted very much to join Valeria, who gave me bad news by cablegram. She had again escaped from Mexico, but not peacefully, as we had planned; instead, she had abducted her son in a plane.

Perhaps even Montalvo himself was unable to assemble a good collection of books, and could not surround himself with those little luxuries in the way of beautiful things that any mediocre writer acquires if he has the good luck to be born outside the accursed militarized regions of our continent. There is much more atmosphere in the house of Jorge Isaacs in Colombia. The people who form the

Montalvo Society are educated, enthusiastic, devoted to the great man, but they have no power; they, like the rest of the country, are affected by the ups and downs of the military cliques that take turns in power and make a pretense of democracy and culture but are really incapable of creating or even preserving and understanding a message like that of Montalvo. Our contemporaries may read his violent pages and even applaud what they read, but they do not realize that these passages are still directed against them, against present as well as past militarism. Visiting Ambata brings on a boundless moral depression, for it is a mass of impoverished Creoles, tired of dreaming noble dreams that always fail.

And we thought, "If Montalvo reappeared, people like the ones he knew would again throw him out. They do not tackle Zaldumbide, because he is an aesthete. If he began to preach, they would send him abroad, but without a salary."

Oh, terrible climates of Hispanic America! How I should like to see the best of the Anglo-Saxon race engaged in the fight with the tropics, sure as I am that they would fare worse than the descendants of the Spaniards.

The cynical propaganda of my enemies actually turned out to be useful in my present task of teaching the South Americans about the future that awaited nations which surrender their souls and not merely their property to foreigners.

CUBA   The lesson Mexico taught about pretorianism is one that I learned literally and in detail from Machado. Feigned interest in the people, and merciless tyranny; dishonest business, and socialistic preaching; opening new highways, and throwing political prisoners to the sharks. An evil trio of dictators spelled dishonor for America: the Dean was Juan Vicente, in Venezuela; the teacher, Calles, in Mexico; the pupil, Machado, in Cuba. Machado lacked Yankee support and was the first to fall. The local proconsul demanded more and more; he was of the Morrow type, a banker first and a diplomat *per accidens*. Nor did Machado fully satisfy the aims of the Poinsett gang; he did not persecute the Church, and he imprisoned and killed communists. Hence, they directed at him manifestos with the signature of Waldo Frank and other literati who condemn Mussolini as a despot, but never Stalin. *The New York Times* and *The New Republic* also came out against Machado; to put an end to priests and American Spaniards what was needed was a Mexican-type regime. Actually, the Army was bribed, barracks were set up, officers came to be governed by sergeants. Poor Cuba! Months before all this, I lived in Havana, talked to the leaders of different groups, advised the workers to be careful, warned the communists that they would be what they were in Mexico, an excuse for the interference of Washington.

Quickly I wound up my series of lectures. The papers behaved very generously, and gave me their reports on each session in the Theatre to correct and expand. Then in an apartment along the Vedado, I set to work on the *Ethics*. I did not want to tackle the *Aesthetics*, which was stirring in my mind, without first crossing the bridge of the *Ethics*. By way of preparation, I set to work to review whatever would be useful or essential in my work. The Director of the Library, a true Spanish gentleman, recognized me one morning in the general reading room, approached, took me to his office, and invited me to make use of a little private room. About midday, he would call me to his office. At that hour he brought together the most distinguished of the readers for some conversation; doctors who were looking up cases; lawyers who were preparing briefs. And since they were all Cubans, you can imagine the fervor of the talk, which was cultivated, often learned, and always cordial. After this meeting, I would eat good rice and chickpeas in some restaurant; then I rested for three-quarters of an hour, and then sat down at my typewriter to copy my morning's notes. But this hard-working tranquility was often interrupted. The times were stormy and I did not escape the lightning flashes. My best friends and daily callers were embattled with Machado's police at the doors of the University, which was closed and partially burned.

As for me, the news from my family was not all good. My daughter was happily ensconced in Mexico; Herminio was having difficulty getting on among the Ortiz riff-raff, without accepting favors from them. But my son was wasting his time in the University of California. Who has not wasted one or two years in dissipation, in the foolish, burning passions of youth? The worst of it was that, being in a prohibition country, he and his friends, artists and movie extras, were imbibing the worst kinds of alcohol. I decided to bring the boy with his mother to Havana. As soon as he arrived, I sat him down in front of a bottle of good sherry. "If you acquire a taste for this," I said, "you will never again drink that rot-gut alcohol that burns the palate and produces idiotic, savage drunkenness." And so it turned out; there is no danger, but only goodness in fermented wine; but distilled liquor is always pestilential.

Another problem of more importance was piercing my heart. Valeria was in New Orleans. I wanted to join her, but I did not want to undertake the responsibility of her child who had a well-to-do father, and whom I could not protect. If she had been alone, nothing would have been simpler than to be together openly and start a new life; no one would be better than she at the spiritual tasks we would share. But she would not yield in the bitter fight over her divorce.

Time passed, and the situation in Mexico, far from bursting into purifying flames, tended to stablize itself with all the stagnation of a swamp. The cynical attitude of the usurpers knew no bounds. They gave Morrow a special train to the border and an honor guard of the ugliest, most shameless-looking police. About a year later, when the Proconsul died, after retiring from diplomacy, some highly placed wretches in the administration dedicated a plaque to his memory and named some streets for him.

When I was left alone after the afternoon's work, I walked from the Vedado at the end of the Malecón to the port. Provocative women passed me; months of total continence suddenly hit me; in my mind, I put out my arms and felt Valeria palpitating within them! Then the breeze, laden with spray, wet and whipped my face and dissipated my delusion. Experiencing desire for one of the fair or dark Spanish women I met would have seemed like infidelity, disloyalty, but the Negresses! Pneumatic bodies and flashing eyes, "frank voluptuousness," as Valeria had written of the Negroes of Harlem, using a phrase somewhat like Gide's.

The demands of the flesh, powerful demands that cannot be denied, and that afterward leave our souls humiliated and penitent! To achieve inner cleansing, we feel the desire to enter a Church at dusk, the proper time for meditation. I could not bring myself to do so, deterred by both timidity and shame, since I was in a state of mortal sin, according to right standards of conduct, and had not made up my mind to have done with it. I had no intention of severing my ties with Valeria. I had not felt such intimate and close moral and physical identification with any woman. My epoch denied that a sincere relationship could be sinful; one sacrificed everything to positive happiness; the only thing our code at the time required was that there should be no pretense, that every inclination should be confessed and should be legalized as soon as possible. Why not? Perhaps in the future, when both of us were free, Valeria and I could have a life together that would be fertile—not in children, but in work! An implacable tragedy would have to destroy one of these bonds, apparently so legitimate, for me to learn finally that some lives are

marked by the spirit and must serve the spirit above all. This choice
deprives them of everyday happiness. If I had been born in Egypt,
surely I should not have been a warrior or a Pharaoh or a scribe; I
should have been a priest. And a priest with family cares is a Protestant monstrosity. A priest without a wife may constitute a danger to
society, but the few who conquer, redeem the world.

After re-reading paragraphs of Schopenhauer's *The World as Will,*
to put myself in tune, I wrote a chapter which was to form part of
my *Ethics,* but I misplaced it and could never do it over; I suffered
the distress of losing something that was of doubtful value, but irreplaceable.

A recommendation from the Honduran consul in Havana assured
me of safe transit through Honduras. A vague correspondence with
the president of a literary society in San Pedro Sula guaranteed me a
paid lecture half way across the country. But it was sad to keep wandering, leaving my house on the beach, without hope of a dignified
return to my country, with my family scattered, half in Mexico, my
son and my wife trying to find a comfortable place in New York or
near there, so that the boy could go on with his engineering studies.
And Valeria, God knows where in Europe. What new obstacles
awaited us all? When could I end this intellectual begging, today in
one country, tomorrow in another? Midnight, above a dark sea, was
hardly the time and place for optimism, no matter how rosy the future, how secure the present. My mind yielded to anxiety, to the
desire to put an end to the struggle, even if it were by means of apparently accidental death. On the other hand, the realization that
others need us finally straightens us out.

What came next is today a rapid succession of faded engravings.

They offered me a big dinner in San Pedro, with plenty of strong
drink. At the time for toasts before the thirty or forty people seated
there, I had a rather strange surprise. "Honduras," said the orator,
"received me with open arms, but it had one reservation to make re-
garding me; shortly before my arrival a rumor had gone around that I,
admirer of Argentina and Colombia, great Americanist, nevertheless, felt contempt for the Central American countries; now they were
humble, but they had great hearts, etc."

Unhappily I rose to reply, and I took my revenge by accusing
North American agents of this calumny; I included their disgraceful
allies, the emissaries of the Mexican government, whom I labeled the
creatures of Yankee-made constabularies that were attempting to

wipe out true patriots. "Show me a single line in my writings," I cried, "give me a single proof of what has just been asserted, and I will leave this room, considering myself unworthy of the hospitality you are extending to me!" A unanimous acclamation cut short my speech; as soon as the noise quieted down, I continued, "As for me, Mexican imperialist that I am, I declare to you that I dream of seeing a united Central America. Mexico does not aspire to any trading posts in the South like those of United Fruit; it wants to see a great, united country, which can be its ally, not its vassal, and much less, a piece in the collection of tiny nations that the United States manipulates."

Democracy was a fact in Honduras under its great administrations. Later it would see United Fruit, which could not resign itself to losing its ascendancy, once more creating a military dictatorship, and once more, and for an indefinite time to come, plunging the country into the depths.

I sent greetings to the patriots of Nicaragua who had telegraphed me in Tegucigalpa inviting me to visit them. But the nation was occupied by the Yankee Marines, and the press was muzzled; my presence there would only have served as an excuse for intensifying the persecution of Sandino's followers. Sandino's Hymn was then the favorite song of the patriots of Central America. The Sandino case was feverishly discussed in Honduras, in El Salvador, some considering him a patriot, a hero, while others claimed to have proof that he was working hand in glove with the Yankees in order to provide a reason for prolonging the Marine occupation and their occupation of land for a projected canal. The fact that he repeatedly and publicly crossed from Nicaragua to Mexico without being molested, and his continuing friendship with the government people in Mexico and with the radicals of *The New Republic* and *The Nation* in the United States made him suspect; but on balance, I sang his praises.

EL SALVADOR   Cultivated land encroaching on the jungle; up-to-date railways; new highways; active small industry in the cities; the proud carriage and the frank and easy manner of the people, the push in business life, general optimism—all these things contribute to produce an impression in El Salvador of collective force and of a racial temper which leads the traveler to imagine that peoples, too, can be divided, on the basis of their hormones, into masculine and feminine.

Plans were made for what I was to do in the country. One week in the capital, as a guest of the University, then a trip to Santa Ana, where they told me I would be the guest of a fan who had bought forty copies of my *Metaphysics* to share with his friends. Would I be willing to have the Mexican Minister present at the affair? He was a good fellow and had shown eagerness to cooperate. "Pardon me," I explained, "I don't want to know even what his name is; he is the representative of bandits, and that is enough."

I returned to Honduras to embark for New York.

In New York snow was falling. We spent Christmas Eve together. My son had signed up for a course in automobile mechanics. We decided to go to Europe, but I devoted the month of January to research in the library to complete the material for my *Ethics*. I took notes on lots of books which only there can be obtained easily. In addition, I formed a North and South American Directorate for the Review we were planning to start. Hard work on note-taking and reading made those days in New York pass almost unnoticed. By chance, rumors reached my ears of the activities of Mexican officialdom in the great port of New York; banquets and festivities in honor of Ministers and generals who arrived laden with gold, while the people paid with their misery for their failure to secure a decent government. As I explained to someone, my country no longer hurt me in my heart, but rather, made me sick at my stomach.

Gabriela Mistral was teaching at Columbia, and one day she came to our humble quarters on Riverside Drive. Days before, I had seen her name among those present at a banquet at which the Consul of Mexico had been toastmaster.

"You are making a mistake, Counselor, in going to Europe. What are you going to do there? I know no one would trouble you if you went back to Mexico; that's what you should do. You won't deny that Ortiz Rubio is better than Calles."

"Well, Gabriela, I thought that in his time, Calles did not seem at all bad to you."

She smiled, apparently without being offended, and insisted, "You ought not to meddle with this business of being a candidate. That is for soldiers. You are no soldier!"

I bore with her patiently.

A Valeria in rebellion was worth all of the hired intellectuals put together. Deambrosis, who still represented my literary interests in Paris, wrote that he had made a contract with *La Prensa* of Buenos Aires for one article a month with a thousand francs as honorarium. That meant the cost of a house in Europe.

Paris, as usual, was sunless. A kind of gray dampness, favorable to quiet sleep, floated in the air and penetrated everything, including the soul. At times it snowed, but not too much; the cold was not bothersome to anyone who came from New York. Everything encouraged voluptuous day-dreaming and self-indulgence. Still, in my lodging in the Place de la Sorbonne, there were shadows without and within. I was waiting for a reply to the message I sent on arrival: "Am here, beg you come at once." I also telegraphed Deambrosis inviting him to come along on the trip. The magazines I bought ceased to interest me. The replies were held up; finally, Deambrosis replied, "See you soon." From Valeria, nothing. In periods of insomnia on board ship, I had imagined that I would see her on the dock at Le Havre, since she knew my itinerary. Her silence was disturbing, and hurt me. About eight o'clock I woke up to the fact that I was deserted. Whom should I notify? To whom should I telephone? No name came to mind. Old friends; would they be free? Were they still friends? In any case, everyone knows that in Paris you must make appointments a week in advance. A sudden idea, a curiosity led me to call a certain number.

"Charito?"

She replied herself: "Yes, here I am. I have nothing to do. Come on over."

I hesitated; I didn't like the idea of seeing her in the house of her dead husband.

"No, not there," I objected. "If you like, I'll wait for you in that restaurant where we used to . . ."

"Restaurant so and so? All right . . ."

At two in the morning, worn out, I put her in a taxi, and sought refuge in my hotel.

In general, Hispano-American culture in Paris does not attain the level of that of the *metic*, of the white immigrant, but remains *mestizo*. It is the alien immigrant, the individual of white race coming from Rumania or Poland or Greece, who astonishes us by reaching a position at the summit of French culture. At the beginning of their careers the geniuses like Madame de Noailles, the Rumanian, and Madame Curie, the Pole, were immigrants; Hispano-American immigrants are far below the level needed to produce great figures. And anyway, I hope that on the day when our race produces such great figures, we shall not see them assimilated into another culture, but rooted in our environment, representing something we can call our own. But, in any case, the *metic* enjoys a kind of consideration that we

simple mestizos do not attain. Such an "immigrant," for example, is
the Spaniard, Madariaga, who writes in French and succeeds by
means of affirming that he knows his Voltaire well. *Mon Voltaire*, he
says, and at the same time reminds us that he was brought up in
France. We, who do not even know French properly, as we claim to,
occupy the lowest intellectual level in Paris. Nevertheless, the Hispano-American intellectual market has its importance for the writers
of France. No papers in the world pay better than those of Buenos
Aires. And they pay no one so well as they do top-flight Parisian
writers. Often you will come upon discussions by people who know
their Latin America well. Some of them manage to secure a discreet
fame for the Spanish American writers who have previously had their
work translated into French and who respectfully concern themselves with some great French figure. Anyone who does not render
such obsequious service will pass unnoticed or will, at the most,
arouse astonishment.

In those days they were talking in the cafés about the problem of
Spanish America.

It is only fair to say that not all writers are as orthodox and closed-
minded as I have indicated. There are generous ones like Miomand-
dre, who after paying me some courteous attention, talked to me for a
long while. At the time, he was much impressed by Lawrence's *The
Plumed Serpent*. He asked me how right the mystico-gloomy interpretation of the famous English novelist was. One cannot deny, I
told him, that this is a case where there are insights of real genius; to
such a point that certain predictions which made me angry when the
book appeared were later confirmed, convincing me that I was the
mistaken one, having been misled by excessive patriotic optimism.
Other writers devoted to Spanish subjects, like Jean Cassou, for example, are interested in learning about Mexico. But one problem
which no one attacks optimistically is that of race mixture and what
might be called "Indology." For while the United States, on account
of their policy of breaking down the Spanish tradition, encourages the
admiration of all that is pure Indian, in Europe, on the other hand,
the Indian stuff convinces no one, and it is looked upon rather as a
nightmare; you can see this in books like Siegfried's about Latin
America. No one speaks well about mestizo subjects, either, and
writers avoid the problem because courtesy forbids them to say
what they think. It is high time we realized how close Europe and the
United States are in this matter of looking down on the mestizo. A
work like mine, contained in books like *La Raza Cósmica*, defensive

and hopeful about race mixture, arouses neither surprise nor annoyance, but I would say quite simply, astonishment. And few would have found out about it, except for the fact that a French traveler decided to pass through Brazil and referred in articles he wrote to the success that my thesis on race mixture was enjoying in Brazil. At the same time, he set out to overthrow my theory.

Brazil was the country which had been willing to take my thesis seriously. Brazil has been gaining the rank of a Power.

The demon of sincerity whispered in my ear: "Who built modern Brazil? Is São Paulo not the work of Italians and Portuguese, of Europeans, in short? In Brazil the backward provinces are precisely those, like Bahia, that are mostly peopled by mulattoes."

A conversation with an Englishwoman, who had traveled in Africa, cast at least a momentary light on my problem. She told me about the most recent African studies, according to which the high point of Egyptian culture corresponds to a period of mixture of Negro and white, but one that had been matured by eight hundred years of experience and effort. At the beginning, in Egypt, too, race mixture produced decadence. So there is my race mixture theory, postponed by eight centuries. The problem, then, is whether we will survive for another four centuries in relative independence, or be swept away before then by races that will make the New World powerful without taking us into account, leaving us reduced to the status of pariahs, like the Mexicans of Texas and California.

Very early, I enjoyed the surprise of seeing Valeria and Deambrosis enter my bedroom unannounced. They had made the trip from Bordeaux by night and were tired out, but after a bath they would be ready. I got them separate quarters in the same hotel, and an hour later, we were having coffee with cream and toast, the light French breakfast, which leaves the appetite undisturbed for the formal midday lunch. And we were exchanging opinions.

We walked under the arcades of the Rue de Rivoli, beyond the Joan of Arc, once, twice, without finding what I was looking for, an old Portuguese liquor store that sold Port and Sherry—drawn from casks, classified by year and brand—by the glass for from ten to twenty francs, according to age. By asking questions, we found out that the famous establishment had closed a year before. In its place, we found a modern perfume store. What a disappointment! Paris was losing its real cosmopolitanism and in exchange was being filled with cocktail bars. North Americanization did not even respect la ville lumière. Duhamel was right in expressing alarm in his book

Scènes de la vie future, Voyage par l'Amérique du nord. We made
plans to translate parts of that book for the Spanish American public.

Deambrosis proposed that we see a film everyone was talking about.
Valeria wanted to take a walk through the Latin Quarter. We left
Deambrosis at the door of the movie, then we lost ourselves, behind
St. Séverin, going toward Ste. Geneviève and the university streets,
which at that hour were deserted. The regular pace and the light,
pleasant rubbing of hips which binds bodies together, unite the souls
of two people who have been joined in the illusion that it is for
eternity.

Deambrosis and I went up to my room. In a quarter of an hour the
phone rang. It was the Consulate; the consul himself speaking. Ar-
turo Pani told me, "I have been trying to reach you for more than an
hour. Do you know about Valeria?"

"No, what? I mean . . . you frighten me! . . . What has happened?"

Pani's voice trembled and he stammered, "She has just died! Police
headquarters notified me. I think we should go there together. I'll
pick you up at once."

"Yes, very well, I'll wait for you. Thanks. . . ."

The police had told Pani, "A Mexican lady has shot herself in
Notre Dame. She left a letter for you."

She was in the morgue, at no one knows how many degrees below freezing, in her black dress that had fitted her so well that morning. How cold her bones must be! My own, out of sympathy, shivered.
From the morgue she was seeking the warmth of my living bones and
that is why they, too, were cold. She needed my help to pass over.

She had deserted her son. There was no excuse for it. How could
she have left her son alone in Bordeaux! Here again I had been the
one who did not see, who did not suspect; but she ought to have
known that eliminating herself meant giving the child back to his
father, and it meant the loss of a considerable fortune just when she
was ruined and could not bring him up. Nevertheless, my sorrow
had not yet reached the period of finding excuses; it clamored and
condemned.

It must have been a week after Valeria's death, two or three days
after the burial, when Charito appeared, sweeping aside all obstacles.
When I looked up, she was seated there in front of me, in a simple
street dress, saying with her painted, eloquent lips, "Get out of this

tomb; I have come for you. Don't worry; if you don't want to be seen in a restaurant, we can eat in my apartment; come on, you need to get away from all this!" And I went with her.

"Come on, I'll lend you pajamas so you can be comfortable. I'm going to take a bath; perhaps you would like one, too, a warm bath would do you good."

"No, thanks, thank you very much; go ahead and do as you like."

She went into the adjoining bedroom and began to undress, interrupting herself to appear and tell me, as she saw me turning the pages of a beautiful book, or picking up some bibelot, "Gomarella bought that in Italy; the other thing is a present from so and so."

She walked across the room in her silk dressing gown; then after the shower, she appeared naked, came over to my chair and putting her hand on my shoulder, asked with a smile, "What is the matter with you? Well, it must be true that *'vous l'avez dans la peau!'* "

It was the first time she had referred to the dead woman; we had never talked about her; and we did not mention her again, but I felt Valeria sitting quietly there beside me. And beside Charito I saw Gomarella, also very quiet. So there were four of us and not two. But Charito seemed not to see anything, and I felt like making her keep quiet by telling her, "But they will hear you!" I restrained myself, for she would not have understood; she would have thought I was delirious.

She rubbed my forehead, my hands, "You are cold," she said. "Don't you want something strong? Cognac? Whiskey?"

"No, nothing, thank you." She ran to the bedroom and called me a minute later. In her pajamas, under the covers, she proposed: "If you don't want to lie down, sit here beside me, I want to read you some wonderful pages." And with her clear diction, but in a voice that was beginning to sound rough, she read in impeccable French the story of a plane flight through the night, half fantasy, half reality, by a poet-aviator who was a great soul.

"What is this?" I asked. "It sounds marvelous."

"I knew you would like it; but how stupid of you not to know; one can see you come from Yankeeland. Don't you know what this is? It won the chief literary prize of the year—it's my fiancé's novel."

"Your fiancé?"

"Don't you remember what I told you the other night? I'm going to be married; my friend is the author, look!" And she pointed to the name of the prize-winner. "He is on his way; within a few days he'll be in Paris, I'll introduce him to you." And she went on reading with delight.

So, I thought, for her, Gomarella and I and all the past is simply over and gone—can be looked at objectively. Her whole soul was looking toward the future. Her destiny was ever upward, with the author of that noble literature. Surprise made me speechless. A few minutes later I insisted on leaving, not wishing to see her again.

Her last advice, after she had rung the bell which tells them downstairs to open the door, was "Give my concierge five francs, so that she won't give me a black look tomorrow for waking her up at all hours."

Altogether, I told myself in the street, there is no doubt that as a soul she is insignificant. She hasn't one, I remember she told me once. And yet, the fates selected her to receive a series of marvelous pieces of luck.

Oh, how incomprehensible life is, what a Sphinx!

And a kind of satisfaction filled my breast with calm, because an instinctive posthumous fidelity had enabled me to resist the flesh.

Reading the encouraging words of Labarca's article about me, I felt distressed at the thought of my notes on *Ethics* lying abandoned in the bottom of suitcases that were constantly moving about. And the time that I still had to give to the sterile, stupid struggle of Mexican politics; but that struggle was something I was honor-bound to carry on, and was the only way to redeem the sacrifice of those who had died for the regeneration of our country.

The first bomb resounded in the Sorbonne.

By good fortune, my Venezuelans dominated the Federation of Latin American students. In the Sorbonne, the authorities at first refused a room for my lecture; but the students threatened and won out, and we were granted a rather spacious hall in the central building. It was pompously announced that all Latin peoples, including the French, would be interested in hearing my talk on the methods of Monroeism against the Latins of the New World.

I explained the last presidential elections in Mexico, the fall of Obregón at the hands of the people's vengeance, the use that Morrow, the Yankee Ambassador, made of the ensuing confusion to consolidate the power of Calles, his tool. I continued with the creation of an official party, starting with a junta of generals, all of them men grown rich on the government and under the protective mantle of a proletarian revolution; the murder of my partisans; the denial of suffrage by means of an Army converted into a constabulary of the Yankee Embassy; the haste with which the Wall Street bankers published a fantastic computation of the voting, favorable to Morrow's candidate, even before the voting was officially concluded; and the essence of the treaties of Bucareli, which oblige us to pay the Yankee for expropriated land, without giving the Mexicans an equivalent guarantee. During such a succint account of facts implying treason to the country in every case, no one dared interrupt; it seemed as though the audience were holding its breath in order to learn more about the situation; but the communists were there in a distant gallery watching for their chance. They found it in the question of the land; and one of them rose to ask if I was in agreement with the distribution, the collectivization of property, or if I accepted the bourgeois thesis of small properties. The communists are so stupid, and their theories are so worn and well-known, that anybody can answer them at once, but the tone of the question irritated me, and I, in turn, asked, "Who are you? Tell me that first, so that the audience can know who is asking questions." And since I suspected that the Mexican Consulate had sent them, I added, pointing to the one who raised the issue, "For instance, what do you live on?"

In a moment the place was in an indescribable uproar.

The next day it came out that the discussion had gone on more violently after my departure, and that the custodians in alarm had put out the lights, leading to a riot that resulted in the breaking of several chairs and one or more windows.

Aside from the material for the *Review,* my *Ethics* was once more occupying my attention. My original plan had been to publish the *Ethics* and all my future books myself. But experience led me to give them once more to Spanish publishing houses. With Aguilar I worked out a contract that seemed advantageous enough. Only in appearance, however, for there is no way to guarantee the number of copies printed unless they are numbered, and none of the Spanish publishers would accept this arrangement. Anyway, having a contract which forces the publisher to pay us for the book when we hand over the manuscript is a good stimulus for getting it done. So it was, that in order not to miss the opportunity, and while I was finishing my *Ethics,* I put together a volume of articles and tales which came out in Madrid with the title of *Pesimismo Alegre.* A Madrid critic suggested the change to *Pesimismo Heróico,* and I was sorry I had not used that title.

One day the Secretary of the Mexican Embassy, a young fellow named Quintanilla, turned up; I was glad to see him because of my memory of friendship with his father. He said, "I bring you greetings from the Minister, who says that political questions do not concern him, and that he is your friend." "I am very sorry," I replied, "not to be able to reciprocate; no member of the government merits greetings from me."

Our review, La Antorcha, came out with irreproachable punctuality, but full of errata. What is more, we would correct a page twice, and the third printing would contain brand new errors; the typesetters did not know a word of Spanish, but where was I to find another printing shop?

Alcides Argüedas came to talk from time to time. This excellent Bolivian friend had given up the Legation in Bogotá, was situated in Paris as Consul, and was working on his great History of Bolivia.

In the auto there was talk about the festival that General Lyautey was preparing on the grounds of the Colonial Exposition. . . . The last number was performed by ballet girls from the Opéra, elegant blondes, in the arms of Nubian athletes of Herculean strength, and wonderfully supple. We thought, "What would they say in the United States at the sight of these couples of mixed black and white? This is a great general, a real Marshall, among free civilized peoples." Lyautey, already old and sure of immortality, could afford to disagree with parties and politicians.

From its second or third number, La Antorcha began to publish writings by Valeria. The success of her political narrative series could be seen in the growth in sales and in letters of warm praise, signed by cultivated friends in San Salvador and Colombia. "Who is this extraordinary writer?" they asked. And it broke my heart to have to keep silent and not tell them: she was the conscience of Mexico, who preferred to end her life rather than endure ignominy. This impression that her suicide was the protest of the soul of the nation was confirmed by the news that reached me from Mexico of other suicides and deaths.

Notre Dame caused such deep feelings of horror in me that I endeavored not to pass it, except once out of necessity and without turning my head toward the church. But that did not interfere with the imperative need that was ultimately to lead me into it to pray for the dead woman! I allowed the days to pass as if a certain interval was necessary to put an end to the spell under which we both had fallen. At the same time, I was convinced that a sort of rite of expiation was necessary. The chance came with the announcement of a memorable function, presided over by the Cardinal Archbishop, in which the Vatican Choir enthralled Paris by their singing of the *Marcellus Mass* of Palestrina. At a price of I don't know how many francs, there was not a seat left, nor even standing room. A crowded mass of humanity remained more than an hour with souls uplifted and minds refreshed by the marvel of this purely vocal orchestration of plainsong and sublime counterpoint. My idea that counterpoint is the aesthetic equivalent of the syllogism, but superior in that it is synthetic, became firmer that morning, and I decided to take it as one of the bases of my future work. With every lamp lit, the Gothic edifice shone in all its magnificence; nevertheless, it did not succeed in winning over my dislike of the ogival style. This gave me a theme for the chapter on the superiority of the basilica style. Music releases the flow of consciousness. A torrent of ideas and feelings is connected with the development of the ceremonial. And although I was not actually thinking of the dead woman, she was within me, thinking with me, until I reached the point of thinking of the terrible beyond. Where was she really? How was she? Dissolved into nothingness, like an animal? Suffering in the shade? Enjoying luminous peace?

At the time of the elevation of the host, when the heart expresses its most secret longings, I felt that the essence of the Christian message is the revelation and liberation of the power inherent in pity. A soul that sinned could not be in any inferno, if the sin was only to demand of life a maximum of nobility, and to rebel against evil and crime. And even if she sinned gravely, the love of the Father was there, the love in which she had trusted, a love very different from the angry justice of Jehovah.

In any case, the Spanish Republic came at the right time, and perhaps it would succeed in arousing national pride; it would offer a task to the intellectuals, and we would see the Mother Country governed like France by its thinkers and not its soldiers. We should have forseen that a negative, skeptical generation, subject to foreign influence, could never carry out a really constructive transformation. From the very beginning, envy divided the distinguished men. Second-rate politicians like Azaña usurped the roles that belonged by right to men like Unamuno. And the worst of it was that Azaña did not stick to politics, but with a sudden burst of vanity, brought about by his unmerited success, began to claim to be an intellectual; he put on theatrical works, dreamt of competing with major talents, acted like a superman.

They did not dare undertake any large scale plan. My *Antorcha* told them, "Create a mystique of this historical moment, think and act like an Empire, and in America you will reconquer at least a spiritual leadership."

I had moved to Madrid to complete the arrangements for printing and distributing my *Antorcha* in Spain rather than in France. Prices in Spain were much lower than in France, and besides, I wanted to live in a country where people spoke my own language. I have always thought that those years are lost that one spends perforce in a foreign country. And a country is foreign primarily because they don't speak your own language there.

When would I get six months or so to sit down and at last write my book on Aesthetics?

And why, instead of going again into exile, did we not return to Mexico? Perhaps it was because of the hope of a revolution, although the government declared that that was impossible.

The worst of it was that because of the fatigue of the people, and as a result of endless propaganda, the public had lost its feeling of slavery. The press, controlled by officialdom, produced its daily paeans of praise of the glorious revolution that had saved the country. The greatest criminals, the most idiotic leaders, were acclaimed as heroes, exalted as statesmen.

As my mind became clearer, I went back to thinking about my important books. The writing of my *Ethics* was finished. For relaxation, and in order to see things in better perspective, I decided not to begin the *Aesthetics* right away. Between it and the *Ethics,* I would get out a book that I had long wanted to write. A novel, and what could be better than one based on my own wanderings and passions? I began to scribble *A Mexican Ulysses.*

In the bookstores one saw nothing but the screaming covers of Marxist editions. Communism, which was already being put on the shelf in France, was bursting forth in Spain. At first the socialists fought it valiantly.

Indisputable proof confirmed the stories of horror in Mexico; but the international gang continued to cry out against the tyranny of Machado in Cuba, against Mussolini, even against Vicente Gómez, but never against Mexican militarism.

There was talk about the domination of Mexico's government by the United States, working through false friends like Morrow, and about the possibility that the new Spanish Republic might support a movement of cultural emancipation in the New World. "Ah, but we can't get involved in that!" confessed Américo Castro, and he went on to express what we afterward called The Triangle Theory. "You see," the technician Castro (whose first name, "Américo," seemed to relate to North America rather than South), affirmed in didactic fashion, "you see, we here in Spain are located in one of the corners of the triangle, Madrid, New York, Buenos Aires, and we have obligations to the North as well as to the South; interests in Spanish America, to be sure, but also interests in the United States."

"And what interests are those?" someone asked. "And how can they be compared to those in Spanish America?"

"Ah," observed don Américo, "you don't know, you are not well informed, you don't look on these matters from the technical point of view. Look, there are three hundred thousand students of Spanish in the United States, scattered among universities which pay excellent salaries to professors who specialize in Spanish language and literature. Through the *Instituto Libre de Enseñanza* we get those posts; no appointment is made over there without consulting us, and without the approval of our representatives. No, we cannot get involved in the disputes of you Spanish Americans with the Yankees, we would lose the advantage of a situation which has cost us long years of hard work."

The monopoly of a hundred or two hundred positions as teachers of Spanish meant more to some of those men than the moral reconquest of a whole Continent for their mother country.

But is this not, after all, the Marxist criterion? First come material interests, and down with all that humbug about race, mother country, culture—all merely secondary products of economic evolution!

Later, the aid from the Methodists in the United States that all these leftists received to maintain themselves in power (a support more important in men and resources than even Russia's) proved the strength of the underground ties that bound them to the United States. My theory, scarcely suspected at the time, that in the case of Spain you were dealing with a Yankee Methodist intervention identical with that sponsored by Gómez Farías and Benito Juárez in Mexico, has become clearer and is fully confirmed today. In the United States itself there is today a reaction against sending money and volunteers to the Spanish Civil War.

For the very reason that the roots of Spanish tradition were fought and denied on its native soil, it was pleasant to feel oneself in Madrid. The strata of the population that were not contaminated kept up the old-fashioned customs and habits. The imperishable strength of a concept, a mode of life, was enough to defeat the most powerful conspiracy. This resistance movement struck me in all phases of life: it gave me subject matter for my *Aesthetics*. For example, it appeared in the closed clique of the Germanophile phenomenologists led by Ortega y Gasset, and by Unamuno, the philosophical dilettante. Although these two differed in almost everything, they were one in their aim of centering philosophical thought in the famous anxiety of the Swedish Protestant Kierkegaard. A mystic without faith, or the negation of mysticism.

Unamuno took as his point of departure the mental poverty (so like his own) of that arid monk, Kierkegaard, to support his *Agonía del Christianismo* and his *Sentimiento Trágico de la Vida*, doctrines of negation in a style full of labored commonplaces. And Ortega, for his part, came to the discovery of Bergson, whom he read in German translations, twenty years late.

At noon, the Avenida that goes from Castellana to the Puerta del Sol gives the impression of a vast open-air drawing room. Pretty women and the masculine population, dressed with a careless and graceful luxury, circulate happily, but still with gravity and dignity. Over the little tables they talk or read the papers. The sherry shines in big glasses; the hors d'oeuvre are seafood and olives. Certain cafés boast of opening a fresh bottle to serve each client. Not even in France is there a wine comparable to Tío Pepe, a sherry that was much in demand at the time. In the matter of table wines, especially red wines, no one can equal the French, with their Bordeaux, Burgundies, and Chateaux of Provence; but in apéritifs, the French themselves give in to Port and Sherry, the wines of the Peninsula. The groups talking over the little tables break up at two in the afternoon. Then comes an abundant meal, and after that the siesta, and back to work. At night, once again the cafés receive the population to talk and display themselves. Theatre performances start late so that people can enjoy their suppers and a chance to talk. Even after midnight, when the theatres with their superb women, let out, people go back to their cafés to talk about the events of the day, sipping thick, delicious chocolate, with little cinnamon-covered rolls, so light and tasty. No European capital amuses itself for so many hours a day as Madrid did in the years before the Civil War.

Very near our house, the beautiful Western Park was the paradise of children. Every morning they used to take my little granddaughter there to enjoy the sun. Tuberculosis, which threatens the children of England and France, is no great danger in Spain.

Segovia is a dream, with its aqueduct, and La Granja, and its waterfalls. And the gardens of Aranjuez, the most beautiful in the world; without the French craze for geometric design, but still with an artistic order in the arrangement of the beds; lawns with statues, and carpets of flowers in bloom. Splendor in the vegetable kingdom to match the splendor of the aristocracy. And in the ancient royal mansion such riches of pictures, maps, prints, rugs, Majolica; a princely ostentation that surpasses all that the courts of other empires have left behind them in Europe! Nobility without obsequiousness characterizes the Spaniards, with their "hidalgo" temperament, that exists in both master and man; strength without the barbarity of the Germans, or the stinginess of the English. Only Italy, which has everything in a superlative degree, produces a similar sensation of magnificent human beings.

When I learned that the overthrow of Ortiz Rubio—which should have been the signal for general armed uprising against the gang which thus made a mockery of its own work—had led, on the contrary, to public shouts of joy for the impossible new President, I decided to stop the publication of La Antorcha. It was prostituting the written word, I thought, to use it in the face of a situation which no longer needed to be condemned, its infamy was so obvious. The only right course of action was rebellion. And since this did not come, the honorable minority had no other recourse than scornful silence before such vileness.

In Mexico, a group of the old opponents of re-election took advantage of the inauguration of the new executive to go into action once more. Forgetting that I was the Chief of the Party, they held meetings and took serious action without even informing me that they were getting together. When I protested against this procedure in La Antorcha, they replied by expelling me from the party on the pretext that "I had abandoned my partisans," and because I did not appear in Mexico, undoubtedly to accompany them to the antechambers of the President.

"Why do you want me in Mexico?" I replied. "To go through the farce of political opposition with you, after I have preached armed revolt?"

The betrayal by a group of fellow-enthusiasts would not have worried me at all; such things are frequent in politics. What got under my skin was the attitude of the public, which, subconsciously moved by its own abject condition, took the side of the cheaters.

When the treason of the little group of anti-re-electionists took place, there was not a club or society in the whole country that took

up my defense. The government succeeded in breaking up the opposition and divorcing it from the man who was its Chief and should
have gone on being Chief for the whole time of the struggle, without
making any deals with the usurpers. The opposition has paid for its
crime as I foresaw it would, with disorientation, fragmentation, and
loss of face. They will not find an honest man to accept candidacy
for them in the future, I predicted; and once more I turned out to be
a good prophet.

All the publicity and the enthusiasm with which numerous Spanish
groups rolled out the red carpet for visitors from America led to frequent invitations for us to visit this or that region of Spain. I refused
most of these opportunities, because I did not want to incur expense
and because I had all my time taken up with the preparation of *A
Mexican Ulysses* and the study of topics for my *Aesthetics*.

Mass production is without any doubt contrary to nature. The system used in California, which stunts the trunk in order to increase the
quantity of fruit, gains in numbers and loses in quality. The same
thing, perhaps, happens in all the orders of natural production. The
peoples characterized by genuine aristocracy, "quality" peoples like
the French, the Spanish, never reach a hundred million inhabitants.
On the other hand, in the United States, with its hundred and thirty
million, they are prematurely approaching Chinafication. Quantity
keeps increasing, at the cost of lower quality. And, quite aside from
these considerations, the quality of Spain is a matter of the atmosphere and of the very soul.

Mexico remained at peace. "The peace of the cemetery," we used
to call it under Madero, speaking of the Díaz period; what came later
might be called "the peace of ignominy." In it, mine was the only
voice raised in protest. One after another more friends quarreled with
me or turned their backs on me as they came to terms with iniquity.
My enemies prospered, and I could have no confidence in my friends.
The few who remained faithful lived under oppression.

The new puppet that the Calles group raised to the Presidency
was even worse than Ortiz Rubio. A man who had never dared to be a
candidate, not even for the office of deputy, who would not have
stood up to the heckling of a single public meeting, Abelardo Rodríguez, became president by unanimous vote. He spoke English
badly, but Spanish even worse, and had become a millionaire as an
administrator or governor of Baja California, where there is no busi-

ness other than sentry boxes, houses of prostitution, and an International Casino. Sharing his take with two or three presidents, he moved up the ladder.

Summer came upon us quickly. The writing of *Ulysses* was almost done, and I began to use the services of Taracena to place the book in installments in some American periodical. Taracena did what he could and finally found an acceptable deal in Havana; they gave a carbon copy to a paper in Mexico which paid poorly. The wealthy papers of Mexico in those days did not mention my name except to attack me.

The clique that called itself the Anti-re-electionist Party slandered and expelled me; even my friend Ortiz voted for my expulsion, and then tried to defend his action by saying that I, too, had committed many errors. He did not tell me what the errors were. And I limited myself to telling him that I found friendship with him incompatible considering his cooperation with my enemies. The one sure thing is that the whole country wanted to be comfortable, tried to adapt itself to the situation, and felt annoyed with what it called my stubbornness, my ambition, my obstinacy. Every one of those who backed down felt called upon to justify his apostasy to himself by finding defects and faults in the Chief. And since we are men and not gods, is it not possible to write or think slanderous things about anyone?

From the beginning I turned my eyes toward Argentina. That country would be my refuge, perhaps indefinitely, perhaps permanently.

Robles wrote me that Dr. José Peco, Dean of the Faculty of Social Sciences in the University of La Plata, and an independent and generous-minded man, would guarantee me about two thousand pesos for some lectures to be given before the end of the year.

Nobody talked of contributing anything to enable me to carry on the plan of open struggle and of preaching armed rebellion against the government. In spite of this, the majority of our friends thought I should run again as a candidate in the coming election. And these were the very same men who had carried out the electoral fiction of 1929, who now invited the people to take part in a new election! And old party men, converted into accomplices of this farce, alleged that if I did not present myself as a candidate, renouncing my rebellious attitude, I would be showing lack of tenacity and proving that I was afraid of a fight! In a word, I sent a cable to Robles, saying: "I accept and sail in a month."

Very early in the morning we left Gijón, sped on our way by

Angelín, accompanied as far as Oviedo by my friend Rodríguez. In Oviedo, we came to the parting of the ways. My wife and son took the road toward the French frontier; my daughter, Herminio, my granddaughter, and I took the bus to La Coruña. Beside the bus, through the window misted over by the fog, I saw for the last time the face of my friend, streaked with the tears he made no effort to conceal. It was very likely that we would never see each other again; life had on various occasions brought us together, and then separated us by great distances; this absurd game has a fatal end in old age and death. What bitter thoughts would my wife and my son hold, isolated in Europe, without friends, condemned to an ostracism which would last for at least a couple of years! And what trials awaited us in a land that was new to us, new and strange, and one in which we would have to fight our way?

LIST OF NAMES

LIST OF NAMES

Adriana   Vasconcelos' mistress

Aguascalientes, The Military Convention of   Opened Oct. 10, 1914
in a neutral city to settle differences between the various revolutionary groups; Carranza's refusal to give up his position to the
Provisional President elected by the Convention led to its failure

Agüero, José de la Riva   Peruvian companion of Vasconcelos

Aguirre Benavides, General Eugenio   Sub-secretary of War in Gutiérrez's cabinet

Ahumada, Herminio   Vasconcelos' son-in-law

Alberdi, Juan Bautista   Political philosopher (1810–84) whose *Bases*
is a most influential landmark in Argentine intellectual history

Alessio Robles, Miguel   Villista and Secretary of Justice in Carranza's
cabinet

Almanza, Mateo   A general and member of Gutiérrez's cabinet

Altamirano, Ignacio   Nineteenth-century fighter for liberty and learning

Argüedas, Alcides   Bolivian historian

Arroyo, César   Colombian friend whom Vasconcelos encountered in
Europe

Asunsolo, Ignacio   Sculptor whose works appear on the Palace of
Education

Azaña, Manuel   Spanish Republican statesman (1880–1940)

Blanco, Lucio   Minister of *Gobernación* in Gutiérrez's cabinet

Blanquet, General Aurelio   Huertista general and Minister of War

Bouquet, General Carlos   Career military man trusted by Vasconcelos, later shot in Nogales

Bucareli, treaties of (1923)   Guarantees of payment of indemnities
to foreigners whose property was expropriated

Calles, Plutarco Elías   Obregón's successor as the Mexican president
(1924–28), remained a political strong man through 1934

Cárdenas, Lázaro   President (1934–40)

Carrillo Puerto, Felipe   Labor leader, governor of Yucatán under

Obregón; as head of Socialist Party of the Southeast, supported Calles

Carranza, Venustiano The First Chief, who preferred that title and its informality to the restrictions of constitutional government, was President from 1917–20

Caso, Antonio Mexico's most famous professor of philosophy (1883–1946)

Cassou, Jean Novelist, art critic, and Director of the Paris Museum of Modern Art

Citadel, The Pact of the Agreement forcing out Madero and opening the way for Huerta

Chacón y Calvo, José María Cuban critic and philologist (1893—)

Corrales, Juanito Vasconcelos follower

Cuauhtemoc Last prince of the Aztecs

Dávila, General Vicente Constitutionalist general who took Monterrey from Villa in May, 1915

Díaz, Porfirio Ruled Mexico for a quarter of a century until 1911

Díaz Lombardo, Miguel Madero's minister in Paris

Díaz Soto y Gama, Antonio Zapatista leader, delegate to Aguascalientes Convention

Escobar, José Editor of local paper in Guaymas, later candidate for President

Fanny Fanny Atinúa, an opera singer

Field Jurado, Francisco Campeche Senator, assassinated on Obregón's orders

Fombona, Blanco Venezuelan novelist and publicist

Gama, Valentín Secretary for Commerce in Gutiérrez's cabinet

Gastélum, Dr. Bernardo J. Mexican ambassador to Uruguay, Minister of Education, later of Health under Obregón

Gómez, Juan Vicente Venezuelan dictator

Gomez Farías, Valentín Vice President under Santa Anna; a radical reformer

Góngora, Victorio President of Vasconcelos' Anti-Re-election Party

González Prada, Manuel Leading Peruvian intellectual (1844–1918)

Guadalupe, The Plan of The vague agreement (signed in March, 1913) which named Carranza First Chief

Gutiérrez, Eulalio   Provisional President (1914–15) under the Convention of Aguascalientes
Guzmán, Eulalia   Woman archaeologist

Haya de la Torre, Henriquez   Peruvian political leader; founder of APRA (Alianza Popular Revolucionara Americana)
Henríquez Ureña   Dominican man of letters who became an American figure through his residence in the United States, Mexico, and Argentina
Huerta, Adolfo de la   Provisional President (1920)
Huerta, Victoriana   General who defected from Madero to follow him in power (1913–14)

Ibáñez, Blasco   Spanish novelist
Inman, Samuel Guy   One-time missionary, later writer and lecturer on Latin America
Isaacs, Jorge   Author of *María* (1837–95)

Juárez, Benito   Indian revolutionary and constitutional leader who became President in 1861 (d. 1872)

Labarca, Guillermo   Chilean writer and politician
Lamont, Thomas William   American banker (1870–1948), in Mexico on funding the debt in 1921
Lizárrega, Nacho   Head of student group in Guadalajara
Lombardo Toledano, Vicente   Leftist labor leader and Director of Preparatory School
Lyautey, Louis Hubert   Marshal and French colonial administrator in Morocco, from 1912–16 and 1917–25

Madariaga, Salvador de   Spanish writer and professor, long a resident abroad
Madero, Emilio   Brother of the President
Madero, Francisco I.   Succeeded in ending Díaz's long rule of Mexico and served as President from 1911 until he was assassinated on February 22, 1913, after which he became a national hero
Madero, Raul   Revolutionary general (brother of the President), exiled in New York, accompanied Vasconcelos to dismiss Villa from his command
Maldonado, Calixto   Lawyer who concluded that there was no valid election in Vasconcelos' campaign
Maytorena, José M.   General and Governor of Sonora
Menéndez y Pelayo, Marcelino   Eminent Spanish philologist and critic

Mistral, Gabriela   Chilean poetess (1889–1957) and honorary consul, Nobel prize winner

Montalvo, Juan   Ecuadorian writer and social critic (1832–89)

Morrow, Dwight W.   (1873–1931) Morgan partner, appointed Ambassador to Mexico in 1927; American historians hold that he inaugurated better relations between the two countries

Muñoz, Romano   Prefect in Preparatory School

Obregón, Alvaro   General who won out over Zapata and Villa and on the death of Carranza became the leader of his country (1920–24)

Orozco, José Clemente   One of the great three Mexican mural painters

Ortega y Gasset, José   Spanish philosopher (d. 1955) who has had more influence in Mexico than any other recent philosopher

Ortiz Rubio, Pascual   President (1930–32)

Palma, Ricardo   Peruvian man of letters (1833–1919), author of *Tradiciones Peruanas*

Pansi, Alberto J.   Official under Carranza, astutely defects from him, becomes Minister to France

Paredes, Antonio de Jesús   Vicar-general of the archdiocese of Mexico City

Pedrero, Andrés   Eloquent student partisan of Vasconcelos who remained a close friend

Pellicer, Carlos (Carlitos)   Mexican literary man and orator

Peralto, Miguel   Engineer and Secretary of Administration under Obregón, Zapatista official in Education Ministry

Pino Suárez, José María   Vice President under Madero

Plagianini, Felix   Minister of Education under Carranza

Poinsett, Joel   (1779–1851) First American minister to Mexico, accused of meddling; the flower bears his name

Portes Gil, Emilio   Provisional President (1928–30)

Prieto Laurens, Jorge   Party chief (Co-operative Party) and President of the Council of the Capital, but a brutal and corrupt politician, according to Vasconcelos

Queiroz, Eça de   Portuguese nineteenth-century writer

Ramírez, Ignacio   Nineteenth-century Mexican Voltaire (1818–79)

Reed, John   Harvard graduate who became a well-known leftist reporter of the Mexican and Russian revolutions; author of *Ten Days that Shook the World*

Reyes, Alfonso   Outstanding Mexican intellectual and diplomatic

Warren, Charles B. American Commissioner; received by Obregón
Wilson, Henry Lane American Ambassador to Mexico who undermined the position of Madero

Zaldumbide, Gonzalo Colombian writer and diplomat
Zapata, Emiliano Unlettered Southern leader from Morelos; paradoxically it is his ideas that ultimately triumphed